THE SAVAGE MIND

There is no one on earth like savages, peasants, and provincials for examining their affairs from every angle; what's more, when they move from thought to action, you can see they have worked things out completely.

H. de Balzac, *Le Cabinet des Antiques*
(Bibl. de la Pléiade, vol. IV, pp. 400–401).

THE SAVAGE MIND

Claude Lévi-Strauss

THE UNIVERSITY OF CHICAGO PRESS

THE NATURE OF HUMAN SOCIETY SERIES
Editors: Julian Pitt-Rivers and Ernest Gellner

International Standard Book Number:
0-226-47484-4 [paperback]
Library of Congress Catalog Card Number: 66-28197

THE UNIVERSITY OF CHICAGO PRESS, CHICAGO 60637
WEIDENFELD AND NICOLSON LTD., LONDON

Translated from the French, *La Pensée sauvage*

Published 1966
Printed in the United States of America

99 98 97 96 95 94 13 14 15

To the Memory
of
Maurice Merleau-Ponty

CONTENTS

PREFACE xi

1 THE SCIENCE OF THE CONCRETE 1

2 THE LOGIC OF TOTEMIC CLASSIFICATIONS 35

3 SYSTEMS OF TRANSFORMATIONS 75

4 TOTEM AND CASTE 109

5 CATEGORIES, ELEMENTS, SPECIES, NUMBERS 135

6 UNIVERSALIZATION AND PARTICULARIZATION 161

7 THE INDIVIDUAL AS A SPECIES 191

8 TIME REGAINED 217

9 HISTORY AND DIALECTIC 245

BIBLIOGRAPHY 271

INDEX 283

ILLUSTRATIONS

(Between pages 148 and 149)

1 Francois Clouet. Portrait of Elizabeth of Austria. (*Photo: Musée du Louvre*)
2 Club used for killing fish (*Photo: Huillard*)
3 The opposite of totemism: Naturalized Man. Sketch by Le Brun
4 Humanized Nature. Sketch by Grandville (*Bibl. Nationale*)
5 Alphabet of Birds (*Musée National des Arts et Traditions Populaires. Photo: Huillard*)
6 Society of Animals (*Musée National des Arts et Traditions Populaires. Photo: Huillard*)
7 Australian Churinga (*Photo: Bandy*)
8 Aranda water-colours (*Photos: Australian Information Service*)

PREFACE

This book is complete in itself, but the problems it discusses are closely linked to those which I surveyed more hastily in a recent work entitled *Totemism* (trans. Rodney Needham, London, 1964). Without wishing to oblige the reader to refer to it, it is proper to draw his attention to the connection between the two: the first forms a kind of historical and critical introduction to the second. I have not, therefore, deemed it necessary to return, here, to the theories, definitions and facts which have already been dealt with at sufficient length.

Nevertheless the reader should know what is expected of him on opening these pages: that he acquiesce in the negative conclusion which the first volume reached in regard to totemism; for, once it is clear why I believe that the anthropologists of former times were the prey to an illusion, it is time for me to explore totemism's positive side.

No one will suppose that, by placing the name of Maurice Merleau-Ponty on the first page of a book whose final chapter is devoted to a work of Sartre, I have intended to oppose them to one another. Those who were close to Merleau-Ponty and myself during recent years know some of the reasons why it was natural that this book which develops freely certain themes of my lectures at the *Collège de France* should be dedicated to him. It would have been, in any case, had he lived, as the continuation of a dialogue whose opening goes back to 1930 when, in company with Simone de Beauvoir, we were brought together by our teaching activities, on the eve of receiving our final degrees. And, since death has torn him from us, may this book at least remain devoted to his memory as a token of good faith, gratitude and affection.

If I have felt obliged to give expression to my disagreement with Sartre regarding the points which bear on the philosophical fundaments of anthropology, I have only determined to do so after several readings of the work in question which occupied my pupils at the *Ecole des Hautes Etudes* and myself during many sessions of the year 1960–1. Over and above our inevitable divergences I hope that Sartre will recognize above all that a discussion to which so much care has been given constitutes on behalf of all of us a homage of admiration and respect.

I would like to express my warm thanks to my colleague, Jacques Bertin, professor at the *Ecole des Hautes Etudes* who was kind enough to make some of the diagrams for me in his laboratory; I. Chiva and J. Pouillon whose notes recalled to me some improvised points which were otherwise lost; Mme Edna H. Lemay who typed the manuscript; Mlle Nicole Belmont who helped me with the tasks of assembling the documentation and making the bibliography and the index; and my wife who aided me in rereading the text and correcting the proofs.

CHAPTER ONE

THE SCIENCE OF THE CONCRETE

It has long been the fashion to invoke languages which lack the terms for expressing such a concept as 'tree' or 'animal', even though they contain all the words necessary for a detailed inventory of species and varieties. But, to begin with, while these cases are cited as evidence of the supposed ineptitude of 'primitive people' for abstract thought, other cases are at the same time ignored which make it plain that richness of abstract words is not a monopoly of civilized languages. In Chinook, a language widely spoken in the north-west of North America, to take one example, many properties and qualities are referred to by means of abstract words: 'This method', Boas says, 'is applied to a greater extent than in any other language I know.' The proposition 'The bad man killed the poor child' is rendered in Chinook: 'The man's badness killed the child's poverty'; and for 'The woman used too small a basket' they say: 'She put the potentilla-roots into the smallness of a clam basket' (Boas 2, pp. 657–8).

In every language, moreover, discourse and syntax supply indispensable means of supplementing deficiencies of vocabulary. And the tendentious character of the argument referred to in the last paragraph becomes very apparent when one observes that the opposite state of affairs, that is, where very general terms outweigh specific names, has also been exploited to prove the intellectual poverty of Savages:

> Among plants and animals he [the Indian] designates by name only those which are useful or harmful, all others are included under the classification of bird, weed, etc. (Krause, p. 104).

A more recent observer seems in the same way to believe that the native gives names and forms concepts solely in accordance with his needs:

> I well remember the hilarity of Marquesian friends . . . over the (to them) fatuous interest of the botanist of our expedition in 1921, who was collecting nameless ('useless') 'weeds' and asking their names (Handy and Pukui, Part VI, p. 127n).

However, Handy compares this indifference to that which specialists in our civilization show towards phenomena which have no immediate bearing on their own field. When his native collaborator stressed the fact that in Hawaii 'every botanical, zoological or inorganic form that is known to have been named (and personalized), was *some thing* . . . used', she is careful to add 'in some way'. She goes on to say that the reason why 'there was an infinite variety of living things in forest and sea, of meteorological or marine phenomena, which were unnamed' was that they were regarded as being of no 'use or interest' – terms which are not equivalent, as 'use' concerns practical, and 'interest' theoretical, matters. What follows confirms this by concentrating on the latter aspect at the expense of the former: 'Living was experience fraught with exact and definite significance' (id., p. 126–7).

In fact, the delimitation of concepts is different in every language, and, as the author of the article 'nom' in the *Encyclopédie* correctly observed in the eighteenth century, the use of more or less abstract terms is a function not of greater or lesser intellectual capacity, but of differences in the interests – in their intensity and attention to detail – of particular social groups within the national society: 'In an observatory a *star* is not simply a star but β of Capricorn or γ of Centaur or ζ of the Great Bear, etc. In stables every *horse* has a proper *name* – *Diamond*, *Sprite*, *Fiery*, etc.' Further, even if the observation about so-called primitive languages referred to at the beginning of the chapter could be accepted as it stands, one would not be able to conclude from this that such languages are deficient in general ideas. Words like 'oak', 'beech', 'birch', etc., are no less entitled to be considered as abstract words than the word 'tree'; and a language possessing only the word 'tree' would be, from this point of view less rich in concepts than one which lacked this term but contained dozens or hundreds for the individual species and varieties.

The proliferation of concepts, as in the case of technical languages, goes with more constant attention to properties of the world, with an interest that is more alert to possible distinctions which can be introduced between them. This thirst for objective knowledge is one of the most neglected aspects of the thought of people we call 'primitive'. Even if it is rarely directed towards facts of the same level as those with which modern science is concerned, it implies comparable intellectual application and methods of observation. In both cases the universe is an object of thought at least as much as it is a means of satisfying needs.

Every civilization tends to overestimate the objective orientation of its thought and this tendency is never absent. When we make the mistake of thinking that the Savage is governed solely by organic or economic needs, we forget that he levels the same reproach at us, and that to him his own desires for knowledge seems more balanced than ours:

> These native Hawaiians' utilization of their available natural assets was well-nigh complete – infinitely more so than that of the present commercial era which ruthlessly exploits the few things that are financially profitable for the time being, neglecting and often obliterating the rest (Handy and Pukui, Part VIII, p. 62).

Cash-crop agriculture is hardly to be confused with the science of the botanist. But, in ignoring the latter and taking only the former into account, the old Hawaiian aristocrat is simply repeating, and turning to the advantage of a native culture, a mistake of the same kind that Malinowski made when he claimed that primitive peoples' interest in totemic plants and animals was inspired by nothing but the rumbling of their stomachs.

Tessman (Vol. 2, p. 192) mentions 'the accuracy with which (the Fang of the Gabon) identify the slightest differences between species of the same genus'. The two authors quoted above make a similar observation about Oceania:

> The acute faculties of this native folk noted with exactitude the generic characteristics of all species of terrestial and marine life, and the subtlest variations of natural phenomena such as winds, light and colour, ruffling of water and variation in surf, and the currents of water and air (Handy and Pukui, Part VI, p. 126).

Among the Hanunóo of the Philippines a custom as simple as that of betel chewing demands a knowledge of four varieties of areca nut and eight substitutes for them, and of five varieties of betel and five substitutes (Conklin, 3):

> Almost all Hanunóo activities require an intimate familiarity with local plants and a precise knowledge of plant classification. Contrary to the assumption that subsistence level groups never use but a small segment of the local flora, ninety-three per cent of the total number of native plant types are recognized by the Hanunóo as culturally significant (Conklin I, p. 249).

This is equally true of fauna:

> The Hanunóo classify all forms of the local avifauna into seventy-five categories . . . (they) distinguish about a dozen kinds of snakes . . . sixty-odd types of fish . . . more than a dozen . . . types of fresh and salt water crustaceans . . . a similar number of . . . types of arachnids and myriapods . . . The thousands of insect forms present are grouped by the Hanunóo into a hundred and eight named categories, including thirteen for ants and termites . . . Salt water molluscs . . . of more than sixty classes are recognized by the Hanunóo, while terrestrial and fresh water types number more than twenty-five . . . Four distinct types of bloodsucking leeches are distinguished . . .: altogether 461 animal types are recorded (id., pp. 67–70).

A biologist writes the following about pygmies of the Philippines:

> Another characteristic of Negrito life, a characteristic which strikingly demarcates them from the surrounding Christian lowlanders, is their inexhaustible knowledge of the plant and animal kingdoms. This lore includes not only a specific recognition of a phenomenal number of plants, birds, animals, and insects, but also includes a knowledge of the habits and behaviour of each. . . .
>
> The Negrito is an intrinsic part of his environment, and what is still more important, continually studies his surroundings. Many times I have seen a Negrito, who, when not being certain of the identification of a particular plant, will taste the fruit, smell the leaves, break and examine the stem, comment upon its habitat, and only after all of this, pronounce whether he did or did not know the plant.

The natives are also interested in plants which are of no direct use to them, because of their significant links with the animal and insect world, and having shown this, the same author continues:

> The acute observation of the pygmies and their awareness of the interrelationships between the plant and animal life . . . is strikingly pointed out by their discussions of the living habits of bats. The *tididin* lives on the dry leaves of palms, the *dikidik* on the underside of the leaves of the wild banana, the *litlit* in bamboo clumps, the *kolumboy* in holes in trees, the *konanaba* in dark thickets, and so forth. In this manner, the Pinatubo Negritos can distinguish the habits of more than fifteen species of bats. Of course, the classification of bats, as well as of insects, birds, animals, fish and plants, is determined primarily by their actual physical differences and/or similarities.
>
> Most Negrito men can with ease enumerate the specific or descriptive

names of at least four hundred and fifty plants, seventy-five birds, most of the snakes, fish, insects, and animals, and of even twenty species of ants . . .* and the botanical knowledge of the *mananambal*, the 'medicine men and women, who use plants constantly in their practice, is truly astounding (R. B. Fox, pp. 187–8).

Of a backward people of the Tyukyu archipelago, we read:

Even a child can frequently identify the kind of tree from which a tiny wood fragment has come and, furthermore, the sex of that tree, as defined by Kabiran notions of plant sex, by observing the appearance of its wood and bark, its smell, its hardness, and similar characteristics. Fish and shellfish by the dozen are known by individually distinctive terms, and their separate features and habits, as well as the sexual differences within each type, are well recognized (Smith, p. 150).

Several thousand Coahuila Indians never exhausted the natural resources of a desert region in South California, in which today only a handful of white families manage to subsist. They lived in a land of plenty, for in this apparently completely barren territory, they were familiar with no less than sixty kinds of edible plants and twenty-eight others of narcotic, stimulant or medicinal properties (Barrows). A single Seminol informant could identify two hundred and fifty species and varieties of plants (Sturtevant). Three hundred and fifty plants known to the Hopi Indians and more than five hundred to the Navaho have been recorded. The botanical vocabulary of the Subanun of the Southern Philippines greatly exceeds a hundred terms (Frake) and that of the Hanunóo approaches two thousand.† Sillans, working with a single informant in the Gabon, recently published an ethno-botanical list of about eight thousand terms, distributed between the languages or dialects of twelve or thirteen neighbouring tribes (Walker and Sillans). The, for the most part unpublished, results of Marcel Griaule and his co-workers in the Sudan promise to be equally impressive.

Their extreme familiarity with their biological environment, the passionate attention which they pay to it and their precise knowledge of it has often struck inquirers as an indication of attitudes and preoccupations which distinguish the natives from their white visitors. Among the Tewa Indians of New Mexico:

* Also at least forty-five types of edible ground-mushrooms and ear-fungi (l.c., p. 231) and on the technological plane, more than fifty types of arrows (id., pp. 265–8).

† See below, pp. 138, 153.

Small differences are noted . . . they have a name for every one of the coniferous trees of the region; in these cases differences are not conspicuous. The ordinary individual among the whites does not distinguish (them) . . . Indeed, it would be possible to translate a treatise on botany into Tewa . . . (Robbins, Harrington and Freire-Marreco, pp. 9, 12).

E. Smith Bowen scarcely exaggerates in the amusing description she gives of her confusion when, on her arrival in an African tribe, she wanted to begin by learning the language. Her informants found it quite natural, at an elementary stage of their instruction, to collect a large number of botanical specimens, the names of which they told her as they showed them to her. She was unable to identify them, not because of their exotic nature but because she had never taken an interest in the riches and diversities of the plant world. The natives on the other hand took such an interest for granted.

These people are farmers: to them plants are as important and familiar as people. I'd never been on a farm and am not even sure which are begonias, dahlias, or petunias. Plants, like algebra, have a habit of looking alike and being different, or looking different and being alike; consequently mathematics and botany confuse me. For the first time in my life I found myself in a community where ten-year-old children weren't my mathematical superiors. I also found myself in a place where every plant, wild or cultivated, had a name and a use, and where every man, woman and child knew literally hundreds of plants . . . (my instructor) simply could not realize that it was not the words but the plants which baffled me (Smith Bowen, p. 19).

The reaction of a specialist is quite different. In a monograph in which he describes nearly three hundred species or varieties of medicinal or toxic plants used by certain peoples of Northern Rhodesia, Gilges writes:

It has always been a surprise to me to find with what eagerness the people in and around Balovale were ready and willing to talk about their medicines. Was it that they found my interest in their methods pleasing? Was it an exchange of information amongst colleagues? Or was it to show off their knowledge? Whatever the reason, information was readily forthcoming. I remember a wicked old Luchozi who brought bundles of dried leaves, roots and stems and told me about their uses. How far he was a herbalist and how far a witch-doctor I could never fathom, but I regret that I shall never possess his knowledge of African psychology and his art in the treatment of his fellow men, that, coupled with my scientific medical knowledge, might have made a most useful combination (Gilges, p. 20).

Conklin quotes the following extract from his field notes to illustrate the intimate contact between man and his environment which the native is constantly imposing on the ethnologist:

> At 0600 and in a light rain, Langba and I left Parina for Binli . . . At Aresaas, Langba told me to cut off several 10 x 50 cm. strips of bark from an *anapla kilala* tree (*Albizzia procera* (Roxb.) Benth.) for protection against the leeches. By periodically rubbing the cambium side of the strips of sapanceous (and poisonous: Quisumbling, 1947, 148) bark over our ankles and legs – already wet from the rain-soaked vegetation – we produced a most effective leech-repellent lather of pink suds. At one spot along the trail near Aypud, Langba stopped suddenly, jabbed his walking stick sharply into the side of the trail and pulled up a small weed, *tawag kugum buladlad* (*Buchnera urticifolia* R. Br.) which he told me he will use as a lure . . . for a spring-spear boar trap. A few minutes later, and we were going at a good pace, he stopped in a similar manner to dig up a small terrestrial orchid (hardly noticeable beneath the other foliage) known as *líyamlíyam* (*Epipogum roseum* (D. Don.) Lindl.). This herb is useful in the magical control of insect pests which destroy cultivated plants. At Binli, Langha was careful not to damage those herbs when searching through the contents of his palm leaf shoulder basket for *apug* 'slaked lime' and *tabaku* (*Nicotiana tabacum* L.) to offer in exchange for other betel ingredients with the Binli folk. After an evaluative discussion about the local forms of betel pepper (*Piper betle* L.) Langba got permission to cut sweet potato (*Ipomoea batatas* (L.) Poir.) vines of two vegetatively distinguishable types, *kamuti inaswang* and *kamuti lupaw* . . . In the camote patch, we cut twenty-five vine-tip sections (about 75 cm. long) of each variety, and carefully wrapped them in the broad fresh leaves of the cultivated *saging saba* (*Musa sapientum compressa* (Blco. Teoforo) so that they would remain moist until we reached Langba's place. Along the way we munched on a few stems of *tubu minuma*, a type of sugar cane (*Saccharum officinarum* L.), stopped once to gather fallen bunga area nuts (*Areca catechu* L.), and another time to pick and eat the wild cherrylike fruits from some *bugnay* shrubs (*Antidesma brunius* (L.) Spreng). We arrived at the Mararim by mid-afternoon having spent much of our time on the trail discussing changes in the surrounding vegetation in the last few decades! (Conklin I, pp. 15–17).

This knowledge and the linguistic means which it has at its disposal also extend to morphology. In Tewa there are distinct terms for all or almost all the parts of birds and mammals (Henderson and Harrington, p. 9). Forty terms are employed in the morphological description of the leaves of trees or plants, and there are fifteen distinct terms for the different parts of a maize plant.

The Hanunóo have more than a hundred and fifty terms for the parts and properties of plants. These provide categories for the identification of plants and for 'discussing the hundreds of characteristics which differentiate plant types and often indicate significant features of medicinal or nutritional value' (Conklin I, p. 97). Over six hundred named plants have been recorded among the Pinatubo and 'in addition to having an amazing knowledge of plants and their uses, . . . (they) employ nearly one hundred terms in describing the parts or characteristics of plants' (R. B. Fox, p. 179).

Knowledge as systematically developed as this clearly cannot relate just to practical purposes. The ethnologist who has made the best study of the Indians of the north-eastern United States and Canada (the Montagnais, Naskapi, Micmac, Malecite, Penobscot) emphasizes the wealth and accuracy of their zoological and botanical knowledge and then continues:

> Such knowledge, of course, is to be expected with respect to the habits of the larger animals which furnish food and the materials of industry to primitive man. We expect, for instance, that the Penobscot hunter of Maine will have a somewhat more practical knowledge of the habits and character of the moose than even the expert zoologist. But when we realize how the Indians have taken pains to observe and systematize facts of science in the realm of lower animal life, we may perhaps be pardoned a little surprise.
>
> The whole class of reptiles . . . affords no economic benefit to these Indians; they do not eat the flesh of any snakes or batrachians, nor do they make use of other parts except in a very few cases where they serve in the preparation of charms against sickness or sorcery (Speck I, p. 273).

And nevertheless, as Speck has shown, the north-eastern Indians have developed a positive herpetology, with distinct terms for each genus of reptile and other terms applying to particular species and varieties.

The precise definition of and the specific uses ascribed to the natural products which Siberian peoples use for medicinal purposes illustrate the care and ingeniousness, the attention to detail and concern with distinctions employed by theoretical and practical workers in societies of this kind. We find, for instance: spiders and whiteworms swallowed as a cure for sterility among the Helmene and Iakoute; fat of black beetle (Ossete, hydrophobia); squashed cockroach, chicken's gall (Russians of Sourgout, abscesses and hernias); macerated redworms (Iakoute, rheumatism); pike's gall (Bouriate, eye complaints); loach and crayfish swallowed alive (Russians of Siberia, epilepsy and all diseases); contact with a woodpecker's beak, blood of a woodpecker, nasal insufflation of the powder of a mummified woodpecker, gobbled egg of the bird *koukcha* (Iakoute, against toothache, scrofula, high fevers and tuberculosis respectively); partridge's blood, horse's sweat (Oïrote, hernias and warts); pigeon broth (Bouriate, coughs); powder made of the crushed feet of the bird *tilegous* (Kazak, bite of mad dog); dried bat worn round the neck (Russians of the Altaï, fever); instillation of water from an icicle hanging on the nest of the bird *remiz* (Oïrote, eye complaints). Taking just the case of bears among the Bouriate: the flesh of bears has seven distinct therapeutic uses, the blood five, the fat nine, the brains twelve, the bile seventeen, the fur two. It is also the bear's frozen excretions which the Kalar collect at the end of the winter season to cure constipation (Zelenine, pp. 47–59). An equally extensive list for an African tribe can be found in a study by Loeb.

Examples like these could be drawn from all parts of the world and one may readily conclude that animals and plants are not known as a result of their usefulness; they are deemed to be useful or interesting because they are first of all known.

It may be objected that science of this kind can scarcely be of much practical effect. The answer to this is that its main purpose is not a practical one. It meets intellectual requirements rather than or instead of satisfying needs.

The real question is not whether the touch of a woodpecker's beak does in fact cure toothache. It is rather whether there is a point of view from which a woodpecker's beak and a man's tooth can be seen as 'going together' (the use of this congruity for therapeutic purposes being only one of its possible uses), and whether some initial order can be introduced into the universe by means of these groupings. Classifying, as opposed to not classifying, has a value of its own, whatever form the classification may take. As a recent theorist of taxonomy writes:

> Scientists do tolerate uncertainty and frustration, because they must. The one thing that they do not and must not tolerate is disorder. The whole aim of theoretical science is to carry to the highest possible and conscious degree the perceptual reduction of chaos that began in so lowly and (in all probability) unconscious a way with the origin of life. In specific instances it can well be questioned whether the order so achieved is an objective characteristic of the phenomena or is an artifact constructed by the scientist. That question comes up time after time in animal

> taxonomy . . . Nevertheless, the most basic postulate of science is that nature itself is orderly. . . . All theoretical science is ordering and if, systematics is equated with ordering, then systematics is synonymous with theoretical science (Simpson, p. 5).

The thought we call primitive is founded on this demand for order. This is equally true of all thought but it is through the properties common to all thought that we can most easily begin to understand forms of thought which seem very strange to us.

A native thinker makes the penetrating comment that 'All sacred things must have their place' (Fletcher *2*, p. 34). It could even be said that being in their place is what makes them sacred for if they were taken out of their place, even in thought, the entire order of the universe would be destroyed. Sacred objects therefore contribute to the maintenance of order in the universe by occupying the places allocated to them. Examined superficially and from the outside, the refinements of ritual can appear pointless. They are explicable by a concern for what one might call 'micro-adjustment' – the concern to assign every single creature, object or feature to a place within a class. The ceremony of the Hako among the Pawnee is particularly illuminating in this respect, although only because it has been so well analysed. The invocation which accompanies the crossing of a stream of water is divided into several parts, which correspond, respectively, to the moment when the travellers put their feet in water, the moment when they move them and the moment when the water completely covers their feet. The invocation to the wind separates the moment when only the wet parts of the body feel cool: 'Now, we are ready to move forward in safety' (id., pp. 77–8). As the informant explains: 'We must address with song every object we meet, because Tira'wa (the supreme spirit) is in all things, everything we come to as we travel can give us help . . . ' (id., pp. 73, 81).

This preoccupation with exhaustive observation and the systematic cataloguing of relations and connections can sometimes lead to scientifically valid results. The Blackfoot Indians for instance were able to prognosticate the approach of spring by the state of development of the foetus of bison which they took from the uterus of females killed in hunting. These successes cannot of course be isolated from the numerous other associations of the same kind which science condemns as illusory. It may however be the case that magical thought, that 'gigantic variation on the theme of the principle of Causality' as Hubert and Mauss called it (2, p. 61), can be distinguished from science not so much by any ignorance or contempt of determinism but by a more imperious and uncompromising demand for it which can at the most be regarded as unreasonable and precipitate from the scientific point of view.

> As a natural philosophy it (witchcraft) reveals a theory of causation. Misfortune is due to witchcraft co-operating with natural forces. If a buffalo gores a man, or the supports of a granary are undermined by termites so that it falls on his head, or he is infected with cerebro-spinal meningitis, Azande say that the buffalo, the granary, and the disease, are causes which combine with witchcraft to kill a man. Witchcraft does not create the buffalo and the granary and the disease for these exist in their own right, but it is responsible for the particular situation in which they are brought into lethal relations with a particular man. The granary would have fallen in any case, but since there was witchcraft present it fell at the particular moment when a certain man was resting beneath it. Of these causes the only one which permits intervention is witchcraft, for witchcraft emanates from a person. The buffalo and the granary do not allow of intervention and are, therefore, whilst recognized as causes, not considered the socially relevant ones (Evans-Pritchard *I*, p. 418–19).

Seen in this way, the first difference between magic and science is therefore that magic postulates a complete and all-embracing determinism. Science, on the other hand, is based on a distinction between levels: only some of these admit forms of determinism; on others the same forms of determinism are held not to apply. One can go further and think of the rigorous precision of magical thought and ritual practices as an expression of the unconscious apprehension of the *truth of determinism*, the mode in which scientific phenomena exist. In this view, the operations of determinism are divined and made use of in an all-embracing fashion before being known and properly applied, and magical rites and beliefs appear as so many expressions of an act of faith in a science yet to be born.

The nature of these anticipations is such that they may sometimes succeed. Moreover they may anticipate not only science itself but even methods or results which scientific procedure does not incorporate until an advanced stage of its development. For it seems to be the case that man began by applying himself to the most difficult task, that of systematizing what is immediately presented to the senses, on which science for a long time turned its back and which it is only beginning to bring back into its purview. In the history of scientific thought this 'anticipation-effect', has, incidentally, occurred repeatedly. As Simpson (pp. 84–5) has shown with the help of an example drawn from nineteenth-century biology, it is due to the fact that, since scientific explanation is always the discovery of an 'arrangement', any attempt of this type, even one inspired by non-scientific principles, can hit on true arrangements. This is even to be foreseen if one grants that the number of structures is by definition finite: the 'structuring' has an intrinsic effectiveness of its own whatever the principles and methods which suggested it.

Modern chemistry reduces the variety of tastes and smells to different combinations of five elements: carbon, hydrogen, oxygen, sulphur and nitrogen. By means of tables of the presence and absence of the elements and estimates of proportions and minimum amounts necessary for them to be perceptible, it succeeds in accounting for differences and resemblances which were previously excluded from its field on account of their 'secondary' character. These connections and distinctions are however no surprise to our aesthetic sense. On the contrary they increase its scope and understanding by supplying a basis for the associations it already divined; and at the same time one is better able to understand why and in what conditions it should have been possible to discover such associations solely by the systematic use of intuitive methods. Thus to a logic of sensations tobacco smoke might be the intersection of two groups, one also containing broiled meat and brown crusts of bread (which are like it in being composed of nitrogen) and the other one to which cheese, beer and honey belong on account of the presence of diacetyl. Wild cherries, cinnamon, vanilla and sherry are grouped together by the intellect as well as the senses, because they all contain aldehyde, while the closely related smells of wintergreen, lavender and bananas are to be explained by the presence of ester. On intuitive grounds alone we might group onions, garlic, cabbage, turnips, radishes and mustard together even though botany separates liliaceae and crucifers. In confirmation of the evidence of the senses, chemistry shows that these different families are united on another plane: they contain sulphur (W.K.). A primitive philosopher or a poet could have effected these regroupings on the basis of considerations foreign to chemistry or any other form of science. Ethnographic literature reveals many of equal empirical and aesthetic value. And this is not just the result of some associative madness destined sometimes to succeed simply by the law of chance. Simpson advances this interpretation in the passage quoted above; but he displays more insight when he shows that the demand for organization is a need common to art and science and that in consequence 'taxonomy, which is ordering par excellence, has eminent aesthetic value' (loc. cit., p. 4). Given this, it seems less surprising that the aesthetic sense can by itself open the way to taxonomy and even anticipate some of its results.

I am not however commending a return to the popular belief (although it has some validity in its own narrow context) according to which magic is a timid and stuttering form of science. One deprives oneself of all means of understanding magical thought if one tries to reduce it to a moment or stage in technical and scientific evolution. Like a shadow moving ahead of its owner it is in a sense complete in itself, and as finished and coherent in its immateriality as the substantial being which it precedes. Magical thought is not to be regarded as a beginning, a rudiment, a sketch, a part of a whole which has not yet materialized. It forms a well-articulated system, and is in this respect independent of that other system which constitutes science, except for the purely formal analogy which brings them together and makes the former a sort of metaphorical expression of the latter. It is therefore better, instead of contrasting magic and science, to compare them as two parallel modes of acquiring knowledge. Their theoretical and practical results differ in value, for it is true that science is more successful than magic from this point of view, although magic foreshadows science in that it is sometimes also successful. Both science and magic however require the same sort of mental operations and they differ not so much in kind as in the different types of phenomena to which they are applied.

These relations are a consequence of the objective conditions in which magic and scientific knowledge appeared. The history of the latter is short enough for us to know a good deal about it. But the fact that modern science dates back only a few centuries raises a problem which ethnologists have not sufficiently pondered. The Neolithic Paradox would be a suitable name for it.

It was in neolithic times that man's mastery of the great arts of civilization – of pottery, weaving, agriculture and the domestication of animals – became firmly established. No one today would any longer think of attributing these enormous advances to the fortuitous accumulation of a series of chance discoveries or believe them to have been revealed by the passive perception of certain natural phenomena.*

Each of these techniques assumes centuries of active and methodical observation, of bold hypotheses tested by means of endlessly repeated experiments. A biologist remarks on the rapidity with which plants from the New World have been acclimatized in the Philippines and adopted and named by the natives. In many cases they seem even to have rediscovered their medicinal uses, uses identical with those traditional in Mexico. Fox's interpretation is this:

> ... plants with bitter leaves or stems are commonly used in the Philippines for stomach disorders. If an introduced plant is found to have this characteristic, it will be quickly utilized. The fact that many Philippine groups, such as the Pinatubo Negritos, constantly experiment with plants hastens the process of the recognition of the potential usefulness, as defined by the culture, of the introduced flora (R. B. Fox, pp. 212–13).

To transform a weed into a cultivated plant, a wild beast into a domestic animal, to produce, in either of these, nutritious or technologically useful properties which were originally completely absent or could only be guessed at; to make stout, water-tight pottery out of clay which is friable and unstable, liable to pulverize or crack (which, however, is possible only if from a large number of organic and inorganic materials, the one most suitable for refining it is selected, and also the appropriate fuel, the temperature and duration of firing and the effective degree of oxidation); to work out techniques, often long and complex, which permit cultivation without soil or alternatively without water; to change toxic roots or seeds into foodstuffs or again to use their poison for hunting, war or ritual – there is no doubt that all these achievements required a genuinely scientific attitude, sustained and watchful interest and a desire for knowledge for its own sake. For only a small proportion of observations and experiments (which must be assumed to have been primarily inspired by a desire for knowledge)

* An attempt has been made to discover what would happen if copper ore had accidentally found its way into a furnace: complex and varied experiments have shown that nothing happens at all. The simplest method of obtaining metallic copper which could be discovered consisted in subjecting finely ground malachite to intense heat in a pottery dish crowned with an inverted clay pot. This, the sole result, restricts the play of chance to the confines of the kiln of some potter specializing in glazed ware (Coghlan).

could have yielded practical and immediately useful results. There is no need to dwell on the working of bronze and iron and of precious metals or even the simple working of copper ore by hammering which preceded metallurgy by several thousand years, and even at that stage they all demand a very high level of technical proficiency.

Neolithic, or early historical, man was therefore the heir of a long scientific tradition. However, had he, as well as all his predecessors, been inspired by exactly the same spirit as that of our own time, it would be impossible to understand how he could have come to a halt and how several thousand years of stagnation have intervened between the neolithic revolution and modern science like a level plain between ascents. There is only one solution to the paradox, namely, that there are two distinct modes of scientific thought. These are certainly not a function of different stages of development of the human mind but rather of two strategic levels at which nature is accessible to scientific enquiry: one roughly adapted to that of perception and the imagination: the other at a remove from it. It is as if the necessary connections which are the object of all science, neolithic or modern, could be arrived at by two different routes, one very close to, and the other more remote from, sensible intuition.

Any classification is superior to chaos and even a classification at the level of sensible properties is a step towards rational ordering. It is legitimate, in classifying fruits into relatively heavy and relatively light, to begin by separating the apples from the pears even though shape, colour and taste are unconnected with weight and volume. This is because the larger apples are easier to distinguish from the smaller if the apples are not still mixed with fruit of different features. This example already shows that classification has its advantages even at the level of aesthetic perception.

For the rest, and in spite of the fact there is no necessary connection between sensible qualities and properties, there is very often at least an empirical connection between them, and the generalization of this relation may be rewarding from the theoretical and practical point of view for a very long time even if it has no foundation in reason. Not all poisonous juices are burning or bitter nor is everything which is burning and bitter poisonous. Nevertheless, nature is so constituted that it is more advantageous if thought and action proceed as though this aesthetically satisfying equivalence also corresponded to objective reality. It seems probable, for reasons which are not relevant here, that species possessing some remarkable characteristics, say, of shape, colour or smell give the observer what might be called a 'right pending disproof' to postulate that these visible characteristics are the sign of equally singular, but concealed, properties. To treat the relation between the two as itself sensible (regarding a seed in the form of a tooth as a safeguard against snake bites, yellow juices as a cure for bilious troubles, etc.) is of more value provisionally than indifference to any connection. For even a heterogeneous and arbitrary classification preserves the richness and diversity of the collection of facts it makes. The decision that everything must be taken account of facilitates the creation of a 'memory bank'.

It is moreover a fact that particular results, to the achievement of which methods of this kind were able to lead, were essential to enable man to assail nature from a different angle. Myths and rites are far from being, as has often been held, the product of man's 'myth-making faculty',* turning its back on reality. Their principal value is indeed to preserve until the present time the remains of methods of observation and reflection which were (and no doubt still are) precisely adapted to discoveries of a certain type: those which nature authorised from the starting point of a speculative organization and exploitation of the sensible world in sensible terms. This science of the concrete was necessarily restricted by its essence to results other than those destined to be achieved by the exact natural sciences but it was no less scientific and its results no less genuine. They were secured ten thousand years earlier and still remain at the basis of our own civilization.

There still exists among ourselves an activity which on the technical plane gives us quite a good understanding of what a science we prefer to call 'prior' rather than 'primitive', could have been on the plane of speculation. This is what is commonly called 'bricolage' in French. In its old sense the verb 'bricoler' applied to ball games and billiards, to hunting, shooting and riding. It was however always used with reference to some extraneous movement: a ball rebounding, a dog straying or a horse swerving from its direct course to avoid an obstacle. And in our own time the 'bricoleur' is still someone who works with his hands and uses devious means

* The phrase is from Bergson, op. cit., 'fonction fabulatrice' (trans. note).

compared to those of a craftsman.* The characteristic feature of mythical thought is that it expresses itself by means of a heterogeneous repertoire which, even if extensive, is nevertheless limited. It has to use this repertoire, however, whatever the task in hand because it has nothing else at its disposal. Mythical thought is therefore a kind of intellectual 'bricolage' – which explains the relation which can be perceived between the two.

Like 'bricolage' on the technical plane, mythical reflection can reach brilliant unforeseen results on the intellectual plane. Conversely, attention has often been drawn to the mytho-poetical nature of 'bricolage' on the plane of so-called 'raw' or 'naive' art, in architectural follies like the villa of Cheval the postman or the stage sets of Georges Méliès, or, again, in the case immortalized by Dickens in *Great Expectations* but no doubt originally inspired by observation, of Mr Wemmick's suburban 'castle' with its miniature drawbridge, its cannon firing at nine o'clock, its bed of salad and cucumbers, thanks to which its occupants could withstand a siege if necessary . . .

The analogy is worth pursuing since it helps us to see the real relations between the two types of scientific knowledge we have distinguished. The 'bricoleur' is adept at performing a large number of diverse tasks; but, unlike the engineer, he does not subordinate each of them to the availability of raw materials and tools conceived and procured for the purpose of the project. His universe of instruments is closed and the rules of his game are always to make do with 'whatever is at hand', that is to say with a set of tools and materials which is always finite and is also heterogeneous because what it contains bears no relation to the current project, or indeed to any particular project, but is the contingent result of all the occasions there have been to renew or enrich the stock or to maintain it with the remains of previous constructions or destructions. The set of the 'bricoleur's' means cannot therefore be defined in terms of a project (which would presuppose besides, that, as in the case of the engineer, there were, at least in theory, as many sets of tools and materials or 'instrumental sets', as there are different kinds of projects). It is to be defined only by its potential

* The 'bricoleur' has no precise equivalent in English. He is a man who undertakes odd jobs and is a Jack of all trades or a kind of professional do-it-yourself man, but, as the text makes clear, he is of a different standing from, for instance, the English 'odd job man' or handyman (trans. note).

use or, putting this another way and in the language of the 'bricoleur' himself, because the elements are collected or retained on the principle that 'they may always come in handy'. Such elements are specialized up to a point, sufficiently for the 'bricoleur' not to need the equipment and knowledge of all trades and professions, but not enough for each of them to have only one definite and determinate use. They each represent a set of actual and possible relations; they are 'operators' but they can be used for any operations of the same type.

The elements of mythical thought similarly lie half-way between percepts and concepts. It would be impossible to separate percepts from the concrete situations in which they appeared, while recourse to concepts would require that thought could, at least provisionally, put its projects (to use Husserl's expression) 'in brackets'. Now, there is an intermediary between images and concepts, namely signs. For signs can always be defined in the way introduced by Saussure in the case of the particular category of linguistic signs, that is, as a link between images and concepts. In the union thus brought about, images and concepts play the part of the signifying and signified respectively.

Signs resemble images in being concrete entities but they resemble concepts in their powers of reference. Neither concepts nor signs relate exclusively to themselves; either may be substituted for something else. Concepts, however, have an unlimited capacity in this respect, while signs have not. The example of the 'bricoleur' helps to bring out the differences and similarities. Consider him at work and excited by his project. His first practical step is retrospective. He has to turn back to an already existent set made up of tools and materials, to consider or reconsider what it contains and, finally and above all, to engage in a sort of dialogue with it and, before choosing between them, to index the possible answers which the whole set can offer to his problem. He interrogates all the heterogeneous objects of which his treasury* is composed to discover what each of them could 'signify' and so contribute to the definition of a set which has yet to materialize but which will ultimately differ from the instrumental set only in the internal disposition of its parts. A particular cube of oak could be a wedge to make up for the inadequte length of a plank of pine or it could be a pedestal – which would allow the grain and polish of the old wood

* Cf. 'Treasury of ideas' as Hubert and Mauss so aptly describe magic (2, p. 136).

to show to advantage. In one case it will serve as extension, in the other as material. But the possibilities always remain limited by the particular history of each piece and by those of its features which are already determined by the use for which it was originally intended or the modifications it has undergone for other purposes. The elements which the 'bricoleur' collects and uses are 'pre-constrained' like the constitutive units of myth, the possible combinations of which are restricted by the fact that they are drawn from the language where they already possess a sense which sets a limit on their freedom of manoeuvre (Lévi-Strauss, 5, p. 35). And the decision as to what to put in each place also depends on the possibility of putting a different element there instead, so that each choice which is made will involve a complete reorganization of the structure, which will never be the same as one vaguely imagined nor as some other which might have been preferred to it.

The engineer no doubt also cross-examines his resources. The existence of an 'interlocutor' is in his case due to the fact that his means, power and knowledge are never unlimited and that in this negative form he meets resistance with which he has to come to terms. It might be said that the engineer questions the universe, while the 'bricoleur' addresses himself to a collection of oddments left over from human endeavours, that is, only a sub-set of the culture. Again, Information Theory shows that it is possible, and often useful, to reduce the physicists' approaches to a sort of dialogue with nature. This would make the distinction we are trying to draw less clearcut. There remains however a difference even if one takes into account the fact that the scientist never carries on a dialogue with nature pure and simple but rather with a particular relationship between nature and culture definable in terms of his particular period and civilization and the material means at his disposal. He is no more able than the 'bricoleur' to do whatever he wishes when he is presented with a given task. He too has to begin by making a catalogue of a previously determined set consisting of theoretical and practical knowledge, of technical means, which restrict the possible solutions.

The difference is therefore less absolute than it might appear. It remains a real one, however, in that the engineer is always trying to make his way out of and go beyond the constraints imposed by a particular state of civilization while the 'bricoleur' by inclination or necessity always remains within them. This is another way of saying that the engineer works by means of concepts and the 'bricoleur' by means of signs. The sets which each employs are at different distances from the poles on the axis of opposition between nature and culture. One way indeed in which signs can be opposed to concepts is that whereas concepts aim to be wholly transparent with respect to reality, signs allow and even require the interposing and incorporation of a certain amount of human culture into reality. Signs, in Peirce's vigorous phrase 'address somebody'.

Both the scientist and 'bricoleur' might therefore be said to be constantly on the look out for 'messages'. Those which the 'bricoleur' collects are, however, ones which have to some extent been transmitted in advance – like the commercial codes which are summaries of the past experience of the trade and so allow any new situation to be met economically, provided that it belongs to the same class as some earlier one. The scientist, on the other hand, whether he is an engineer or a physicist, is always on the look out for *that other message* which might be wrested from an interlocutor in spite of his reticence in pronouncing on questions whose answers have not been rehearsed. Concepts thus appear like operators *opening up* the set being worked with and signification like the operator of its *reorganization*, which neither extends nor renews it and limits itself to obtaining the group of its transformations.

Images cannot be ideas but they can play the part of signs or, to be more precise, co-exist with ideas in signs and, if ideas are not yet present, they can keep their future place open for them and make its contours apparent negatively. Images are fixed, linked in a single way to the mental act which accompanies them. Signs, and images which have acquired significance, may still lack comprehension; unlike concepts, they do not yet possess simultaneous and theoretically unlimited relations with other entities of the same kind. They are however already *permutable*, that is, capable of standing in successive relations with other entities – although with only a limited number and, as we have seen, only on the condition that they always form a system in which an alteration which affects one element automatically affects all the others. On this plane logicians' 'extension' and 'intension' are not two distinct and complementary aspects but one and the same thing. One understands then how mythical thought can be capable of generalizing and so be scientific, even though it is still entangled in imagery. It too works by analogies and comparisons even though its creations, like those of the 'bricoleur', always really consist of a new arrangement of elements, the nature of which is unaffected by whether they figure in the instrumental set or in the final arrangement (these being the same, apart from the internal disposition of their parts): 'it would seem that mythological worlds have been built up, only to be shattered again, and that new worlds were built from the fragments' (Boas I, p. 18). Penetrating as this comment is, it nevertheless fails to take into account that in the continual reconstruction from the same materials, it is always earlier ends which are called upon to play the part of means: the signified changes into the signifying and vice versa.

This formula, which could serve as a definition of 'bricolage', explains how an implicit inventory or conception of the total means available must be made in the case of mythical thought also, so that a result can be defined which will always be a compromise between the structure of the instrumental set and that of the project. Once it materializes the project will therefore inevitably be at a remove from the initial aim (which was moreover a mere sketch), a phenomenon which the surrealists have felicitously called 'objective hazard'. Further, the 'bricoleur' also, and indeed principally, derives his poetry from the fact that he does not confine himself to accomplishment and execution: he 'speaks' not only *with* things, as we have already seen, but also through the medium of things: giving an account of his personality and life by the choices he makes between the limited possibilities. The 'bricoleur' may not ever complete his purpose but he always puts something of himself into it.

Mythical thought appears to be an intellectual form of 'bricolage' in this sense also. Science as a whole is based on the distinction between the contingent and the necessary, this being also what distinguishes event and structure. The qualities it claimed at its outset as peculiarly scientific were precisely those which formed no part of living experience and remained outside and, as it were, unrelated to events. This is the significance of the notion of primary qualities. Now, the characteristic feature of mythical thought, as of 'bricolage' on the practical plane, is that it builds up structured sets, not directly with other structured sets* but by using the

* Mythical thought builds structured sets by means of a structured set, namely, language. But it is not at the structural level that it makes use of it: it builds ideological castles out of the debris of what was once a social discourse.

remains and debris of events: in French 'des bribes et des morceaux', or odds and ends in English, fossilized evidence of the history of an individual or a society. The relation between the diachronic and the synchronic is therefore in a sense reversed. Mythical thought, that 'bricoleur', builds up structures by fitting together events, or rather the remains of events,* while science, 'in operation' simply by virtue of coming into being, creates its means and results in the form of events, thanks to the structures which it is constantly elaborating and which are its hypotheses and theories. But it is important not to make the mistake of thinking that these are two stages or phases in the evolution of knowledge. Both approaches are equally valid. Physics and chemistry are already striving to become qualitative again, that is, to account also for secondary qualities which when they have been explained will in their turn become means of explanation. And biology may perhaps be marking time waiting for this before it can itself explain life. Mythical thought for its part is imprisoned in the events and experiences which it never tires of ordering and re-ordering in its search to find them a meaning. But it also acts as a liberator by its protest against the idea that anything can be meaningless with which science at first resigned itself to a compromise.

The problem of art has been touched on several times in the foregoing discussion, and it is worth showing briefly how, from this point of view, art lies half-way between scientific knowledge and mythical or magical thought. It is common knowledge that the artist is both something of a scientist and of a 'bricoleur'. By his craftsmanship he constructs a material object which is also an object of knowledge. We have already distinguished the scientist and the 'bricoleur' by the inverse functions which they assign to events and structures as ends and means, the scientist creating events (changing the world) by means of structures and the 'bricoleur' creating structures by means of events. This is imprecise in this crude form but our analysis makes it possible for us to refine it. Let us now look at this portrait of a woman by Clouet and consider the reason for the very profound aesthetic emotion which is, apparently inexplicably, aroused by the highly realistic, thread by thread, reproduction of a lace collar (Plate 1).

The choice of this example is not accidental. Clouet is known to

* 'Bricolage' also works with 'secondary' qualities, i.e. 'second hand'.

have liked to paint at less than life-size. His paintings are therefore, like Japanese gardens, miniature vehicles and ships in bottles, what in the 'bricoleur's' language are called 'small-scale models' or 'miniatures'. Now, the question arises whether the small-scale model or miniature, which is also the 'masterpiece' of the journeyman may not in fact be the universal type of the work of art. All miniatures seem to have intrinsic aesthetic quality – and from what should they draw this constant virtue if not from the dimensions themselves? – and conversely the vast majority of works of art are small-scale. It might be thought that this characteristic is principally a matter of economy in materials and means, and one might appeal in support of this theory to works which are incontestably artistic but also on a grand scale. We have to be clear about definitions. The paintings of the Sistine Chapel are a small-scale model in spite of their imposing dimensions, since the theme which they depict is the End of Time. The same is true of the cosmic symbolism of religious monuments. Further, we may ask whether the aesthetic effect, say, of an equestrian statue which is larger than life derives from its enlargement of a man to the size of a rock or whether it is not rather due to the fact that it restores what is at first from a distance seen as a rock to the proportions of a man. Finally even 'natural size' implies a reduction of scale since graphic or plastic transposition always involves giving up certain dimensions of the object: volume in painting, colour, smell, tactile impressions in sculpture and the temporal dimension in both cases since the whole work represented is apprehended at a single moment in time.

What is the virtue of reduction either of scale or in the number of properties? It seems to result from a sort of reversal in the process of understanding. To understand a real object in its totality we always tend to work from its parts. The resistance it offers us is overcome by dividing it. Reduction in scale reverses this situation. Being smaller, the object as a whole seems less formidable. By being quantitatively diminished, it seems to us qualitatively simplified. More exactly, this quantitative transposition extends and diversifies our power over a homologue of the thing, and by means of it the latter can be grasped, assessed and apprehended at a glance. A child's doll is no longer an enemy, a rival or even an interlocutor. In it and through it a person is made into a subject. In the case of miniatures, in contrast to what happens when we try to understand an object or living creature of real dimensions, knowledge of the whole precedes knowledge of the parts. And even if this is an illusion, the point of the procedure is to create or sustain the illusion, which gratifies the intelligence and gives rise to a sense of pleasure which can already be called aesthetic on these grounds alone.

I have so far only considered matters of scale which, as we have just seen, imply a dialectical relation between size (i.e. quantity) and quality. But miniatures have a further feature. They are 'man made' and, what is more, made by hand. They are therefore not just projections or passive homologues of the object: they constitute a real experiment with it. Now the model being an artefact, it is possible to understand how it is made and this understanding of the method of construction adds a supplementary dimension. As we have already seen in the case of 'bricolage', and the example of 'styles' of painters shows that the same is true in art, there are several solutions to the same problem. The choice of one solution involves a modification of the result to which another solution would have led, and the observer is in effect presented with the general picture of these permutations at the same time as the particular solution offered. He is thereby transformed into an active participant without even being aware of it. Merely by contemplating it he is, as it were, put in possession of other possible forms of the same work; and in a confused way, he feels himself to be their creator with more right than the creator himself because the latter abandoned them in excluding them from his creation. And these forms are so many further perspectives opening out on to the work which has been realized. In other words, the intrinsic value of a small-scale model is that it compensates for the renunciation of sensible dimensions by the acquisition of intelligible dimensions.

Let us now return to the lace collar in Clouet's picture. Everything that has been said applies in this case, for the procedure necessary to represent it as a projection, in a particular space, of properties whose sensible dimensions are fewer and smaller than that of the object is exactly the reverse of that which science would have employed had it proposed, in accordance with its function, to produce (instead of reproducing) not only a new, instead of an already known, piece of lace but also real lace instead of a picture of lace. Science would have worked on the real scale but by means of inventing a loom, while art works on a diminished scale to produce an image homologous with the object. The former approach is of a metonymical order, it replaces one thing by another thing, an effect by its cause, while the latter is of a metaphorical order.

This is not all. For if it is true that the relation of priority between structure and event is exactly the opposite in science and 'bricolage', then it is clear that art has an intermediate position from this point of view as well. Even if, as we have shown, the depiction of a lace collar in miniature demands an intimate knowledge of its morphology and technique of manufacture (and had it been a question of the representation of people or animals we should have said: of anatomy and physical attitudes), it is not just a diagram or blueprint. It manages to synthesize these intrinsic properties with properties which depend on a spatial and temporal context. The final product is the lace collar exactly as it is but so that at the same time its appearance is affected by the particular perspective. This accentuates some parts and conceals others, whose existence however still influences the rest through the contrast between its whiteness and the colour of the other clothes, the reflection of the pearly neck it encircles and that of the sky on a particular day and at a particular time of day. The appearance of the lace collar is also affected by whether it indicates casual or formal dress, is worn, either new or previously used, either freshly ironed or creased, by an ordinary woman or a queen, whose physiognomy confirms, contradicts or qualifies her status in a particular social class, society, part of the world and period of history . . . The painter is always mid-way between design and anecdote, and his genius consists in uniting internal and external knowledge, a 'being' and a 'becoming', in producing with his brush an object which does not exist as such and which he is nevertheless able to create on his canvas. This is a nicely balanced synthesis of one or more artificial and natural structures and one or more natural and social events. The aesthetic emotion is the result of this union between the structural order and the order of events, which is brought about within a thing created by man and so also in effect by the observer who discovers the possibility of such a union through the work of art.

Several points are suggested by this analysis. In the first place, the analysis helps us to see why we are inclined to think of myths both as systems of abstract relations and as objects of aesthetic contemplation. The creative act which gives rise to myths is in fact exactly the reverse of that which gives rise to works of art. In the case of works of art, the starting point is a set of one or more objects and one or more events which aesthetic creation unifies by revealing a common structure. Myths travel the same road but start from the other end. They use a structure to produce what is itself an object consisting of a set of events (for all myths tell a story). Art thus proceeds from a set (object + event) to the *discovery* of its structure. Myth starts from a structure by means of which it *constructs* a set (object + event).

The first point tempts one to generalize the theory. The second might seem to lead to a restriction of it. For we may ask whether it is in fact the case that works of art are always an integration of structure and event. This does not on the face of it seem to be true for instance of the cedarwood Tlingit club, used to kill fish, which I have in front of me on my bookshelf (Plate 2). The artist who carved it in the form of a sea monster intended the body of the implement to be fused with the body of the animal and the handle with its tail, and that the anatomical proportions, taken from a fabulous creature, should be such that the object could *be* the cruel animal slaying helpless victims, at the same time as an easily handled, balanced and efficient fishing utensil. Everything about this implement – which is also a superb work of art – seems to be a matter of structure: its mythical symbolism as well as its practical function. More accurately, the object, its function and its symbolism seem to be inextricably bound up with each other and to form a closed system in which there is no place for events. The monster's position, appearance and expression owe nothing to the historical circumstances in which the artist saw it, in the flesh or in a dream, or conceived the idea of it. It is rather as if its immutable being were finally fixed in the wood whose fine grain allows the reproduction of all its aspects and in the use for which its empirical form seems to pre-determine it. And all this applies equally to the other products of primitive art: an African statue or a Melanesian mask ... So it looks as if we have defined only one local and historical form of aesthetic creation and not its fundamental properties or those by means of which its intelligible relations with other forms of creation can be described.

We have only to widen our explanation to overcome this difficulty. What, with reference to a picture of Clouet's, was provisionally defined as an event or set of events now appears under a broader heading: events in this sense are only one mode of the contingent whose integration (perceived as necessary) into a structure gives rise to the aesthetic emotion. This is so whatever the type of art in question. Depending on the style, place and period the contingent plays a part in three different ways or at three distinct points in artistic creation (or in all of them). It may play a part in the occasion for the work or in the execution of the work or in the purpose for which it is intended. It is only in the first case that it takes the form of an event properly speaking, that is, of contingency exterior and prior to the creative act. The artist perceives it from without as an attitude, an expression, a light effect or a situation, whose sensible and intellectual relations to the structure of the object affected by these modalities he grasps and incorporates in his work. But the contingent can also play an intrinsic part in the course of execution itself, in the size or shape of the piece of wood the sculptor lays hands on, in the direction and quality of its grain, in the imperfections of his tools, in the resistance which his materials or project offer to the work in the course of its accomplishment, in the unforeseeable incidents arising during work. Finally, the contingent can be extrinsic as in the first case but posterior, instead of anterior, to the act of creation. This is the case whenever the work is destined for a specific end, since the artist will construct it with a view to its potential condition and successive uses in the future and so will put himself, consciously or unconsciously, in the place of the person for whose use it is intended.

The process of artistic creation therefore consists in trying to communicate (within the immutable framework of a mutual confrontation of structure and accident) either with the *model* or with the *materials* or with the future *user* as the case may be, according to which of these the artist particularly looks to for his directions while he is at work. Each case roughly corresponds to a readily identifiable form of art: the first to the plastic arts of the West, the second to so-called primitive or early art and the third to the applied arts. But it would be an oversimplification to take these identifications very strictly. All forms of art allow all three aspects and they are only distinguished from one another by the relative proportion of each. Even the most academic of painters comes up against problems of execution, for example. All the so-called primitive arts can be called applied in a double sense: first, because many of their productions are technical objects and, secondly, because even those which seem most divorced from practical preoccupations have a definite purpose. Finally, as we know, implements lend themselves to disinterested contemplation even among ourselves.

With these reservations, it is easy to show that the three aspects are functionally related and that the predominance of any one of them leaves less or no place for the others. So-called professional painting is, or believes itself to be, quite free so far as both execution and purpose are concerned. Its best examples display a complete mastery of technical difficulties – which, indeed, can be considered to have been completely overcome since Van der Weyden; the problems which painters have set themselves since then amount to little more than a game of technical refinement. In the extreme case it is as though, given his canvas, paints and brushes, the painter were able to do exactly what he pleased. On the other hand, he also tries to make his work into an object independent of anything contingent, of value in itself and for itself. This is indeed what the formula of the 'easel picture' implies. Freed from the contingent both with regard to execution and purpose professional painting can, then, bring it to bear upon the occasion of the work, and indeed if this account is correct it is bound to do so. Professional painting can therefore be defined as 'genre' painting if the sense of this expression is considerably widened. For, from the very general viewpoint we are taking, the attempt of a portrait painter – even of a Rembrandt – to recapture on his canvas his model's most revealing expression or secret thoughts belongs to the same genre as that of a painter like Detaille, whose compositions reproduce the hour and order of battle and the number and disposition of the buttons distinguishing the uniforms of each Arm. To use a disrespectful analogy, 'opportunity makes the thief'* in either case. The relative proportions of the three aspects are reversed in the applied arts. In these, first place is given to purpose and execution, contingent factors playing an approximately equal part in each, in the examples we consider the most 'pure', at the same time the occasion of the work plays no part. This can be seen from the fact that a wine cup or goblet, a piece of basket work or a fabric seems to us perfect when its practical value manifestly transcends time and corresponds wholly to its functions for men of different periods and civilizations. If the difficulties of execution are entirely mastered, as is the case when it is entrusted to machines,

* In the original: 'l'occasion fait le larron' (trans. note).

the purpose can become more and more precise and specific and applied art is transformed into industrial art. We call it peasant or folk art if the reverse is the case. Finally, primitive art is the opposite of professional or academic art. Professional or academic art internalizes execution (which it has, or believes itself to have, mastered) and purpose ('art for art's sake' being an end in itself). As a result, it is impelled to externalize the occasion (which it requires the model to provide) and the latter thus becomes a part of the signified. Primitive art, on the other hand, internalizes the occasion (since the supernatural beings which it delights in representing have a reality which is timeless and independent of circumstances) and it externalizes execution and purpose which thus become a part of the signifying.

On a different plane we therefore find once more this dialogue with the materials and means of execution by which we defined 'bricolage'. The essential problem for the philosophy of art is to know whether the artist regards them as interlocutors or not. No doubt they are always regarded as such, although least of all in art which is too professional and most of all in the raw or naive art which verges on 'bricolage', to the detriment of structure in both cases. No form of art is, however, worthy of the name if it allows itself to come entirely under the sway of extraneous contingencies, whether of occasion or purpose. If it did so it would rate as an icon (supplementary to the model) or as an implement (complementary with the material worked). Even the most professional art succeeds in moving us only if it arrests in time this dissipation of the contingent in favour of the pretext and incorporates it in the work, thereby investing it with the dignity of being an object in its own right. In so far as early art, primitive art and the 'primitive' periods of professional painting are the only ones which do not date, they owe it to this dedication of the accidental to the service of execution and so to the use, which they try to make complete, of the raw datum as the empirical material of something meaningful.*

* Pursuing this analysis, one might define non-representational painting by two features. One, which it has in common with 'easel' painting, consists in a total rejection of the contingency of purpose: the picture is not made for a particular use. The other feature characteristic of non-representational painting is its methodical exploitation of the contingency of execution, which is claimed to afford the external pretext or occasion of the picture. Non-representational painting adopts 'styles' as 'subjects'. It claims to give a concrete representation of the formal conditions of all painting. Paradoxically the result is that non-representational painting does not, as it thinks, create works which are as real as,

It is necessary to add that the balance between structure and event, necessity and contingency, the internal and external is a precarious one. It is constantly threatened by forces which act in one direction or the other according to fluctuations in fashion, style or general social conditions. From this point of view, it would seem that impressionism and cubism are not so much two successive stages in the development of painting as partners in the same enterprise, which, although not exact contemporaries, nevertheless collaborated by complementary distortions to prolong a mode of expression whose very existence, as we are better able to appreciate today, was seriously threatened. The intermittent fashion for 'collages', originating when craftsmanship was dying, could not for its part be anything but the transposition of 'bricolage' into the realms of contemplation. Finally, the stress on the event can also break away at certain times through greater emphasis either on transient social phenomena (as in the case of Greuze at the end of the eighteenth century or with socialist realism) or on transient natural, or even meteorological, phenomena (impressionism) at the expense of structure, 'structure' here being understood as 'structure of the same level', for the possibility of the structural aspect being re-established elsewhere on a new plane is not ruled out.

We have seen that there are analogies between mythical thought on the theoretical, and 'bricolage' on the practical plane and that artistic creation lies mid-way between science and these two forms of activity. There are relations of the same type between games and rites.

All games are defined by a set of rules which in practice allow the playing of any number of matches. Ritual, which is also 'played', is on the other hand, like a favoured instance of a game, remembered from among the possible ones because it is the only one which results in a particular type of equilibrium between the two sides. The transposition is readily seen in the case of the Gahuku-Gama of New Guinea who have learnt football but who will play, several days running, as many matches as are necessary for both

if not more real than, the objects of the physical world, but rather realistic imitations of non-existent models. It is a school of academic painting in which each artist strives to represent the manner in which he would execute his pictures if by chance he were to paint any.

sides to reach the same score (Read, p. 429). This is treating a game as a ritual.

The same can be said of the games which took place among the Fox Indians during adoption ceremonies. Their purpose was to replace a dead relative by a living one and so to allow the final departure of the soul of the deceased.* The main aim of funeral rites among the Fox seems indeed to be to get rid of the dead and to prevent them from avenging on the living their bitterness and their regret that they are no longer among them. For native philosophy resolutely sides with the living: 'Death is a hard thing. Sorrow is especially hard'.

Death originated in the destruction by supernatural powers of the younger of two mythical brothers who are cultural heroes among all the Algonkin. But it was not yet final. It was made so by the elder brother when, in spite of his sorrow, he rejected the ghost's request to be allowed to return to his place among the living. Men must follow this example and be firm with the dead. The living must make them understand that they have lost nothing by dying since they regularly receive offerings of tobacco and food. In return they are expected to compensate the living for the reality of death which they recall to them and for the sorrow their demise causes them by guaranteeing them long life, clothes and something to eat. 'It is the dead who make food increase', a native informant explains. 'They (the Indians) must coax them that way' (Michelson I, pp. 369, 407).

Now, the adoption rites which are necessary to make the soul of the deceased finally decide to go where it will take on the role of a protecting spirit are normally accompanied by competitive sports, games of skill or chance between teams which are constituted on the basis of an *ad hoc* division into two sides, Tokan and Kicko. It is said explicitly over and over again that it is the living and the dead who are playing against each other. It is as if the living offered the dead the consolation of a last match before finally being rid of them. But, since the two teams are asymmetrical in what they stand for, the outcome is inevitably determined in advance:

> This is how it is when they play ball. When the man for whom the adoption-feast is held is a Tokana, the Tokanagi win the game. The Kickoagi cannot win. And if it is a Kicko woman for whom the adoption-

* See below, p. 199 n.

feast is given, the Kickoagi win, as in turn the Tokanagi do not win (Michelson I, p. 385).

And what is in fact the case? It is clear that it is only the living who win in the great biological and social game which is constantly taking place between the living and the dead. But, as all the North American mythology confirms, to win a game is symbolically to 'kill' one's opponent; this is depicted as really happening in innumerable myths. By ruling that they should always win, the dead are given the illusion that it is they who are really alive, and that their opponents, having been 'killed' by them, are dead. Under the guise of playing with the dead, one plays them false and commits them. The formal structure of what might at first sight be taken for a competitive game is in fact identical with that of a typical ritual such as the Mitawit or Midewinin of these same Algonkin peoples in which the initiates get symbolically killed by the dead whose part is *played* by the initiated; they feign death in order to obtain a further lease of life. In both cases, death is brought in but only to be duped.

Games thus appear to have a *disjunctive* effect: they end in the establishment of a difference between individual players or teams where originally there was no indication of inequality. And at the end of the game they are distinguished into winners and losers. Ritual, on the other hand, is the exact inverse; it *conjoins*, for it brings about a union (one might even say communion in this context) or in any case an organic relation between two initially separate groups, one ideally merging with the person of the officiant and the other with the collectivity of the faithful. In the case of games the symmetry is therefore preordained and it is of a structural kind since it follows from the principle that the rules are the same for both sides. Asymmetry is engendered: it follows inevitably from the contingent nature of events, themselves due to intention, chance or talent. The reverse is true of ritual. There is an asymmetry which is postulated in advance between profane and sacred, faithful and officiating, dead and living, initiated and uninitiated, etc., and the 'game' consists in making all the participants pass to the winning side by means of events, the nature and ordering of which is genuinely structural. Like science (though here again on both the theoretical and the practical plane) the game produces events by means of a structure; and we can therefore understand why competitive games should flourish in our industrial societies. Rites and myths, on the other hand, like 'bricolage' (which these same societies only tolerate as a hobby or pastime), take to pieces and reconstruct sets of events (on a psychical, socio-historical or technical plane) and use them as so many indestructible pieces for structural patterns in which they serve alternatively as ends or means.

CHAPTER TWO

THE LOGIC OF TOTEMIC CLASSIFICATIONS

There is certainly something paradoxical about the idea of a logic whose terms consist of odds and ends left over from psychological or historical processes and are, like these, devoid of necessity. Logic consists in the establishment of necessary connections and how, we may ask, could such relations be established between terms in no way designed to fulfil this function? Propositions cannot be rigorously connected unless the terms they contain have first been unequivocally defined. It might seem as if in the preceding pages we had undertaken the impossible task of discovering the conditions of an *a posteriori* necessity.

Against this it may be said that, in the first place, these odds and ends appear as such only in relation to the history which produced them and not from the point of view of the logic for which they are used. It is with respect to content alone that they can be regarded as heterogeneous for, so far as form is concerned, there is an analogy between them, which the example of bricolage made it possible to define. The analogy consists in the incorporation in their form itself of a certain amount of content, which is roughly the same for all. The significant images of myth, the materials of the bricoleur, are elements which can be defined by two criteria: they have *had a use*, as words in a piece of discourse which mythical thought 'detaches' in the same way as a bricoleur, in the course of repairing them, detaches the cogwheels of an old alarm clock; and *they can be used again* either for the same purpose or for a different one if they are at all diverted from their previous function.

Secondly, neither the images of myth nor the materials of the bricoleur are products of 'becoming' pure and simple. Previously, when they were part of other coherent sets, they possessed the rigour which they seem to lack as soon as we observe them in their new use. What is more, they still possess this precision in so far as they are not raw materials but wrought products: terms in language or, in the case of the bricoleur, in a technological system. They are therefore condensed expressions of necessary relations which impose constraints with various repercussions at each stage of their employment. Their necessity is not simple and univocal. But it is there nevertheless as the invariance of a semantic or aesthetic order, which characterizes the group of transformations to which they lend themselves, which, as we have seen, are not unlimited.

This logic works rather like a kaleidoscope, an instrument which also contains bits and pieces by means of which structural patterns are realized. The fragments are products of a process of breaking up and destroying, in itself a contingent matter, but they have to be homologous in various respects, such as size, brightness of colouring, transparency. They can no longer be considered entities in their own right in relation to the manufactured objects of whose 'discourse' they have become the indefinable debris, but they must be so considered from a different point of view if they are to participate usefully in the formation of a new type of entity: one consisting of patterns in which, through the play of mirrors, reflections are equivalent to real objects, that is, in which signs assume the status of things signified. These patterns actualize possibilities whose number, though it may be very great, is not unlimited, for it is a function of the possible lay-out and balances which may be effected between bodies whose number itself is finite. Finally, and most important, these patterns produced by the conjunction of contingent events (the turning of the instrument by the person looking through it) and a law (namely that governing the construction of the kaleidescope, which corresponds to the invariant element of the constraints just mentioned) project models of intelligibility which are in a way provisional, since each pattern can be expressed in terms of strict relations between its parts and since these relations have no content apart from the pattern itself, to which no object in the observer's experience corresponds – even though, by such a manoeuvre, particular objective structures, such as those of snow crystals or certain types of radiolaria and diatomaceae might be revealed while their empirical basis were yet unknown, to the observer who had not yet seen them.

One can conceive that such a concrete logic may be possible. It now remains to define its features and the way in which they can be observed in the course of ethnographic enquiry. Both an affective and an intellectual aspect become apparent.

The beings which native thought endows with significance are seen as exhibiting a certain affinity with man. The Ojibwa believe in a universe of supernatural beings:

> Yet to call these beings supernatural slightly misinterprets the Indians' conception. They are a part of the natural order of the universe no less than man himself, whom they resemble in the possession of intelligence and emotions. Like man, too, they are male or female, and in some cases at least may even have families of their own. Some are tied down to definite localities, some move from place to place at will; some are friendly to Indians, other hostile (Jenness 2, p. 29).

Other observations emphasize that the feeling of indentification is stronger than the sense of difference:

> A Hawaiian's oneness with the living aspect of native phenomena, that is, with spirit and God and with other persons as souls, is not correctly described by the word rapport, and certainly not by such words as sympathy, empathy, abnormal, supernormal or neurotic, mystical or magical. It is not 'extra-sensory', for it is partly of-the-sense and not-of-the-senses. It is just a part of natural consciousness for the normal Hawaiian . . . (Handy and Pukui, Part VI, vol. 62, p. 124).

The natives themselves are sometimes acutely aware of the 'concrete' nature of their science and contrast it sharply with that of the whites:

> We know what the animals do, what are the needs of the beaver, the bear, the salmon, and other creatures, because long ago men married them and acquired this knowledge from their animal wives. Today the priests say we lie, but we know better. The white man has been only a short time in this country and knows very little about the animals; we have lived here thousands of years and were taught long ago by the animals themselves. The white man writes everything down in a book so that it will not be forgotten; but our ancestors married the animals, learned all their ways, and passed on the knowledge from one generation to another (Jenness 3, p. 540).

This disinterested, attentive, fond and affectionate lore acquired and transmitted through the attachments of marriage and upbringing is here described with such noble simplicity that it seems superfluous to conjure up the bizarre hypotheses suggested to philosophers by too theoretical a view of the development of human knowledge. Nothing here calls for the intervention of a so-called 'principle of participation' or even for a mysticism embedded in metaphysics which we now perceive only through the distorting lens of the established religions.

The way in which this concrete knowledge works, its means and methods, the affective values with which it is imbued are to be found and can be observed very close to us, among those of our contemporaries whose tastes and profession put them in a situation in relation to animals which, *mutatis mutandis*, comes as close as our civilization allows to that which is usual among all hunting peoples, namely circus people and people working in zoos. Nothing is more instructive in this respect, after the native evidence just quoted, then the account given by the director of the Zürich zoo of his first tête-à-tête – if one may so call it – with a dolphin. He notes 'its exaggerated human eyes, its strange breathing hole, the torpedo shape and colour of its body, the completely smooth and waxy texture of its skin and not least its four impressive rows of equally sharp teeth in its beak-like mouth', but describes his feelings thus:

> Flippy was no fish, and when he looked at you with twinkling eyes from a distance of less than two feet, you had to stifle the question as to whether it was in fact an animal. So new, strange and extremely weird was this creature, that one was tempted to consider it as some kind of bewitched being. But the zoologist's brain kept on associating it with the cold fact, painful in this connection, that it was known to science by the dull name, *Tursiops truncatus* (Hediger, p. 138).

Comment like this from the pen of a man of science is enough to show if indeed it is necessary, that theoretical knowledge is not incompatible with sentiment and that knowledge can be both objective and subjective at the same time. It also shows that the concrete relations between man and other living creatures sometimes, especially in civilizations in which science means 'natural science', colour the entire universe of scientific knowledge with their own emotional tone, which is itself the result of this primitive identification and, as Rousseau saw with his profound insight, responsible for all thought and society. But if a zoologist can combine taxonomy and the warmest affection, there is no reason to invoke distinct principles to explain the conjunction of these two attitudes in the thought of so-called primitive peoples.

Following Griaule, Dieterlen and Zahan have established the extensiveness and the systematic nature of native classification in the Sudan. The Dogon divide plants into twenty-two main families, some of which are further divided into eleven sub-groups. The twenty-two families, listed in the appropriate order, are divided into two series, one of which is composed of the families of odd numbers and the other of those of even ones. In the former, which symbolizes single births, the plants called male and female are associated with the rainy and the dry seasons respectively. In the latter, which symbolizes twin births, there is the same relation but in reverse. Each family is also allocated to one of three categories: tree, bush, grass;* finally, each family corresponds to a part of the body, a technique, a social class and an institution (Dieterlen *I*, 2).

Facts of this kind caused surprise when they were first brought back from Africa. Very similar modes of classification had, however, been described considerably earlier in America, and it was these which inspired Durkheim's and Mauss's famous essay. The reader is referred to it, but it is worth adding a few further examples.

The Navaho Indians, who regard themselves as 'great classifiers', divide living creatures into two categories on the basis of whether they are or are not endowed with speech. The category of creatures without speech consists of animals and plants. Animals are divided into three groups, 'running', 'flying' and 'crawling'. Each of these groups is further divided in two ways: into 'travellers by land' and 'travellers by water' and into 'travellers by day' and 'travellers by night'. The division into species obtained by this means is not always the same as that of zoology. Thus birds grouped in pairs on the basis of a classification into male and female are in fact sometimes of the same sex but of different kinds. For the association is based on the one hand on their relative size and, on the other, on their place in the classification of colours and the function

* Among the Fulani: plants with vertical trunks, climbing plants, creeping plants, respectively subdivided into plants with and without thorns, with and without bark and with or without fruit (Hampaté Ba and Dieterlen, p. 23). Cf. Conklin I, pp. 92–4 for a tripartite classification of the same type in the Philippines ('tree', 'creeper', 'grass') and Colbacchini, p. 202, for one in Brazil among the Bororo ('trees' = land; 'creepers' = air and 'marsh-plants' = water).

assigned to them in magic and ritual (Reichard, 1, 2).* But native taxonomy is often precise and unambiguous enough to allow certain identifications, for instance, the one made only a few years ago of the 'Great Fly', mentioned in myths, with a tachinid *Hystricia pollinosa*.

Plants are named on the basis of three sorts of characteristics: their supposed sex, their medicinal properties and their visual or tactual appearance (prickly, sticky, etc.). Each of these three groups is subdivided into three further groups according to size (large, medium, small). The classification is of the same kind throughout the reserve of some twenty-five thousand square miles, in spite of the dispersion of its sixty thousand occupants over this rather extensive territory (Reichard, Wyman and Harris, Vestal, Elmore).

Each animal or plant corresponds to a natural element, itself dependent on rites whose extreme complexity among the Navaho is well known. The following correspondences are found in the 'Flint-Chant': crane – sky, red songbird – sun; eagle – mountain; hawk – rock; bluebird – tree; hummingbird – plant; cornbeetle – earth; heron – water (Haile, pp. 120–1).

The Hopi, like the Zuni who particularly engaged Durkheim's and Mauss's attention, classify living creatures and natural phenomena by means of a vast system of correspondences. The facing table is based on the information scattered in several authors. It is undoubtedly only a modest fragment of an entire system, many of whose elements are missing.

Similar correspondences are also known among people whose social structure is very much looser than that of the Pueblo: the Eskimo sculptor of salmon uses the wood whose colour is closest to that of their flesh for carving each species: 'All woods, they say, are salmon' (Rasmussen, p. 198).

These are only a few of the examples which might be given. There would be even more examples than there are, had ethnologists not often been prevented from trying to find out about the complex and consistent conscious systems of societies they were studying by the assumptions they made about the simpleness and coarseness of 'primitives'. It did not occur to them that there could be such systems in societies of so low an economic and

* In contrast to the Canela of Brazil, who 'In all known cases, showed themselves to be informed about sexual dimorphism' (Vanzolini, p. 170).

	NORTH-WEST	SOUTH-WEST	SOUTH-EAST	NORTH-EAST	ZENITH	NADIR
COLOURS	yellow	blue, green	red	white	black	multicoloured
ANIMALS	puma	bear	wild cat	wolf	vulture	snake
BIRDS	oriole	blue-bird (*Sialia*)	parrot	magpie	swallow	warbler
TREES	Douglas-fir	white pine	red willow	aspen		
BUSHES	green rabbit-brush (*chrysothamnus*)	sage-brush (*Artemisia*)	cliff-rose (*Cowania stansburiana*)	grey rabbit-brush (*Chrysothamnus*)		
FLOWERS	mariposa lily (*calochortus*)	larkspur (*delphinium*)	(*Castilleja*)	(*Anogra*)		
CORN	yellow	blue	red	white	purple	sweet
BEANS	French bean (*Phaseolus vulg.*)	Butter-bean (*Phas. vulg.*)	dwarf bean	lima bean (*Phaseolus lunatus*	various	

Beans were also subdivided into:

light	light	white	white	blue
black	yellow	black	grey	red
red	brown	spotted	yellow	pink
			red	etc.
			black	

technical level since they made the unwarranted assumption that their intellectual level must be equally low. And it is only just beginning to be realized that the older accounts which we owe to the insight of such rare inquirers as Cushing do not describe exceptional cases but rather forms of science and thought which are extremely widespread in so-called primitive societies. We must therefore alter our traditional picture of this primitiveness. The 'savage' has certainly never borne any resemblance either to that creature barely emerged from an animal condition and still a prey to his needs and instincts who has so often been imagined nor to that consciousness governed by emotions and lost in a maze of confusion and participation. The examples given, and others which could be added, are evidence of thought which is experienced in all the exercises of speculation and resembles that of the naturalists and alchemists of antiquity and the middle ages: Galen, Pliny, Hermes Trismegistus, Albertus Magnus ... From this point of view 'totemic' classifications are probably closer than they look to the plant emblem systems of the Greeks and Romans, which were expressed by means of wreaths of olive, oak, laurel, wild celery, etc., or again to that practised by the medieval church where the choir was strewn with hay, rushes, ivy or sand according to the festival.

Astrological herbalism distinguished seven planetary plants, twelve herbs associated with signs of the zodiac and thirty-six plants assigned to decantates and to horoscopes. Some had to be gathered on a particular day and at a particular time in order to be effective. These were specified for each: Sunday for hazel nut and olive; Monday for rue, clover, peonies and endives; Tuesday for vervain; Wednesday for periwinkle; Thursday for vervain, periwinkle, peonies, laburnum and cinquefoil if these were intended for medicinal use; Friday for endives, mandrake and vervain used for incantations; Saturday for crosswort and plantain. In Theophrastus one even finds a system of correspondence between plants and birds, in which the peony is associated with the woodpecker, centaury with the triorchis and falcon and black hellebore with the eagle (Delatte).

All this, which we are perfectly willing to attribute to a natural philosophy worked out over the years by specialists with a tradition of centuries behind them, is very closely reproduced in exotic societies. The Omaha Indians consider one of the main differences between themselves and the whites to be that 'Indians never pick flowers', that is, never picked them for pleasure. For 'plants have sacred uses known (only) to the secret owners'. Even soapweed which is commonly used for steam baths to cure toothache, earache or rheumatism is lifted as though it were a sacred root:

> In the hole from which the root was withdrawn a pinch of tobacco was left. Often a knife or some money was left there also, and the taker of the root uttered a brief prayer, 'I have taken what you have given, and I am leaving this here for you. I want to lead a long life and to have no harm strike me or my family' (Fortune I, p. 175).

When a medicine man of eastern Canada gathers roots or leaves or bark for medicines, he is careful to propitiate the soul of each plant by placing a tiny offering at its base. For he believes that without the co-operation of the soul the mere 'body' of the plant can work no cures (Jenness I, p. 60).

The Fulani of the Sudan class plants in series, each being related to a day of the week and to one of eight directions:

> The plant . . . must be gathered in accordance with these various classifications . . . Bark, root, leaves or fruits must be collected on the day of the lunar month to which the plant corresponds, the *lare*, the 'guardian spirit' of the flocks which is related to the sequence of the months, must be invoked and the sun must be in the right position. Thus in giving directions the *silatigi* will say for instance: 'To do such and such, you must take the leaf of a thorny climber which is without bark on such and such a day when the sun is in such and such a position, facing in such and such a direction and invoking such and such a *lare*' (Hampaté Ba and Dieterlen, p. 23).

Native classifications are not only methodical and based on carefully built up theoretical knowledge. They are also at times comparable from a formal point of view, to those still in use in zoology and botany.

The Aymara Indians of the Bolivian plateau (who may be descended from the legendary Colla to whom the great civilization of Tiahuanaco is attributed) are able experimenters in the preservation of foodstuffs. It was by direct imitation of their technique of dehydration that the American army was able during the last war to reduce the rations of powdered potatoes sufficient for a hundred meals to the volume of a shoe box. They were also agriculturalists and botanists, and developed the cultivation and taxonomy of the genus *Solanum* (of great importance to the Indians since they live at an altitude of more than twelve thousand feet where maize will not ripen) further than it has perhaps ever been done.

Over two hundred and fifty varieties are still distinguished in native vocabulary and the figure was certainly higher in the past. This taxonomy operates by using a term to designate the variety and adding a qualifying adjective for each subvariety. Thus the variety *imilla* 'girl' is subdivided either according to colour (black, blue, white, red, blood-coloured) or according to other characteristics such as grassy, insipid, egg-shaped and so on. There are about twenty-two main varieties which are subdivided in this way. In addition, there is a general dichotomy between those which may be eaten after simple cooking and those which can only be eaten after being alternately frozen and fermented. A binomial taxonomy also always uses criteria such as form (flat, thick, spiral, like cactus leaf, lumpy, egg-shaped, in the shape of an ox tongue, etc.), texture (mealy, elastic, sticky, etc.), or 'sex' (boy or girl) (La Barre).

It was a professional biologist who pointed out how many errors and misunderstandings, some of which have only recently been rectified, could have been avoided, had the older travellers been content to rely on native taxonomies instead of improvising entirely new ones. The result was that eleven different authors between them applied the scientific name *Canis azarae* to three distinct genera, eight species and nine different sub-species, or again that a single variety of the same species was referred to by several different names. The Guarani of Argentine and Paraguay, on the other hand, work methodically with names composed of one, two or three terms. By this means they distinguish for instance between large, small and medium felines: the *dyagua eté* is the supreme example of the large feline, the *mbarakadya eté* of the small wild cat. The *mini* (small) among the *dyague* (large) correspond to the *guasu* (large) among the *chivi*, that is, the medium-sized felines:

> In general, native terms can be said to constitute a well-conceived system, and, with a pinch of salt, they can be said to bear some resemblance to our scientific nomenclature. These primitive Indians did not leave the naming of natural phenomena to chance. They assembled tribal councils to decide which terms best corresponded to the nature of species, classifying groups and sub-groups with great precision. The preservation of the indigenous terms for the local fauna is not just a matter of piety and integrity; it is a duty to science (Dennler, pp. 234 and 244).

In a large part of the Cape York Peninsula in North Australia foods are distinguished as 'plant' or 'animal' by means of two special morphemes. The Wik Munkan, a tribe living in the valley and estuary of the Archer River on the west coast, refine this division. They prefix the name of every plant or food derived from it with the term *mai* and every animal, as well as flesh or animal food, with the term *min*. Similarly, *yukk* is used as a prefix for all names of trees or terms referring to a stick, a piece of wood or wooden object, *koi* for kinds of string and fibre, *wakk* for grasses, *tukk* for snakes, *kämpan* and *wänk* for straw and string baskets respectively. And the same sort of construction of names with the prefix *ark* allows types of scenery and their association to this or that characteristic flora or fauna to be distinguished: *ark tomp* sandbeach proper, *ark tomp nintän* dune country behind the beaches, *ark pint'l* coastal plains with brackish water, etc.

The natives are acutely aware of the characteristic trees, underscrub and grasses of each distinct 'association area', using this term in its ecological sense. They are able to list in detail and without any hesitation, the characteristic trees in each, and also to record the string, resin, grasses, and other products used in material culture, which they obtain from each association, as well as the mammals and birds characteristic of each habitat. Indeed, so detailed and so accurate is their knowledge of these areas that they note the gradual changes in marginal areas . . . My informants were able to relate without hesitation the changes in fauna and in food supply in each association in relation to the seasonal changes.

The native taxonomy allows the following zoological and botanical genera, species and varieties to be distinguished: *mai' watti'yi* (*Dioscorea sativa var. rotunda*, Bail.); *yukk putta* (*Eucalyptus papuana*) – *yukk pont* (*E. tetrodonta*); *tukk pol* (*python spilotes* – *tukk oingorpän* (*P. amethystinus*); *min pänk* (*Macropus agilis*) – *min ko'impia* (*M. rufus*) – *min lo'along* (*M. giganteus*), etc. It is therefore not too much to say, as the writer in question does, that the arrangement of animals and plants, and the foods or technological materials derived from them, bears some resemblance to a simple Linnaean classification (Thomson pp. 165–7).

In the face of such accuracy and care one begins to wish that every ethnologist were also a mineralogist, a botanist, a zoologist and even an astronomer . . . For Reichard's comment about the Navaho applies not only to the Australians and Sudanese but to all or almost all native peoples:

> Since the Navajo regard all parts of the universe as essential to well-being, a major problem of religious study is the classification of natural objects, a subject that demands careful taxonomical attention. We need a list, with English, scientific (Latin) and Navajo names of all plants, animals – especially birds, rodents, insects and worms – minerals and rocks, shells and stars (Reichard, p. 7).

Indeed, it becomes increasingly apparent as time goes on that it is not possible to interpret myths and rites correctly, even if the interpretation is a structural one (not to be confused with just a formal analysis) without an exact identification of the plants and animals which are referred to or of such of their remains as are directly used. Let us quickly look at two examples, one from botany and the other from zoology.

In the whole, or nearly the whole, of North America, the plant called 'sage' or 'sage-brush' plays a major part in the most diverse rituals, either by itself or associated with and at the same time, as the opposite of other plants: *Solidago*, *Chrysothamnus*, *Gutierrezia*. This all remains anecdotal and unsystematic until one enquires into the exact nature of American 'sage', which is not a labiate but a composite plant. The vernacular term in fact covers several varieties of wormwood (*Artemisia*) (carefully distinguished in native nomenclatures and each given a different ritual function). This identification, which was completed in an enquiry into popular pharmacopoeia all over the world, shows that in North America, as in the Ancient World, artemisia is a plant with a connotation of feminine, lunar, nocturnal, mainly used in the treatment of dysmenorrhoea and difficult child births.* A similar investigation of the other group of plants makes it clear that it consists of the same species under different names or of species assimilated in native thought on account of their yellow flowers and their use as dyes or medicine (for curing disorders of the urinary tract, that is, of the male genitals). We thus have a set, symetrically opposed to the first, with a connotation of male, sun, day, and the quality of sacredness belongs to the pair as a whole rather than to each plant or kind of plant separately. This system has been made explicit in the analysis of some rituals, such as that of eagle hunting among the Hidatsa (though only thanks

* *Artemisia* seems to have had a female connotation in ancient Mexico also since women were adorned with it to dance in the June festivals in honour of the Goddess Huixtociuatl (Reko, pp. 39, 75; Anderson and Dibble, pp. 88–9). Cf. Paso and Troncoso for everything relating to Nahuatl ethnobotany.

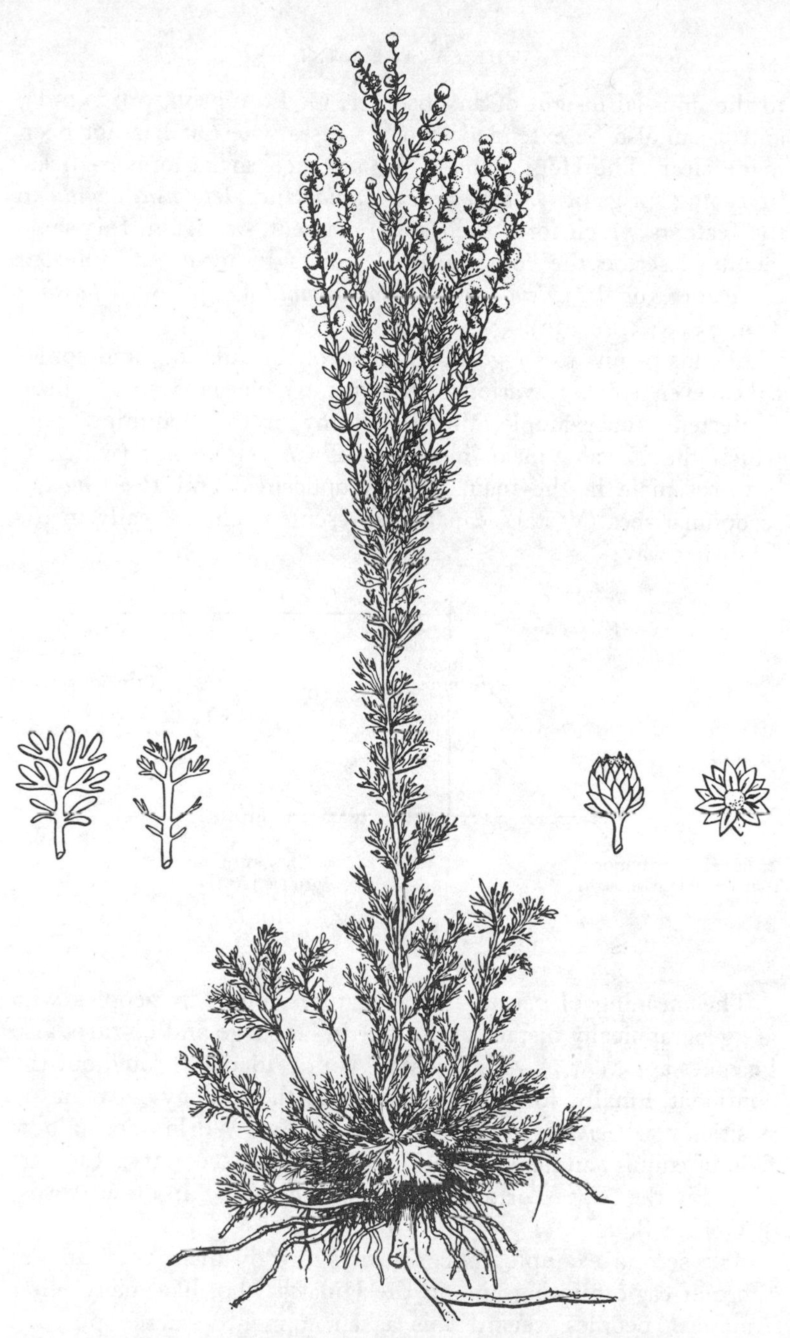

Fig 1 Artemisia frigida (from C. Ledebour, *Icones Plantarum*).

to the unusual insight of an observer, G. L. Wilson, pp. 150–1), and it can also be extended to other cases where it has not been made clear. The Hopi Indians, for instance, make 'prayer-sticks' by typing sprigs of *Gutierrezia euthamiae* and *Artemisia frigida* to the feathers which form their main element, or, again, this same people describe the four cardinal points in terms of different associations of *Artemisia* and *Chrysothamnus* (cf e.g. Voth 1 *passim;* 2, p. 75 sq; 5, p. 130).

All this begins to suggest a method of formulating, and sometimes even solving, various problems which have so far been neglected. For example, the dichotomy of the 'feminine' pole which the Navaho make in terms of *Chrysothamnus* (which is however male in the main pair of opposites) and *Penstemon*, a scrophulariacea (Vestal), can be represented schematically in the following way:

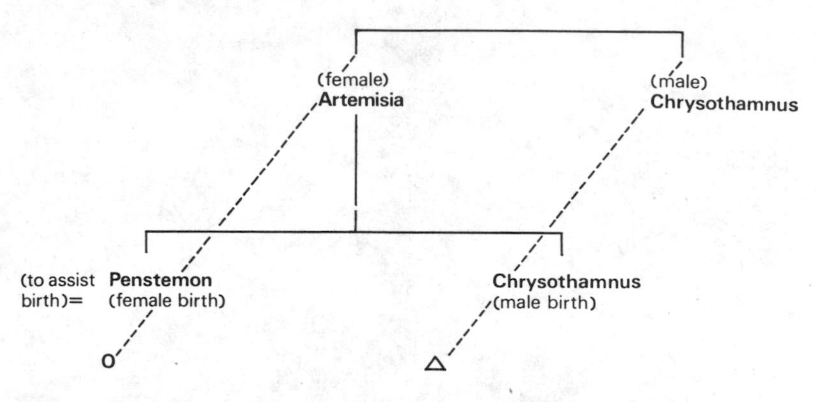

The meaning of certain ritual features found in peoples who are geographically distant and differ in language and culture, also becomes apparent. A rough system is in evidence throughout the continent. Finally, for comparative study the analogy between the position of *Artemisia* in the Old and the New World opens a new field of enquiry and consideration, not least on account of the part played in the New World by *Solidago virga aurea*, in other words, a 'Golden Bough'.

The second example concerns rites already mentioned above: those of eagle hunting among the Hidatsa who, like many other American peoples, regard this as an eminently sacred pursuit. According to the Hidatsa, the hunting of eagles was taught to

Fig 2 Solidago virga aurea (from Torrey Botanical Club).

men by the supernatural animals who originally invented its techniques and procedures. The myths refer to them vaguely as 'bears'.

Informants seem to hesitate between the small black bear and the animal termed glutton, wolverine or carcajou (*Gulo luscus*). The specialists on the Hidatsa, such as Wilson, Densmore, Bowers and Beckwith, did not altogether ignore the problem but they did not attach great importance to it, since it was after all a mythical animal which was in question, and the identification of a mythical animal might seem pointless, if not indeed impossible. In fact, however, the whole interpretation of the ritual depends on this identification. So far as interpretation of eagle hunting ritual is concerned, bears are no help. But wolverines or *carcajous* – a Canadian adaptation of an Indian word meaning 'bad-temper' are a different matter, for they have a very special place in folklore. In the mythology of the Algonkin of the north-east the wolverine is the animal of craft and cunning. It is hated and feared by the Eskimos of Hudson Bay as well as by the western Athapaskan and coastal tribes of Alaska and British Columbia. If one pieces together what is known about all these peoples one arrives at the same explanation as that obtained independently from trappers by a contemporary geographer: 'Gluttons are almost the only members of the weasel family which cannot be trapped. They amuse themselves in stealing not only trapped animals but also the hunter's traps. The only way to get rid of them is to shoot them' (Brouillette, p. 55). Now, the Hidatsa hunt eagles by hiding in pits. The eagle is attracted by a bait placed on top and the hunter catches it with his bare hands as it perches to take the bait. And so the technique presents a kind of paradox. Man *is* the trap but to play this part he has to go down into the pit, that is, to adopt the position of a trapped animal. He is both hunter and hunted at the same time. The wolverine is the only animal which knows how to deal with this contradictory situation: not only has it not the slightest fear of the traps set for it; it actually competes with the trapper by stealing his prey and sometimes even his traps.

It follows, if the interpretation which I have begun to give is correct, that the ritual importance of eagle hunting among the Hidatsa is at least partly due to the use of pits, to the assumption by the hunter of a particular *low* position (literally, and, as we have just seen, figuratively as well) for capturing a quarry which is in the very *highest* position in an objective sense (eagles fly high) and also from a mythical point of view (the eagle being at the top of the mythical hierarchy of birds).

Analysis of the ritual shows that it accords in every detail with the hypothesis that there is a dualism between a celestial prey and a subterranean hunter, which at the same time evokes the strongest possible contrast between high and low in the sphere of hunting. The extreme complexity of the rites which precede, accompany and conclude an eagle hunt is the counterpart of the exceptional position which eagle hunting occupies within a mythical typology which makes it the concrete expression of the widest possible distance between a hunter and his game.

Some obscure features of the ritual become clear at the same time, in particular the significance and meaning of the myths which are told during hunting expeditions. They refer to cultural heroes, capable of being transformed into arrows and masters of the art of hunting with bows and arrows; and therefore, in their guise of wild cats and racoons, doubly inappropriate for the role of bait in eagle hunting. Hunting with bows and arrows involves the region or space immediately above the earth, that is, the atmospheric or middle sky: the hunter and his game meet in the intermediate space. Eagle hunting, on the other hand, separates them by giving them opposite positions: the hunter below the ground and the game close to the empyrean sky.

Another striking feature of eagle hunting is that women have a beneficial effect during their periods. This is contrary to the belief held almost universally by hunting peoples, including the Hidatsa themselves in the case of all except eagle hunting. What has just been said explains this detail also, when it is remembered that in eagle hunting, conceived as the narrowing of a wide gulf between hunter and game, mediation is effected, from the technical point of view, by means of the bait, a piece of meat or small piece of game, the bloodstained carcass of which is destined to rapid decay. A first hunt to procure the bait is necessary in order for the second hunt to take place. One hunt involves the shedding of blood (by means of bows and arrows), the other does not (eagles are strangled without any effusion of blood). The one hunt, which consists in a close union of hunter and game, furnishes the means of effecting a union between what is so distant that it looks at first as if there is a gulf which cannot be bridged – except, precisely, by means of blood.

Menstruation acquires a positive significance from three points of view in a system of this kind. From a strictly formal point of view, since one hunt is the reverse of the other, the role attributed to menstruation is accordingly reversed. It is harmful in one case because its similarity is too great, but it becomes beneficial in the other where it has not only a metaphorical but also a metonymical sense: it evokes the bait as blood and organic decay and the bait is a part of the system. From the technical point of view the bloodstained carcass, soon to be carrion, which is close to the living hunter for hours or even days is the means of effecting the capture, and it is significant that the same native term is used for the embrace of lovers and the grasping of the bait by the bird. Finally, at a semantic level, pollution, at least in the thought of the North American Indians, consists in too close a conjunction between two things each meant to remain in a state of 'purity'. In the hunt at close quarters menstrual periods always risk introducing excessive union which would lead to a saturation of the original relation and a neutralization of its dynamic force by redundancy. In the hunt at a distance it is the reverse. The conjunction is inadequate and the only means to remedy its deficiency is to allow pollution to enter. Pollution appears as *periodicity* on the axis of successions or as *putrefaction* on that of simultaneities.

One of these axes corresponds to the mythology of agriculture and the other to that of hunting. This analysis therefore makes it possible to arrive at a general system of reference allowing the detection of homologies between themes, whose elaborate forms do not at first sight seem related in any way. This result is of great importance in the case of eagle hunting since it is to be found in different forms (though always strongly imbued with ritual) almost all over the American continent and among people of different cultures, some hunters and some agriculturalists. The relatively minor but positive role attributed to pollution by the Hidatsa, the Mandan and the Pawnee (the variations of which can be interpreted as a function of the social organization of each tribe) can therefore be regarded as a particular case of something more general. Another particular case is illustrated by the Pueblo myth of a man betrothed to an eagle-girl. The Pueblo connect this myth with another, that of the 'corpse-girl' and 'ghost-wife'. In this case pollution has a function which is strong (involving the death, instead of the success, of the hunter). For among the Pueblo, as the myths explain, the blood of rabbits who are the prime *object* of the ritual hunt *must not be shed*. Among the Hidatsa, on the other hand, it *must be shed* so that they can be used as the *means* of the ritual hunt par excellence: the hunt of eagles, whose blood may not be shed. The Pueblo indeed capture and rear eagles but they do not kill them and some groups even refrain altogether from keeping them for fear that they should forget to feed them and let them die of hunger.

To return briefly to the Hidatsa: other problems arise in connection with the mythical role of the wolverine further north, in a region at the edge of the major area of the diffusion of this animal species.*

I raise this point to emphasize the fact that historical and geographical problems, as well as semantic and structural ones, are all related to the exact identification of an animal which fulfils a mythical function: *Gulo luscus*. This identification has an important bearing on the interpretation of myths among peoples as far from the region of the wolverine as the Pueblo or even, in the heart of tropical America, the Sherente of Central Brazil who also have the myth of the ghost wife. The suggestion is not however that all these myths were borrowed from a northern culture in spite of the great distance. Any question of this kind could arise only in the case of the Hidatsa in whose myths the wolverine figures explicitly. The most that can be said in the other cases is that analogous logical structures can be constructed by means of different lexical resources. It is not the elements themselves but only the relations between them which are constant.

This last remark leads us to another difficulty which must be considered. The accurate identification of every animal, plant,

* The Hidatsa seem to have lived at various points in the state of North Dakota for as long as their traditions go back.

As for the wolverine: it 'is a circumpolar species belonging to the northern forested areas of both continents. In North America it formerly ranged from the northern limit of trees south to New England and New York, and down the Rocky Mountains to Colorado, and down the Sierra Nevada to near Mount Whitney, California' (Nelson, p. 427). The Common Wolverine is found 'from the Arctic Ocean and Baffin Bay southward and from the Pacific to the Atlantic, reaching the extreme north-eastern United States, Wisconsin, Michigan, Minnesota, North Dakota, and down the Rocky Mountains into Utah and Colorado' (Anthony, p. 111). Species which appear to be synonymous have been reported in the mountains of California and at Fort Union, North Dakota (id.).

stone, heavenly body or natural phenomenon mentioned in myths and rituals is a complex task for which the ethnographer is rarely equipped. Even this is not however enough. It is also necessary to know the role which each culture gives them within its own system of significances. It is of course useful to illustrate the wealth and precision of native observation and to describe its methods: long and constant attention, painstaking use of all the senses, ingenuity which does not despise the methodical analysis of the droppings of animals to discover their eating habits, etc. Of all these minute details, patiently accumulated over the centuries and faithfully transmitted from generation to generation, only a few are however actually employed for giving animals or plants a significant function in the system. And it is necessary to know which, since they are not constant from one society to another so far as the same species is concerned.

The Iban or Sea Dayaks of South Borneo derive omens by interpreting the song and flight of a number of species of birds. The rapid cry of the Crested Jay (*Platylophus galericulatus* Cuvier) is said to resemble the crackling of burning wood and so presages the successful firing of a family's swiddens. The alarm cry of a Trogon (*Harpactes diardi* Temminck) is likened to the death rattle of an animal being slain and augurs good hunting. Again, the alarm cry of the *Sasia abnormis* Temminck is supposed to get rid of the evil spirits which haunt the crops by scraping them off since it resembles the sound of a scraping knife. The 'laugh' of another Trogon (*Harpactes duvauceli* Temminck) is a good omen for trading expeditions and because of its brilliant red breast it is also associated with the renown attending successful war and distant voyages.

It is obvious that the same characteristics could have been given a different meaning and that different characteristics of the same birds could have been chosen instead. The system of divination selects only some distinctive features, gives them an arbitrary meaning and restricts itself to seven birds, the selection of which is surprising in view of their insignificance. Arbitrary as it seems when only its individual terms are considered, the system becomes coherent when it is seen as a whole set: the only birds used in it are ones whose habits readily lend themselves to anthropomorphic symbolism and which are easy to distinguish from each other by means of features that can be combined to fabricate more complex messages (Freeman). Nevertheless when one takes account of the wealth and diversity of the raw material, only a few of the innumerable possible elements of which are made use of in the system, there can be no doubt that a considerable number of other systems of the same type would have been equally coherent and that no one of them is predestined to be chosen by all societies and all civilizations. The terms never have any intrinsic significance. Their meaning is one of 'position' – a function of the history and cultural context on the one hand and of the structural system in which they are called upon to appear on the other.

Vocabulary already shows this selectiveness. In Navaho the wild turkey is the bird which 'pecks' while the woodpecker is the bird which 'hammers'. Worms, maggots and insects are grouped under a generic term, meaning swarming, eruption, boiling, effervescence. Insects are thus thought of in their larval state rather than in their chrysalis or adult form. The name of the lark refers to its extended hind claw while the English term 'horned lark' derives from the protuberant feathers of its head (Reichard I, pp. 10–11).

When he began his study of the classification of colours among the Hanunóo of the Philippines, Conklin was at first baffled by the apparent confusions and inconsistencies. These, however, disappeared when informants were asked to relate and contrast specimens instead of being asked to define isolated ones. There was a coherent system but this could not be understood in terms of our own system which is founded on two axes: that of brightness (value) and that of intensity (chroma). All the obscurities disappeared when it became clear that the Hanunóo system also has two axes but different ones. They distinguish colours into relatively light and relatively dark and into those usual in fresh or succulent plants and those usual in dry or desiccated plants. Thus the natives treat the shiny, brown colour of newly cut bamboo as relatively green while we should regard it as nearer red if we had to classify it in terms of the simple opposition of red and green which is found in Hanunóo (Conklin 2).

In the same way, very closely related animals may often appear in folklore but with a different significance in different instances. The woodpecker and other birds of the same genus are a good example. As Radcliffe-Brown has shown (2), the Australians' interest in the tree-creeper is due to the fact that it inhabits the hollows of trees; but the Indians of the North American prairies pay attention to quite a different feature; the red-headed woodpecker is believed to be safe from birds of prey since its remains are never found (Schoolcraft). The Pawnee of the Upper Missouri, a little further south (in common apparently with the ancient Romans) associate the woodpecker with tempests and storms (Fletcher 2), while the Osage associate it with the sun and stars (La Flesche). The Iban of Borneo mentioned above give a symbolic role to one variety of woodpecker (*Blythipicus rubiginosus* Swainson) because of its 'triumphal' song and the solemn warning character attributed to its alarm cry. It is not of course exactly the same bird which is in question in all these cases but the example helps us to understand how different peoples can use the same animal in their symbolism, employing unrelated characteristics, habitat, meteorological association, cry, etc., the live or the dead animal. Again, each feature can be interpreted in different ways. The Indians of the south-west United States, who are agricult uralists, regard the crow primarily as a garden pest, while the Indians of the north-west Pacific coast, who live entirely by fishing and hunting regard it as a devourer of carrion, and consequently, of excrement. The semantic load of *Corvus* is different in the two cases: plant in one, animal in the other; man's rival when its behaviour is like his own, his enemy when it is the reverse.

Bees are a totemic animal in Africa as well as in Australia. But among the Nuer they are a secondary totem associated with pythons, because the two species have similarly marked bodies. A man who has pythons as a totem also refrains from killing bees or eating their honey. There is an association of the same type between red ants and cobras, because the literal meaning of the latter is 'the brown one' (Evans-Pritchard 2, p. 68).

The semantic position of bees among the Australian tribes of Kimberley is very much more complex. Their languages have noun classes. Thus the Ngarinyin recognize three successive dichotomies: first: into animate and inanimate things, then of the animate class into rational and irrational, and finally, of the former into male and female. In the languages with six classes, the class of manufactured articles included honey as well as canoes on the grounds that honey is 'manufactured' by bees just as canoes are manufactured by men. It is thus understandable that in the languages which have lost some classes animals and manufactured goods have come to be grouped together (Capell).

There are cases in which one can make hypotheses with regard to the logical nature of classification, which appear true or can be seen to cut across the natives' interpretation. The Iroquois peoples were organized into clans whose number and names varied considerably from one to another. It is not however unduly difficult to detect a 'masterplan' which is based on a fundamental distinction between three kinds of clan: water clans (turtle, beaver, eel, snipe, heron), land clans (wolf, deer, bear) and air clans (sparrowhawk, ?ball). But even so the case of aquatic birds is determined arbitrarily for being birds they could belong to the air rather than to the water, and it is not certain that research into the economic life, techniques, mythical imagery and ritual practices would supply an ethnographic context rich enough to decide this point.

The ethnographic data on the central Algonkin and the neighbouring Winnebago suggests a classification into five categories which correspond, respectively, to land, water, the subaquatic world, the sky and the empyream.* The difficulties begin when one tries to classify each clan. The Menomini have fifty clans which seem to be divisible into quadrupeds on dry land (wolf, dog, deer), quadrupeds inhabiting swampy places (elk, moose, marten, beaver, pekan), 'terrestrial' birds (eagle, hawk, raven, crow), aquatic birds (crane, heron, duck, coot) and finally subterranean animals (Hoffman, pp. 41–2). But this last category is particularly recalcitrant as many of the animals included in it (bear, turtle, porcupine) could also be included in other classes. The difficulties would be even greater in the remaining classes.

Australia presents similar problems. Durkheim and Mauss, following Frazer, discussed the global classifications of tribes like the Wotjobaluk, who bury their dead facing in a particular direction which depends on the clan. (See illustration on p. 58.)

* 'Among the Winnebago, a number of other Siouan, and Central Algonkin tribes, there was a fivefold classification; earth animals, sky animals, empyrean animals, aquatic animals, and subaquatic animals. Among the Winnebago the thunderbird belong to the empyrean; the eagle, hawk, and pigeon, to the sky; the bear and wolf, to the earth; the fish, to the water and the water spirit, below the water' (Radin I, p. 186).

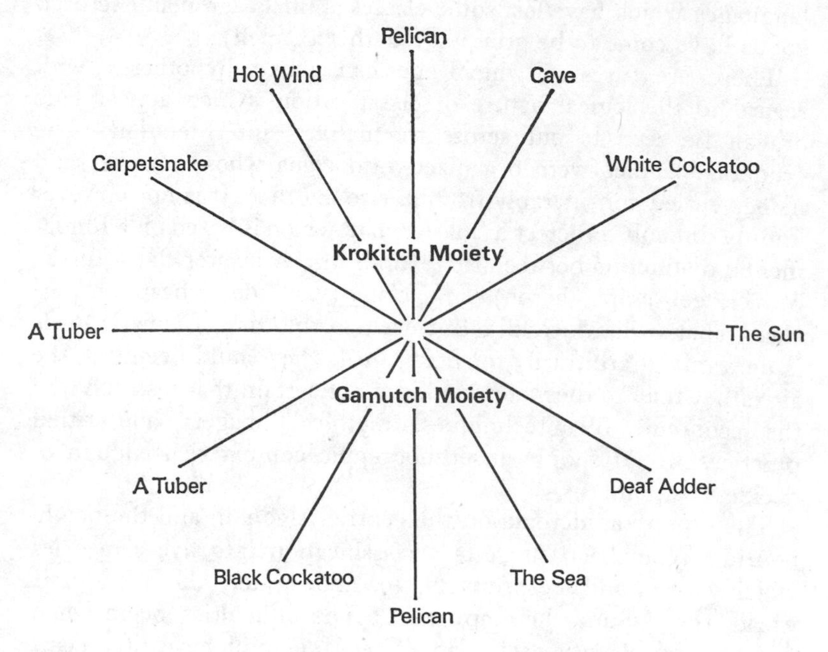

(Frazer, vol. i, p. 455)

The available data are certainly fragmentary, but one cannot fail to notice a rough system, which, indeed, only looks rough to the onlooker because the ethnographic background necessary for its interpretation is almost entirely missing. The white cockatoo, 'diurnal', is next to the sun, and the black cockatoo, which is almost directly opposite, is itself next to the tubers, 'chthonian' plants, and on the same axis as the cave, which is also 'chthonian'. Snakes are on one axis, and the 'sea' creatures, pelican, sea, hot wind, also seem to be grouped according to axes. But does this wind belong to land or sea? We do not know and, as so often, we must go to a geographer or meteorologist or to a botanist, zoologist or geologist, for the solution to this ethnographic problem.

The truth of the matter is that *the principle underlying a classification can never be postulated in advance*. It can only be discovered *a posteriori* by ethnographic investigation, that is, by experience.*

* I here include several pages of a paper intended for the Mélanges Alexandre Koyré.

The case of the Osage, who are southern Sioux, is illuminating because their classifications appear to be systematic. The Osage divide animate and inanimate things into three categories. These are associated respectively with the sky (sun, star, crane, heavenly bodies, night, the constellation of the Pleiad, etc.), with water mussel, turtle, *Typha latifolia* (a type of rush), mist, fishes, etc.) and with dry land (black bear and white bear, porcupine, deer, eagle, etc.). The position of the eagle would be incomprehensible were it not known that in Osage thought eagles are associated with lightning, lightning with fire, fire with coal and coal with the earth. The eagle is thus one of the 'masters of coal', that is, a land animal. Similarly, and with nothing to suggest this in advance, the pelican has a symbolic role on account of the great age it reaches, metal on account of its hardness. The turtle with a serrated tail, an animal of no practical use, is often involved in rites. The reason for its importance could not be understood without the further knowledge that the number thirteen has a mystic value for the Osage. The rising sun emits thirteen rays, which are divided into a group of six and a group of seven corresponding respectively to right and left, land and sky, summer and winter. The tail of this species of turtle is said to have sometimes six and sometimes seven serratures. Its chest therefore represents the vault of the sky and the grey line across it the Milky Way. It would be equally impossible to predict the pan-symbolic function according to the elk, whose body is a veritable *imago mundi*: its coat represents grass, its hams hills, its flanks plains, its backbone the skyline, its neck valleys and its antlers the whole hydrographic network.

A few Osage interpretations can thus be reconstructed, since an enormous amount of documentation is available. The data were collected by La Flesche who was himself the son of an Omaha chief and particularly aware of all the intricacies of native thought. But in the case of an almost extinct tribe like the Creek the difficulties are unsurmountable. The Creek were at one time divided into more than fifty matrilineal totemic clans. These were named mainly after animals but also in some cases after plants or meteorological, geological and anatomical phenomena (dew and wind, salt, pubic hair, respectively). The clans were grouped into phratries, the villages were also divided into two groups possibly corresponding to land animals and sky animals, although there is nothing to suggest this in their designation as 'people of a different speech' and 'white people' or as 'reds' and 'whites'. But why, one may ask, are totems distinguished into 'uncles' and 'nephews' (in the same way that the Hopi distinguish totems into 'mother's brothers' on the one hand and 'father', 'mother' or 'grandmother' on the other)* and why, more particularly, given this division, is it sometimes the less 'important' animal which has the higher position, wolves, for instance, being 'uncles' of bears and wildcats those of the large felines called 'panthers' in the southern United States? Again, why is the clan of the alligator associated with that of the turkey (unless perhaps because both lay eggs) and that of the racoon with the clan of the potato? In Creek thought the side of the 'whites' is that of peace but the fieldworker was given a hopelessly vague explanation: the wind (the name of a 'white' clan) brings good, that is, peaceful, weather; the bear and the wolf are exceedingly watchful animals and therefore useful in the interests of peace, etc. (Swanton I, p. 108 ff.).

The difficulties which these examples illustrate are of two types, extrinsic and intrinsic. The extrinsic difficulties arise from our lack of knowledge of the (real or imaginary) observations and the facts or principles on which classifications are based. The Tlingit Indians say that woodworms are 'clever' and 'neat' and that land otters 'hate the smell of human excretion' (Laguna, pp. 177, 188). The Hopi believe that owls have a favourable influence on peach trees (Stephen, pp. 78, 91, 109). If these attributes were taken into account in classifying these animals we might hunt for the key indefinitely did we not happen to possess these small but precious clues. The Ojibwa Indians of Parry Island number the eagle and squirrel among their 'totems'. Fortunately a native text explains that these animals are included as symbols of the trees they each inhabit: hemlock trees (*Tsuga canadensis*) and cedar trees (*Thuja occidentalis*) respectively (Jenness 2). The interest which the Ojibwa have in squirrels is therefore really an interest in a kind of tree. It has no connection with the great interest which the Asmat of New Guinea also take in squirrels, for different reasons:

* An interpretation has been suggested in the case of an analogous distinction in an African tribe: 'God is the father of the greater spirits of the air, and the lesser of them are said to be children of his sons, of his lineage. The totemic spirits are often said to be children of his daughters, that is, they are not of his lineage, which is the Nuer way of placing them yet lower in the spiritual scale' (Evans-Pritchard 2, p. 119).

> Parrots and squirrels are famous fruiteaters ... and men about to go headhunting feel a relationship to these beings and call themselves their brothers ... (because of the) parallelism between the human body and a tree, the human head and its fruit (Zegwaard, p. 1034).

A different kind of consideration leads to squirrels being forbidden to pregnant women among the Fang of the Gabon. Squirrels shelter in the holes of trees and a future mother who ate their flesh would run the risk of the foetus copying a squirrel and refusing to leave the uterus.* The same reasoning could equally well apply to weasels and badgers, who live in burrows, but the Hopi follow a different line of thought: they hold that the meat of these animals is favourable to child-bearing because of their habit of working their way through the ground and 'getting out' at some other place when they are chased into a hole. They therefore help the baby to 'come out quickly' – as a result of which they can also be called on to make rain fall (Voth I, p. 34 n.).

An Osage ritual incantation makes a puzzling association between a flower – Blazing Star (*Lacinaria pycnostachya*), a plant used for food – maize, and a mammal – the bison. It would be impossible to understand why they associate these things if an independent source did not bring to light the fact that the Omaha, who are closely related to the Osage, hunted bison during the summer until blazing stars were in flower in the plains; they then knew that the maize was ripe and returned to their villages for the harvest (Fortune I, pp. 18–9).

The intrinsic difficulties are of a different kind. They are due not to our lack of knowledge of the objective characteristics used to establish a connection between two or more terms in native thought but to the polyvalent nature of logics which appeal to several, formally distinct types of connection at the same time. The Luapala of Northern Rhodesia provide a good illustration of this feature. Their clans have the names of animals, plants or manufactured articles and they are not 'totemic' in the usual sense

* And not only squirrels: 'The worst danger threatening pregnant women is from animals who live or are caught in any sort of hole (in the ground, in trees). One can positively speak of a *horror vacui*. If a pregnant woman eats an animal of this kind, the child might also want to stay in its hole, "in the belly", and a difficult birth is to be expected. Similarly the parents must not, during this period, take out any birds' nests which have been built into the hollows of trees, and one of my employees, who had made a woman pregnant, absolutely refused to make me a model of a loaf of cassava, on the grounds that it would have to be hollow' (Tessman, vol. 2, p. 193).

of the term, but, as among the Bemba and the Ambo, joking relationships link them in pairs. The reasoning behind this has, from our point of view, the same interest. As I showed in an earlier book and am continuing to establish here, so-called totemism is in fact only a particular case of the general problem of classification and one of many examples of the part which specific terms often play in the working out of a social classification.

The following clans stand in a joking relationship to each other among the Luapula: the Leopard and Goat clans because the leopards eat goats, the Mushroom and Anthill clans because mushrooms grow on anthills, the Mush and Goat clans because men like meat in their mush, the Elephant and Clay clans because women in the old days used to carve out elephants' footprints from the ground and use these natural shapes as receptacles instead of fashioning pots. The Anthill clan is linked with the Snake clan and also with the Grass clan because grass grows tall on anthills and snakes hide there. The Iron clan jokes with all clans with animal names because animals are killed by metal spears and bullets. Reasoning of this kind allows the definition of a hierarchy of clans: the Leopard clan is superior to the Goat clan, the Iron clan to the animal clans and the Rain clan to the Iron clan because rain rusts iron. Moreover the rain clan is superior to all the other clans because animals would die without it, one cannot make mush (a clan name) without it, clay (a clan name) cannot be worked without it, and so on (Cunnison, pp. 62–5).

The Navaho give many different justifications of the virtues they ascribe to medicinal plants and their modes of employing them: the plant grows near a more important medicinal plant; one of the plant's organs looks like a part of the body; the odour (or feel or taste) of the plant is 'right'; the plant makes water the 'right' colour; the plant is associated with an animal (as food, or in habitat, or by contact); the knowledge was revealed by the gods; its uses were learnt from someone else without any explanation: the plant is found near a tree struck by lightning; it is good for a certain ailment in that part of the body or an ailment with similar effects, etc. (Vestal, p. 58). The terms used to differentiate plant names among the Hanunóo belong to the following categories: leaf shape, colour, habitat, size/dimension, sex, habit of growth, plant host, growing time, taste, smell (Conklin I, p. 131).

These examples, together with those given earlier, make it clear that such systems of logic work on several axes at the same time. The relations which they set up between the terms are most commonly based on contiguity (snake and anthill among the Luapula and also the Toreya of South India)* or on resemblance (red ants and cobras which, according to the Nuer, resemble each other in 'colour'). In this they are not formally distinct from other taxonomies, even modern ones, in which contiguity and resemblance also play a fundamental part: contiguity for discovering things which 'belong both structurally and functionally . . . to a single system' and resemblance, which does not require membership of the same system and is based simply on the possession by objects of one or more common characteristics, such as all being 'yellow or all smooth, or all with wings or all ten feet high (Simpson, pp. 3–4).

But other types of relation intervene in the examples we have just examined. Relations may be established, in effect, on either the sensible level (the bodily markings of the bee and the pythons) or on the intelligible level (the function of construction common to the bee and the carpenter): the same animal, the bee, functions, as it were, at different levels of abstraction in two cultures. Again, the connection can be close or distant, synchronic or diachronic (the relation between squirrels and cedars for instance on the one hand, and that between pottery and elephants' footprints on the other), static (mush and goat) or dynamic (fire kills animals, rain 'kills' fire; the flowering of a plant indicates that it is time to return to the village), etc.

It is probable that the number, nature and 'quality' of these logical axes is not the same in every culture, and that cultures could be classified into richer and poorer on the basis of the formal properties of the systems of reference to which they appeal in the construction of their classifications. However, even those which are the least well endowed in this respect employ logics of several dimensions, the listing, analysis and interpretation of which would require a wealth of ethnographic and general information which is all too often lacking.

* 'The members of the sept, at times of marriage, worship anthills, which are the homes of snakes' (Thurston, vol. VII, p. 176). Similarly in New Guinea: 'certain types of plants, as well as the animals and plants parasitic on them, are thought of as belonging to the same mythical and totemic unit' (Wirz, vol. II, p. 21).

Two types of difficulties characteristic of 'totemic' logics have so far been mentioned. The first is that we do not usually know exactly which plants or animals are in question. We have seen that an approximate identification is not adequate since native observations are so precise and finely shaded that the place of each element in the system often depends on a morphological detail or mode of behaviour definable only at the level of varieties or subvarieties. The Eskimos of Dorset carved effigies of animals out of pieces of ivory no bigger than the head of a match with such precision that, when they look at them under microscopes, zoologists can distinguish varieties of the same species such as, for example, the Common Loon and the Red Throated Loon (Carpenter).

The second difficulty mentioned is that each species, variety or subvariety could suitably fill a considerable number of different roles in symbolic systems in which only certain roles are effectively ascribed to them. The range of these possibilities is unknown to us and for an understanding of the choices which are made we need not only ethnographic data but also data from other sources – zoological, botanical, geographical, etc. The rare cases where the data are adequate make it clear that even neighbouring cultures may construct totally different systems out of superficially identical or very similar elements. If North American peoples can regard the sun in some cases as a 'father' and benefactor and in others as a cannibalistic monster thirsting for human flesh and blood, there seems to be no limit to the variety of interpretations to be expected when it is something as specific as the subvariety of a plant or bird which is in question.

A comparison of colour symbolism among the Luvale of Rhodesia and some Australian tribes of the north-east of the state of South Australia provides an example of a case in which the same very simple structure of opposites recurs but the semantic loads are reversed. In the Australian tribes in question, the members of the matrilineal moiety of the deceased paint themselves with red ochre and approach the body, while members of the other moiety paint themselves with white clay and remain at a distance from it. The Luvale also use red and white soil but white clay and white meal are used by them as offerings to ancestral spirits and red clay is substituted on the occasions of puberty rites because red is the colour of life and fertility (C. M. N. White I, pp. 46–7).* White represents the 'unstressed' situation in both cases, while red – the chromatic pole of the opposition – is associated with death in one case and with life in the other. In the Forrest River district of Australia, members of a deceased person's own generation paint themselves black and white and keep away from the corpse while those of other generations do not paint themselves and approach the corpse. The opposition white/red is thus replaced, without any change of semantic load, by an opposition black + white/O. Instead of the values given to white and red being reversed, as in the previous case, the value of white (here associated with black, a non-chromatic colour) remains constant, and it is the content of the opposite pole which is reversed, changing from the 'super-colour' red to the total absence of colour. Finally, another Australian tribe, the Bard, constructs its symbolism by means of the opposition black/red. Black is the colour of mourning for even generations (grandfather, Ego, grandson) and red the colour of mourning for uneven generations (father, son), that is, those which are not assimilated with the generation of the deceased (Elkin 4, pp. 298–9). The opposition between two differently stressed terms – life and death among the Luvale, 'someone else's death and "my" death' in Australia – is thus expressed by pairs of elements taken from the same symbolic chain; absence of colour, black, white, black + white, red (as the supreme presence of colour), etc.

The same fundamental opposition is found among the Fox, but transposed from colour to sound. While the burial ceremony is in progress 'those burying (the dead) talked to each other. But the others did not say a thing to each other' (Michelson I, p. 411). The opposition between speech and silence, between noise and the absence of noise, corresponds to that between colour and the absence of colour or between two chromatisms of different degrees. These observations seem to make it possible to dispose of theories making use of the concepts of 'archetypes' or a 'collective unconscious'. It is only forms and not contents which can be common. If there are common contents the reason must be sought either in the objective properties of particular nature or artificial entities or in diffusion and borrowing, in either case, that is, outside the mind.

* As in China, where white is the colour of mourning and red the colour of marriage.

Another difficulty is due to the natural complexity of concrete logics for which the existence of some connection is more essential than the exact nature of the connections. On the formal plane one might say they will make use of anything which comes to hand. Consequently, we cannot even postulate the formal nature of a connection when we are merely given the two connected terms. Relations between terms, like the terms themselves, must be approached indirectly and, as it were, off the cushion. The same difficulty is found in structural linguistics at the present time, although in a different field, because this also is based on a qualitative logic. It identifies pairs of oppositions made up of phonemes but the spirit of each opposition remains largely hypothetical; it is difficult to avoid a certain impressionism in defining them in the preliminary stages, and several possible solutions to the same problem remain open for a long time. One of the major difficulties of structural linguistics, and one which has not yet been fully overcome, derives from the fact that the reduction which it effects by means of the concept of binary opposition has to be paid for by the diversity of kind which is insidiously reconstituted to the benefit of each opposition. The number of dimensions is reduced on one plane only to be increased on another. It may however be the case that what we have here is not a difficulty of method but a limitation inherent in the nature of particular intellectual operations, whose weakness as well as whose strength is their capacity to be logical while remaining firmly rooted in the qualitative.

A final kind of difficulty must be considered separately. It more particularly concerns the classifications which are called 'totemic' in the fullest sense, that is those which are not only thought but lived. Whenever social groups are named, the conceptual system formed by these names is, as it were, a prey to the whims of demographic change which follows its own laws but is related to it only contingently. The system is given, synchronically, while demographic changes take place diachronically, in other words, there are two determinisms, each operating on its own account and independently of the other.

This conflict between synchrony and diachrony is also found on the linguistic plane. The structural features of a language will probably change if the population using it, which was once numerous, becomes progressively smaller; and it is obvious that a language disappears with the men who speak it. Nevertheless the connection between synchrony and diachrony is not rigid. For, in the first place, all the speakers are, taken as a whole, equivalent (though this would cease to be so if one were to consider specific cases), and secondly, and more important, the structure of the language is to some extent protected by its practical purpose, which is to ensure communication. Language is therefore sensitive to the influence of demographic evolution only up to a point and in so far as its function is not impaired. But the conceptual systems we are studying here are not, or are not primarily, means of communication. They are means of thinking, an activity which is governed by very much less stringent conditions. One either succeeds or not in making oneself understood, but one can think more or less well. Thinking admits of degrees and a way of thinking can degenerate imperceptibly into a way of remembering. This explains why the synchronic structures of so-called totemic systems should be so extremely vulnerable to the effects of diachrony: a mnemotechnic procedure is less trouble to operate than a speculative one which in turn is less exacting than a device for communication.

This point can be illustrated by an only slightly imaginary example. Suppose that a tribe was once divided into three clans, each of which had the name of an animal symbolizing a natural element:

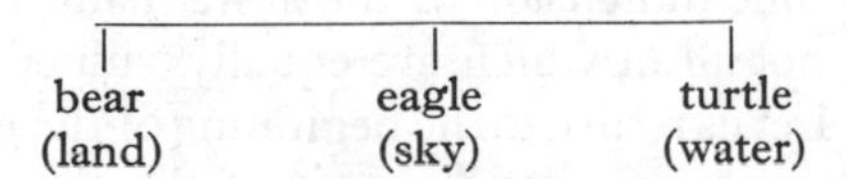

Suppose further that demographic changes led to the extinction of the bear clan and an increase in the population of the turtle clan, and that as a result the turtle clan split into two sub-clans, each of which subsequently gained the status of clans. The old structure will disappear completely and be replaced by a structure of this type:

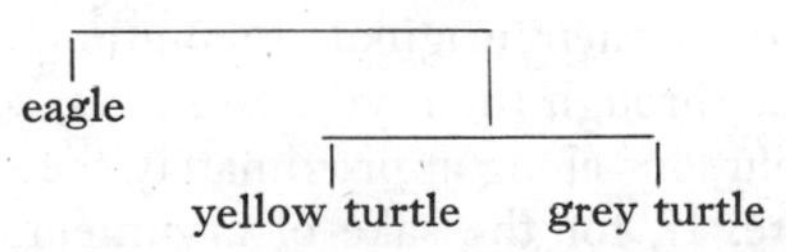

Without further data it would be useless to try to detect the original scheme behind this new structure; it is even possible that any such scheme, whether perceived consciously or not, should have completely disappeared from native thought, and that after this upheaval the three clan names might survive only as traditionally accepted titles with no cosmological significance. This outcome is probably very common and explains why an underlying system can sometimes be posited in theory even though it would be impossible to reconstruct in practice. But it is also frequently the case that things turn out otherwise.

On a first supposition the initial system will be able to survive in the mutilated form of a binary opposition between sky and water. Another solution could be derived from the fact that there were originally three terms and that the number of the terms is still the same at the end. The original three terms expressed an irreducible trichotomy while the final three terms are the result of two successive dichotomies; between sky and water and then between yellow and grey. If this opposition of colour were given a symbolic sense, for instance with reference to day and night, then there would be not one but two binary oppositions: sky/water and day/night, that is a system of four terms.

It can be seen therefore that demographic evolution can shatter the structure but that if the structural orientation survives the shock it has, after each upheaval, several means of re-establishing a system, which may not be identical with the earlier one but is at least formally of the same type. Nor is this all. We have so far considered only one dimension of the system and there are always in fact several, not all of which are equally vulnerable to demographic changes. Let us return to the beginning of the example. When our imaginary society was at the stage of the three elements, the division into three classes did not operate only on the plane of clan names. The system rested on myths of creation and origin and permeated the entire ritual. Even if its demographic basis collapses, this upheaval will not have immediate repercussions on all planes. The myths and rites will change, but only with a time-lag and as if they possessed a certain residual vigour which for a time preserved all or part of their original orientation. This latter will therefore continue through the myths and rites, so as to maintain new structural solutions along approximately the same lines as the previous structure. If, for the sake of argument, we suppose an initial point at which the set of systems was precisely adjusted, then this network of systems will react to any change affecting one of its parts like a motor with a feed-back device: governed (in both senses of the word) by its previous harmony, it will direct the discordant mechanism towards an equilibrium which will be at any rate a compromise between the old state of affairs and the confusion brought in from outside.

Whether they are historically correct or not, the traditional legends of the Osage show that native thought itself may well envisage this sort of interpretation, based on the hypothesis of a structural adjustment of the historical process. When the ancestors emerged from the bowels of the earth they were, according to Osage tradition, divided into two groups, one peace-loving, vegetarian and associated with the left side and the other warlike, carnivorous and associated with the right. The two groups resolved to ally themselves and to exchange their respective foods. In the course of their wanderings, they met a third group, which was ferocious and lived entirely on carrion, with whom they eventually united. Each of the three groups was originally composed of seven clans, making a total of twenty-one clans. In spite of the symmetry of this three-clan division, the system was in disequilibrium since the newcomers belonged to the side of war and there were fourteen clans on one side and seven on the other. In order to remedy this defect and to preserve the balance between the side of war and the side of peace, the number of clans in one of the groups of warriors was reduced to five and that in the other to two. Since then the Osage camps, which are circular in shape with the entrance facing east, consist of seven clans of peace occupying the northern half on the left of the entrance and seven clans of war occupying the southern half on the right of the entrance (J. O. Dorsey *I*, *2*). The legend suggests twin processes. One is purely structural, passing from a dual to a three-fold system and then returning to the earlier dualism; the other, both structural and historical at the same time, consists in undoing the effects of an overthrow of the primitive structure, resulting from historical events, or events thought of as such: migrations, war, alliance. Now, the social organization of the Osage, as it was to be seen in the nineteenth century, in fact integrated both aspects. Although they were each composed of the same number of clans, the side of peace and the side of war were in disequilibrium since one was simply 'sky' while the other, also referred to as 'of the earth', consisted of two groups of clans associated respectively with dry land and water. The system was thus at once historical and structural, composed of two and of three classes, symmetrical and asymmetrical, stable and top heavy . . .

Nowadays the reaction to a difficulty of the same kind is quite different. Consider for instance this agreement to differ with which a recent conference ended:

M. Bertrand de JOUVENEL – M. Priouret, would you like to say a few words in conclusion?

M. Roger PRIOURET – It seems to me that we are faced with two diametrically opposed theories. Raymond Aron follows the views of André Siegfried, according to which there are two basic political attitudes in France. This country is sometimes Bonapartist and sometimes Orleanist. Bonapartism consists in the acceptance and even desire for personal power, Orleanism in leaving the administration of public affairs to representatives. In the face of crises like the defeat of 1871 or a protracted war like the one in Algiers, France changes in attitude, that is, turns from Bonapartism to Orleanism as in 1871 or from Orleanism to Bonapartism, as on 13 May 1958.

In my own view, on the other hand, the actual change, although not entirely independent of these constants in French political temperament, is connected with the upheavals which industrialization brings into society. A different political analogy occurs to me. The coup d'etat of 2 December 1851 corresponds to the first industrial revolution and the coup d'etat of 13 May 1958 to the second. In other words, history shows that upheaval in the conditions of production and consumption seems incompatible with parliamentary government and leads this country to the form of authoritarian power which suits its temperament, namely, personal power' (Sedeis, p. 20).

The Osage would probably have used these two types of opposition, one synchronic and the other diachronic, as a point of departure. Instead of expecting to be able to choose between them they would have accepted both on the same footing and would have tried to work out a single scheme which allowed them to combine the standpoint of structure with that of event.

Considerations of the same kind could undoubtedly provide an intellectually satisfying explanation of the curious mixture of divergencies and parallels characteristic of the social structure of the five Iroquois nations and, on an historically and geographically larger scale, of the similarities and differences exhibited by the Algonkin of the east of the United States. In societies with unilinear exogamous clans, the system of clan names is almost always mid-way between order and disorder. And this, it seems, can only be explained by the combined action of two forces, one of demographic origin which pushes it towards disorganization and the other of speculative inspiration which pushes it towards a reorganization as closely as possible in line with the earlier state of affairs.

The Pueblo Indians provide a good example of this phenomenon. Their villages present so many sociological variations on a theme which looks as if it may be common to all of them. In collecting data on the Hopi, Zuni, Keres and Tanoan, Kroeber at one time believed he could show that 'a single, precise scheme pervades the clan organization of all the Pueblos', even though each village affords only a partial and distorted picture. This scheme was supposed to consist of a structure with twelve pairs of clans: rattlesnake – panther; deer – antelope; squash – crane; cloud – corn; lizard – earth; rabbit – tobacco; Tansey-mustard – Chaparral cock; Katchina (raven – macaw; pine – cotton wood); firewood – coyote; a group of four clans (arrow – sun; eagle – turkey); badger – bear; turquoise – shell or coral (Kroeber *I*, pp. 137–40).

This ingenious attempt to reconstruct a 'master plan' was criticized by Eggan on the basis of fuller and less ambiguous material than Kroeber had at his disposal in 1915–16 when he made his study. Another damaging argument could however also be brought forward, namely that it does not seem possible that a master plan should have survived the different demographic changes in each village. Using Kroeber's own material, let us compare the distribution of clans at Zuni (one thousand, six hundred and fifty inhabitants in 1915 and in two Hopi villages of the first mesa, the number of whose inhabitants Kroeber multiplied by five (result: 1,610) to facilitate the comparison: see p. 72. If one traces a curve showing the distribution of Zuni clans in declining order of population and superimposes a curve of the distribution of Hopi clans of the first mesa, it is clear that the demographic development is different in the two cases and that the comparison does not in principle allow the reconstruction of a common plan (figure 3, p. 72).

In these circumstances and even if we admit that Kroeber's reconstruction may have done violence to the facts at some points, it is none the less remarkable that so many common elements and systematic relations continue to exist in different local organizations. This suggests a rigour, tenacity and fidelity to distinctions

	ZUNI	HOPI (Walpi and Sichumovi)
Sun, Eagle, Turkey	520	90
Dogwood	430	55
Corn, Frog	195	225
Badger, Bear	195	160
Crane	100	nil
Coyote	75	80
Tansey-Mustard, Chaparral Cock	60	255
Tobacco	45	185
Deer, Antelope	20	295
Rattlesnake	nil	120
Lizard, Earth	nil	145
(Of unknown affiliation)	10	nil
Total	1,650	1,610

(Kroeber, *I*, p. 149)

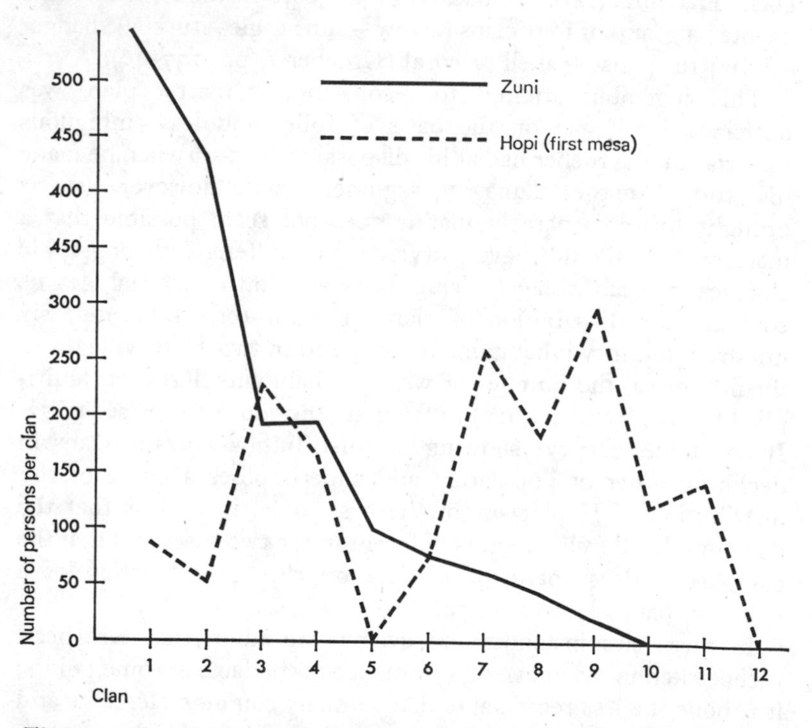

Figure 3. Distribution of the population at Zuni and among the Hopi of the first mesa according to clan.

and differences on the theoretical plane of which a botanist has collected equally convincing proofs on the practical one:

In Mexico I worked almost exclusively with farmers of European or partly European ancestry. Even those who had strikingly Indian features were mostly Spanish-speaking and did not consider themselves Indians. In Guatemala I worked with such people but also with Indians who had retained their old languages and their own cultures. I found, to my surprise, that their cornfields had been more rigidly selected for type than those of their Latin-speaking neighbours. Their fields were quite as true to type as had been prize-winning American cornfields in the great corn-show era when the American farmer was paying exquisite attention to such fancy show points as uniformity. This fact was amazing, considering the great variability of Guatemalan maize as a whole, and the fact that corn crosses so easily. A little pollen blown from one field to another will introduce mongrel germ plasm. Only the most finicky selection of seed ears and the pulling out of plants which are offtype could keep a variety pure under such conditions. Yet for Mexico and Guatemala and our own South-west the evidence is clear: wherever the old Indian cultures have survived most completely the corn is least variable within the variety.

Much later I grew a collection of corn made among an even more primitive people, the Naga of Assam, whom some ethnologists describe as still living in the Stone Age in so far as their daily life is concerned. Each tribe had several different varieties which were sharply different from one another, yet within the variety there were almost no differences from plant to plant. Furthermore, some of the most distinctive of these varieties were grown not only by different families but by different tribes, in different areas. Only a fanatical adherence to an ideal type could have kept these varieties so pure when they were being traded from family to family and from tribe to tribe. It is apparently not true, as has so frequently been stated, that the most primitive people have the most variable varieties. Quite the opposite. It is rather those natives most frequently seen by travellers, the ones who live along modern highways and near big cities, the ones whose ancient cultures have most completely broken down, who have given rise to the impression that primitive peoples are careless plant breeders (Anderson, E., pp. 186–7).

This is a striking example of the concern with differentiating features which pervades the practical as well as the theoretical activities of the people we call primitive. Its formal nature and the 'hold' it has over every kind of content explain how it is that native institutions, though borne along on the flux of time, manage to steer a course between the contingencies of history and the immutability of design and remain, as it were, within the stream of intelligibility. They are always at a safe distance from the Scylla and Charybdis of diachrony and synchrony, event and structure, the aesthetic and the logical, and those who have tried to define them in terms of only one or the other aspect have therefore necessarily failed to understand their nature. Between the basic absurdity Frazer attributed to primitive practices and beliefs and the specious validation of them in terms of a supposed common sense invoked by Malinowski, there is scope for a whole science and a whole philosophy.

CHAPTER THREE

SYSTEMS OF TRANSFORMATIONS

As we have just seen, the practico-theoretical logics governing the life and thought of so-called primitive societies are shaped by the insistence on differentiation. The latter is already evident in the myths underlying totemic institutions (Lévi-Strauss 6, pp. 27–8 and 36–7) and it is also found on the plane of technical activity, which aspires to results bearing the hallmark of permanence and discontinuity. Now, on the theoretical as well as the practical plane, the existence of differentiating features is of much greater importance than their content. Once in evidence, they form a system which can be employed as a grid is used to decipher a text, whose original unintelligibility gives it the appearance of an uninterrupted flow. The grid makes it possible to introduce divisions and contrasts, in other words the formal conditions necessary for a significant message to be conveyed. The imaginary example discussed in the last chapter showed how any system of differentiating features, provided that it is a system, permits the organization of a sociological field which historical and demographic evolution are transforming and which is hence composed of a theoretically unlimited series of different contents.

The logical principle is always to be *able* to oppose terms which previous impoverishment of the empirical totality, provided it has been impoverished allows one to conceive as distinct. *How* to oppose is an important but secondary consideration in relation to this first requirement. In other words, the operative value of the systems of naming and classifying commonly called totemic derives from their formal character: they are codes suitable for conveying messages which can be transposed into other codes, and for expressing messages received by means of different codes in terms of their own system. The mistake of classical ethnologists was to try to reify this form and to tie it to a determinate content when in fact what it provides is a method for assimilating any kind of content. Far from being an autonomous institution definable by its intrinsic characteristic, totemism, or what is referred to as such, corresponds to certain modalities arbitrarily isolated from a formal system, the function of which is to guarantee the convertibility of ideas between different levels of social reality. As Durkheim seems sometimes to have realized, the basis of sociology is what may be called 'socio-logic' (Lévi-Strauss 4, p. 36; p. 137).

In the second volume of *Totemism and Exogamy*, Frazer was particularly concerned with the simple forms of totemic beliefs observed in Melanesia by Codrington and by Rivers. He believed that in them he had discovered the primitive forms which were the origin of the conceptual system of totemism in Australia, whence, in his view, all other types of totemism derived. In the New Hebrides (Aurora) and in the Banks' Islands (Mota) certain people think that their life is associated with that of a plant, animal or inanimate object called *atai* or *tamaniu* in the Banks' Islands and *nunu* at Aurora. The sense of *nunu* and perhaps also of *atai* is roughly that of soul (figure 4).

According to Codrington, a Mota native discovers his *tamaniu* through a vision or with the aid of divining techniques. In Aurora, on the other hand, it is the future mother who believes that a coconut, a bread-fruit tree or some other object is mysteriously connected with the child, who will be a sort of echo of it. Rivers found the same beliefs in Mota where many people observe food prohibitions because they believe themselves to be an animal or fruit which their mother found or noticed while she was pregnant. In such a case, a woman takes the plant, fruit or animal back to her village and asks about the significance of the event. It is explained to her that she will give birth to a child who will resemble, or actually be, the object. She then returns it to the place where she found it and, if it was an animal, builds it a shelter out of stones. She visits and feeds it every day. When the animal disappears, it is because it has entered her body, from which it will reappear in the form of a child.

The child may not eat the plant or animal with which it is identified under pain of illness or death. If it is an inedible fruit

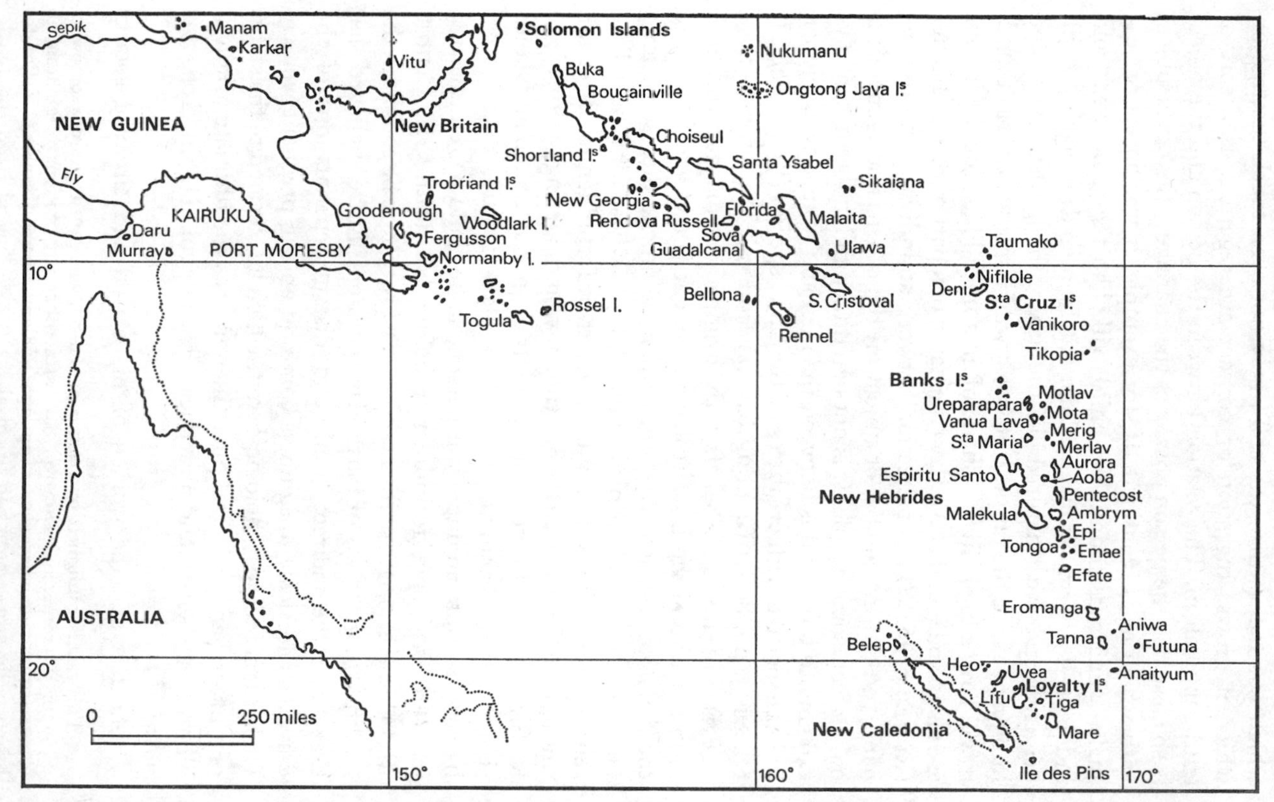

Fig 4 Partial map of Melanesia (Centre documentaire sur l'Oceanie de l'Ecole Pratique des Hautes Etudes).

which was found, then the child may not even touch the tree on which it grows. Ingestion or contact are regarded as a sort of auto-cannibalism. The relation between the person and the object is so close that the person possesses the characteristics of the object with which he is identified. If, for example, it was an eel or sea-snake which was found, the child will, like these, be weak and indolent, if a hermit crab, it will be hot-tempered; or again, it will be gentle and sweet-natured like the lizard, thoughtless, hasty and intemperate like the rat or, if it was a wild apple which was found, it will have a big belly the shape of an apple. These identifications are also to be found at Motlav (the name of a part of Saddle Island) (Rivers, p. 462). The connection between an individual on the one hand and a plant, animal or object on the other is not general; it only affects some people. It is not hereditary and it does not involve exogamous prohibitions between the men and women who happen to be associated with creatures of the same species (Frazer vol. II, pp. 81–3, pp. 89–91 (quoting Rivers), and vol. IV, pp. 286–7).

Frazer regards these beliefs as the origin and explanation of those found at Lifu in the Loyalty Islands and at Ulawa and Malaita in the Solomon Islands. At Lifu a man before he dies sometimes indicates the animal (or bird or butterfly) in whose form he will be reincarnated. All his descendants are then forbidden to eat or kill this animal. 'It is our ancestor', they say, and offerings are made to it. Similarly Codrington observed that in the Solomon Islands (Ulawa) the inhabitants refused to plant banana trees or eat bananas because an important person, so he could be reincarnated in them, had once forbidden it before his death.* In Central Melanesia the origin of food taboos must therefore be sought in the fanciful imaginations of particular ancestors. Frazer believed that they were the indirect result and distant repercussions of the cravings and sickly imaginings common among pregnant women. He held that this psychological trait, which he elevated to the status of a natural and universal phenomenon, was the ultimate origin of all totemic beliefs and practices (Frazer, vol. II, pp. 106–7 *et passim*).

The fact that the women of his period and circle of society

* This fact is confirmed by Ivens, pp. 269–70, who puts forward a somewhat different interpretation. However, he cites other prohibitions originating in reincarnation of an ancestor. Cf. pp. 272, 468 and *passim*. Cf. also C.E. Fox for beliefs of the same type at San Cristoval.

experienced cravings when they were pregnant and that the savage Australian and Melanesian women also did so was enough to convince Frazer of the universality and natural origin of the phenomenon. He would have had otherwise to dissociate it from nature and attribute it to culture, thus admitting that there could in some way be direct, and so alarming, resemblances between late nineteenth century European societies and those of the cannibals. Now, apart from the fact that there is no evidence that pregnant women the world over have cravings, their incidence has diminished considerably in Europe in the last fifty years and they may even have disappeared altogether in some sections of society. They certainly occurred in Australia and Melanesia but in the form of an institutional means of defining in advance certain aspects of the status of persons or groups. And in Europe itself, it is unlikely that the cravings of pregnant women will survive the disappearance of a similar type of belief which fosters them – on the pretext of referring to them – in order to diagnose (not predict) certain physical or psychological peculiarities noticed after (not before) a child's birth. Even if it were the case that the cravings of pregnant women had a natural basis, this latter could not account for beliefs and practices which, as we have seen, are far from being general and which can take different forms in different societies.

Further, it is not clear what made Frazer give the 'sick fancies' of pregnant women priority over those of old men at death's door, except perhaps the fact that people must be born before they can die. But by this reasoning all social institutions should have come into existence in the course of a single generation. Finally, had the system of Ulawa, Malaita and Lifu been derived from that of Motlav, Mota and Aurora, the remains or survivals of the latter should be found in the former. What is striking, however, is that the two systems are exact counterparts of each other. There is nothing to suggest that one is chronologically prior to the other. Their relation is not that of an original to a derivative form. It is rather that between forms symmetrically the reverse of each other, as if system represented a transformation of the same group.

Instead of trying to discern the priorities, let us think in terms of groups and attempt to define their properties. We can summarize these properties as a triple opposition: between birth and death on the one hand, and between the individual or collective nature either of a diagnosis or of a prohibition on the other. It is worth observing that the prohibition follows from a prognostication: anyone eating the forbidden fruit or animal will die.

On the Motlav-Mota-Aurora system, the relevant term in the first opposition is birth. In the Lifu-Ulawa-Malaita system it is death. All the terms in the other oppositions are similarly reversed. In the case where birth is the relevant event, the diagnosis is made collectively and the prohibition (or prognostication) applies to individuals; a woman who is pregnant or about to become so and who finds an animal or fruit on the ground or in her loin cloth, returns to the village where she questions her friends and relatives. The social group collectively (or through the mouthpiece of qualified representatives) gives a diagnosis of the distinctive status of the person about to be born, who will be subject to an individual prohibition.

The whole system is reversed at Lifu, Uwala and Malaita. The relevant event is death, and accordingly the diagnosis is individual since it is made by the dying man and the prohibition is collective, binding as it does all the descendants of the same ancestor and sometimes, as at Ulawa, the whole population.

The two systems are therefore in the position of exact opposites within the same group. This can be seen in the following table where + and — correspond to the first and second member of each pair of opposites respectively:

Significant oppositions:		Motlav-Mota-Aurora	Lifu-Ulawa-Malaita
Birth/death		+	—
Individual/collective	diagnosis:	—	+
	prohibition:	+	—

These facts make it possible to extract a feature which is common to each group and serves to distinguish it as a group from all others of the same set, that is, the set of systems of classification which postulate a homology between natural distinctions and cultural distinctions (an expression to be preferred to 'totemic institutions'). The common feature of the two systems just discussed is their statistical and non-universal nature. Neither applies indiscriminately to all the members of the society: an animal or plant plays a part in the conception of only some children; only some of the dying are reincarnated in a natural species. The domain governed by each system therefore consists of a sample, the selection of which is, at least in theory, left to chance. For this double reason, these systems belong immediately beside the Australian systems of the Aranda type, as Frazer saw although he misunderstood the nature of the relationship – logical and not genetic – which unites them while at the same time recognizing the distinctiveness of each. The Aranda systems are also of a statistical nature but their rule of application is universal since the domain they govern is coextensive with the whole society.

In the course of their passage across Australia, Spencer and Gillen were already struck by the fact that the institutions of the people lying on a south-north axis from the Great Australian Bight to the Gulf of Carpentaria looked as if they formed a coherent system.

> In the Arunta and the Warramunga [socio-religious] conditions are exactly reversed, but, as in other matters, so we find an Intermediate state in the Kaitish (Spencer and Gillen, p. 164).

The Arabanna in the south recognize two exogamous moieties and a number of exogamous totemic clans, all matrilineal. Marriage, shown by Spencer and Gillen to be preferential with the daughter of the mother's elder brother or the father's elder sister, belongs, according to Elkin, to the same type as the Aranda, but complicated by totemic restrictions, which, as we know, the Aranda do not have.

In mythical times (*ularaka*) the totemic ancestors placed the spirit-children (*maiaurli*) in the totemic places. The Aranda have an equivalent belief. But, whereas among the Aranda the spirits regularly return to their place of origin to await a new incarnation, Arabanna spirits change their sex, moiety and totem at each successive incarnation and every spirit therefore regularly passes through a complete cycle of biological and socio-religious statuses (Spencer and Gillen, pp. 146 sq).

If this were a description of the course of events in the real world, the picture presented would be of a system symmetrically the reverse of that of the Aranda. Among the Aranda descent is patrilineal and not matrilineal. Totemic affiliation is determined not by a rule of descent but by the place at which a woman happens to be when she becomes conscious of her pregnancy. In other words, totems are allocated according to a rule among the Arabanna statistically and on the basis of chance among the

Aranda. Totemic groups are strictly exogamous among the Arabanna but play no part in the regulation of marriage among the Aranda; marriage among the Aranda is regulated by a system of eight subsections (and no longer just two moieties), unrelated to totemic affiliations and operating as a cycle which can be represented in the following way (figure 5).*

Simplifying a great deal and confining ourselves for the moment to the older sources, it is tempting to say that the course of events for human beings among the Aranda is the same as the course of events for spirits among the Arabanna. In each generation spirits change their sex and moiety. (I am leaving aside the change of totemic group since totemic affiliation is not relevant in the Aranda system and I am replacing it by a change of subsection, which is the relevant feature.) These two requirements, translated into the terms of the Aranda system, produce the cycle:

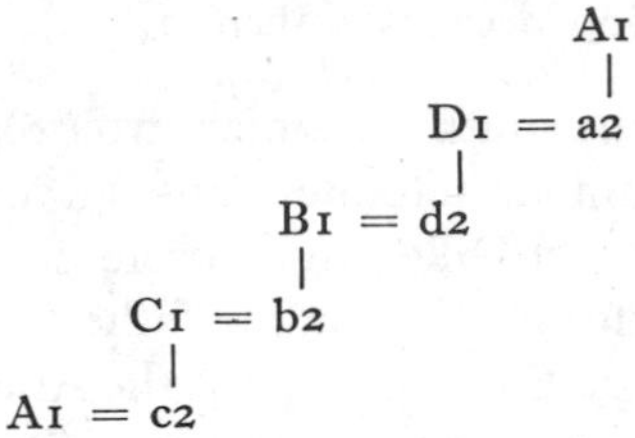

```
                        A1
                        |
                  D1 = a2
                  |
            B1 = d2
            |
      C1 = b2
      |
A1 = c2
```

where capital letters and small letters represent men and women respectively. This cycle corresponds not to the actual structure of Aranda society in which exclusively male and exclusively female cycles are distinguished, but to the procedure, implicit in the terms of the system, by means of which these bits are, as it were, sewn together.

Elkin's criticisms of his predecessors' description should however be taken into account. Elkin believed that Spencer and Gillen had noticed only one form of totemism among the Aranda (Elkin 4, pp. 138–9) when in fact there were two, such as he had himself discovered among the Arabanna: one patrilineal and a matter of cult and the other matrilineal and social and so also exogamous:

> Members of a patrilineal totemic cult-group do perform increase ceremonies, assisted by their 'sisters' sons', and they do ritually hand this cult-totem over to the latter, and through them to others, to eat, but they

* I am indebted to my colleague G. Th. Guilbaud for this mode of diagrammatic representation in the form of annulus.

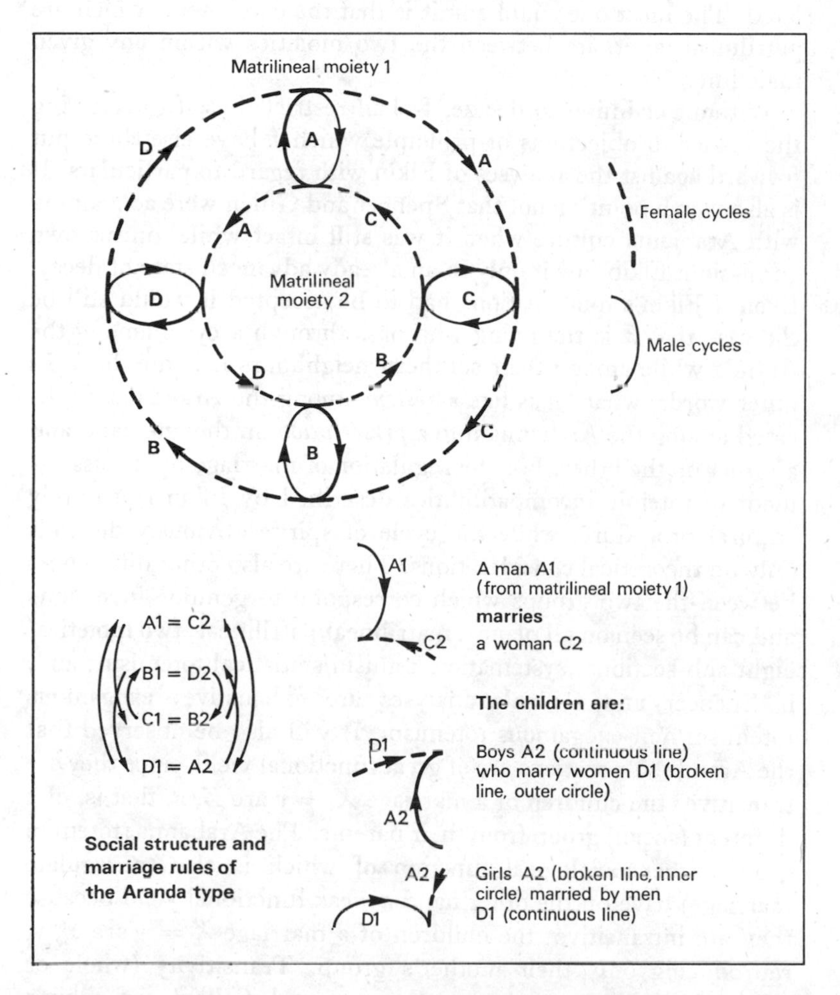

Fig 5 Social structure and marriage rules of the Aranda type (Laboratoire de cartographie de l'Ecole Pratique des Hautes Etudes).

do not henceforth observe a taboo on this totem themselves. On the other hand . . . they do observe a rigid prohibition on eating their *madu*, social totem, which however is not the object of a cult (Elkin 2a, p. 180).

Elkin's objection to Spencer and Gillen's account is therefore that the supposition that the totemic spirits pass through a complete cycle is inconsistent because it would involve a mixture of two forms of totemism which, as he himself holds, cannot be assimilated. The most one could admit is that the cult totems which are patrilineal, alternate between the two moieties within any given male line.

Without claiming to decide, I shall restrict myself to referring the reader to objections of principle which I have elsewhere put forward against the analyses of Elkin with regard to particulars. It is also worth pointing out that Spencer and Gillen were acquainted with Arabanna culture when it was still intact while, on his own admission, Elkin saw it only in an already advanced state of decay. Even if Elkin's qualifications had to be accepted it would still be the case that it is the living who pass through a cycle among the Aranda while among their southern neighbours it is the dead. In other words, what looks like a *system* among the Aranda is duplicated among the Arabanna into a *prescription* on the one hand and a *theory* on the other. For the regulation of marriage by the assessment of totemic incompatibilities described by Elkin is a purely empiral procedure, while the cycle of spirits obviously depends only on theoretical considerations. There are also other differences between the two groups which correspond to genuine inversions and can be seen on all planes: matrilineal/patrilineal; two moieties/eight sub-sections; systematic totemism/statistical totemism; and, if Spencer and Gillen's analyses are exhaustive: exogamous totemism/non-exogamous totemism. It will also be observed that the Aranda sub-sections are of great functional yield, since they are transitive: the children of a marriage $X = y$ are Z, z, that is, of a different (social) group from their parents. The Arabanna (totemic) groups (the sociological function of which is also to regulate marriage) have on the other hand a weak functional yield because they are intransitive: the children of a marriage $X = y$ are Y, y, reproducing only their mother's group. Transitivity (whole or partial according to whether Spencer and Gillen's or Elkin's account is adopted) occurs only in the Arabanna spirit world where a society similar to that of the living among the Aranda is reproduced.

Finally, the same inversion can be seen in the role which territoriality plays in each tribe. The Aranda treat it as having a real and absolute value. It is the only clearly meaningful content in their system for from the beginning of time each place has always belonged to one and only one totemic species. Among the Arabanna, due to the spirits' ability to move through a cycle, locality loses much of its significance and the value accorded to it is relative and formal. The totemic places are ports of call rather than ancestral homes.

Let us now compare the social structure of the Aranda with that of the Warramunga, a people further north who are also patrilineal. Among the Warramunga totems are connected with moieties, that is, their function is the reverse of the one which they have among the Aranda and analogous (although in a different way) to that which they have among the Arabanna, whose geographical position is also the reverse in relation to the Aranda, the Warramunga being the Aranda's northern, while the Arabanna are their southern, neighbours. Like the Arabanna, the Warramunga have paternal and maternal totems, but, in contrast to what occurs among the Arabanna, it is the paternal totems which are prohibited absolutely. The maternal totems are permitted through the agency of the opposite moiety. Among the Arabanna, on the other hand, it is the paternal totems which are allowed to the opposite moiety through the offices of the cult groups belonging to the same moiety.

The role given to the opposite moiety indeed lends itself to an analysis by transformation. There is no reciprocity between moieties in the rites of increase among the Aranda: each cult group performs its rites as it pleases for the benefit of other groups who are themselves free to eat the food made more abundant only through the auspices of the officiating group. Among the Warramunga, on the other hand, the moiety which eats the food actively intervenes to make the other moiety perform the ceremonies from which it benefits.

This difference leads to other related ones. In one case the rites of increase are an individual, in the other a group, affair. Among the Aranda the performance of the rites of increase, which is left to the initiative of the man whose property they are, is of a statistical nature: a person officiates when he wishes without co-ordinating his efforts with those of others. Among the Warramunga on the other hand there is a calendar of ritual, and ceremonies succeed each other in a prescribed order. We thus find again, on the ritual plane, an opposition between periodic and non-periodic structures which we noticed earlier (in the case of the Aranda and Arabanna) and which appeared to be characteristic of the community of the living and the community of the dead. The same formal opposition exists between the Aranda on the one side and the Warramunga and Arabanna on the other but this time it manifests itself on a different plane. Simplifying a good deal, we could say that in both these respects the position among the Warramunga is symmetrical with that prevailing among the Arabanna, with the difference that descent is patrilineal in one case and matrilineal in the other. The Aranda, on the other hand, who are patrilineal like the Warramunga, can be opposed to their northern and southern neighbours by the statistical nature of their performance of rituals which contrasts with the periodic celebration of rituals among the latter.*

Furthermore, the Arabanna and Warramunga think of their totemic ancestors as single individuals who are half-human half-animal and have an air of completeness. The Aranda on the other hand favour the idea of a multiplicity of ancestors (for each totemic group), who are, however, incomplete human beings. As Spencer and Gillen have shown, the groups lying between the Aranda and Warramunga, the Kaitish and Unmatjera, provide an intermediate case in this respect, for their ancestors are represented in myths as a mixture of incomplete human beings and fully fledged men. In general, the distribution of beliefs and customs on a north–south axis shows sometimes a gradual change from one extreme type to its reverse form and sometimes the recurrence of the same forms at the two poles but in that case expressed in a reverse context: patrilineal or matrilineal; the structural inversion then occurs in the centre, that is, among the Aranda:

* Among the Aranda 'there was no set order . . . each separate ceremony is the property of some special individual' but among the Warramunga 'the ceremonies connected with a given totem are performed in a regular sequence: A, B, C, D' (Spencer and Gillen, p. 192–3).

	SOUTH			NORTH
	Arabanna	Aranda	Kaitish, Unmatjera	Warramunga
Totemic ancestors	complete beings, half-human half-animal single	incomplete human beings multiple	incomplete human beings + fully developed men multiple	complete beings, half-human half-animal single
Social organization	exogamous totemism	totems and moieties do not coincide non-exogamous totemism		totems and moieties coincide exogamous totemism
Ritual		reciprocal exclusivism of moieties	initiative of totemic group + assistance moiety	reciprocity of moieties: initiative of opposite moiety
Totemic ceremonies		individual property		collective property
Performance		non-periodic		periodic

We see therefore that going from the Aranda to the Warramunga, one passes from a system with a collective mythology (multiplicity of ancestors) but an individualized ritual to the reverse system of an individualized mythology but a collective ritual. Similarly the properties ascribed to the earth are religious (associated with totems) among the Aranda and social among the Warramunga (territory is divided between the moieties). Finally, the churinga progressively disappears as one goes north. What has already been said might almost have led one to expect this, since in the Aranda context the churinga serves to bring unity into multiplicity: it represents the physical body of an ancestor and is held by a series of successive individuals as proof of their genealogical descent, and it bears witness to the continuity of the individual over time, the possibility of which might seem to be excluded by the Aranda conception of mythical times.*

All these transformations could be systematically set out. The Karadjera among whom a *man dreams* the totemic affiliation of his future child, furnish an instance of a case the reverse of the Aranda where it is the *woman* who *experiences* it. The increasingly exacting nature of totemic prohibitions in North Australia provide a sort of 'culinary' equivalent of the restraints on marriage imposed by a system with eight exogamous sub-sections. Thus some peoples forbid a man, conditionally or absolutely, to eat not only his own totem but also those of his father, his mother, his father's father (or mother's father). Among the Kauralaig of the islands north of Cape York Peninsula a person recognizes as a totem not only his own but also those of his father's mother, mother's father and mother's mother; and marriage is forbidden in the four corresponding clans (Sharp, p. 66). The eating prohibitions resulting from the belief that an ancestor is reincarnated in a species of animal or plant were discussed above. The same type of structure is found in the Melville and Bathurst islands but this time on the linguistic plane. All the homophones of the name of the deceased are avoided by his descendants even if they are terms in current use with only a remote phonetic resemblance to it.† It is words rather than bananas which are forbidden. The same ideas appear and disappear in different societies either identical or transposed from one level of consumption to another, sometimes applying to the treatment of women, sometimes to that of foods, sometimes to the words used in speech.

It is perhaps because Spencer and Gillen's material related to a comparatively limited number of Australian tribes and was at the same time remarkably full for each, that they were more acutely aware than their successors of the systematic relations between the different types. Later specialists' horizons came to be confined to the small area which they themselves were studying; and the sheer quantity of data, together with their own caution, deterred even those who did not abandon the idea of synthesis from looking for

* Cf. below, p. 238.

† As in various Indian tribes where the prohibition on uttering the names of parents-in-law extends to all the words of which these names were composed. Cf. below, p. 176.

laws. The greater our knowledge, the more obscure the overall scheme. The dimensions multiply, and the growth of axes of reference beyond a certain point paralyses intuitive methods: it becomes impossible to visualize a system when its representation requires a continuum of more than three or four dimensions. But the day may come when all the available documentation on Australian tribes is transferred to punched cards and with the help of a computer their entire techno-economic, social and religious structures can be shown to be like a vast group of transformations.

The idea is the more attractive since it is at least possible to see why Australia should be a particularly favourable field for such an experiment, more so than any other continent. In spite of the contact and inter-change with the outside world which has also taken place in Australia, Australian societies have probably developed in isolation more than appears to have been the case elsewhere. Moreover, this development was not undergone passively. It was desired and conceptualized, for few civilizations seem to equal the Australians in their taste for erudition and speculation and what sometimes looks like intellectual dandyism, odd as this expression may appear when it is applied to people with so rudimentary a level of material life. But lest there be any mistake about it: these shaggy and corpulent savages whose physical resemblance to adipose bureaucrats or veterans of the Empire makes their nudity yet more incongruous, these meticulous adepts in practices which seem to us to display an infantile perversity – manipulation and handling of the genitals, tortures, the industrious use of their own blood and their own excretions and secretions (like our own more discreet and unreflecting habit of moistening postage stamps with saliva) – were, in various respects, real snobs. They have indeed been referred to as such by a specialist, born and brought up among them and speaking their language (T. G. H. Strehlow, p. 82). When one considers them in this light, it seems less surprising that as soon as they were taught accomplishments of leisure, they prided themselves on painting the dull and studied water-colours one might expect of an old maid (Plate 8).

Granting that Australia has been turned in on itself for hundreds of thousands of years,* that theorizing and discussion was all the

* With the undoubted exception of the northern regions and these were not without contact with the rest of the continent. This is therefore only an approximation.

rage in this closed world and the influence of fashion often paramount, it is easy to understand the emergence of a sort of common philosophical and sociological style along with methodically studied variations on it, even the most minor of which were pointed out for favourable or adverse comment. Each group was no doubt actuated by the only apparently contradictory incentives of being like others, as good as others, better than others and different from others, that is, of constantly elaborating themes only the general outlines of which were fixed by tradition and custom. In short, in the field of social organization and religious thought, the Australian communities behaved like the peasant societies of Europe in their manner of dressing in the late eighteenth and early nineteenth centuries. That each community had its own dress and that this was composed of roughly the same elements for men and women respectively was never called in question. It was in wealth or ingenuity of detail alone that people tried to distinguish themselves from, and to outdo, the neighbouring village. All women wore coifs but they were different in different regions. In France marriage rules of an endogamous kind were expressed in terms of coifs ('Marry within the coif') just as Australian rules (of an exogamous kind) were expressed in terms of sections or totemism. Here, as elsewhere, among the Australian aborigines as in our own peasant societies the combination of general conformity (which is a feature of a closed world) with the particularism of the parish results in culture being treated like themes and variations in music.

It is therefore conceivable that the favourable historical and geographical conditions outlined have led to Australian cultures standing in a relation of transformation with each other, possibly more completely and systematically than those of other regions of the world. But this external relation must not make us neglect the same relation, this time internal, which exists, in a very much more general fashion, between the different levels of a single culture. As I have already suggested, ideas and beliefs of the 'totemic' type particularly merit attention because, for the societies which have constructed or adopted them, they constitute codes making it possible to ensure, in the form of conceptual systems, the convertibility of messages appertaining to each level, even of those which are so remote from each other that they apparently relate solely to culture or solely to society, that is, to men's relations with each other, on the one hand, or, on the other, to phenomena of a technical or economic order which might rather seem to concern man's relations with nature. This mediation between nature and culture, which is one of the distinctive functions of the totemic operator, enables us to sift out what may be true from what is partial and distorted in Durkheim's and Malinowski's accounts. They each attempted to immure totemism in one or other of these two domains. In fact however it is pre-eminently the means (or hope) of transcending the opposition between them.

This has been brought out very clearly by Lloyd Warner in the case of the Murngin of Arnhem Land. These North Australians explain the origin of things by a myth which is also the basis of an important part of their ritual. At the beginning of time the Wawilak sisters set off on foot towards the sea, naming places, animals and plants as they went. One of them was pregnant and the other carried her child. Before their departure they had both indeed had incestuous relations with men of their own moiety.

After the birth of the younger sister's child, they continued their journey and one day stopped near a water hole where the great snake Yurlunggur lived who was the totem of the Dua moiety to which the sisters belonged. The older sister polluted the water with menstrual blood. The outraged python came out, caused a deluge of rain and a general flood and then swallowed the women and their children. When the snake raised himself the waters covered the entire earth and its vegetation. When he lay down again the flood receded.

As Warner explains, the Murngin consciously associate the snake with the rainy season which causes the annual inundation. In this area the various seasonal changes are so regular that, as a geographer points out, they can be predicted almost to the day. Rainfall is often as high as fifty or sixty inches in two or three months. It increases from just two inches in October to some ten inches in December and fifteen in January. The dry season comes equally rapidly. The graph of the rainfall recorded at Port Darwin over a period of forty-six years might be a picture of the snake Yurlunggur raised above his water hole with his head in the sky and flooding the earth (figure 6, p. 92).

This division of the year into two contrasting seasons, one of seven months and extremely dry and the other of five months with heavy rainfall and great tides which flood the coastal plains for

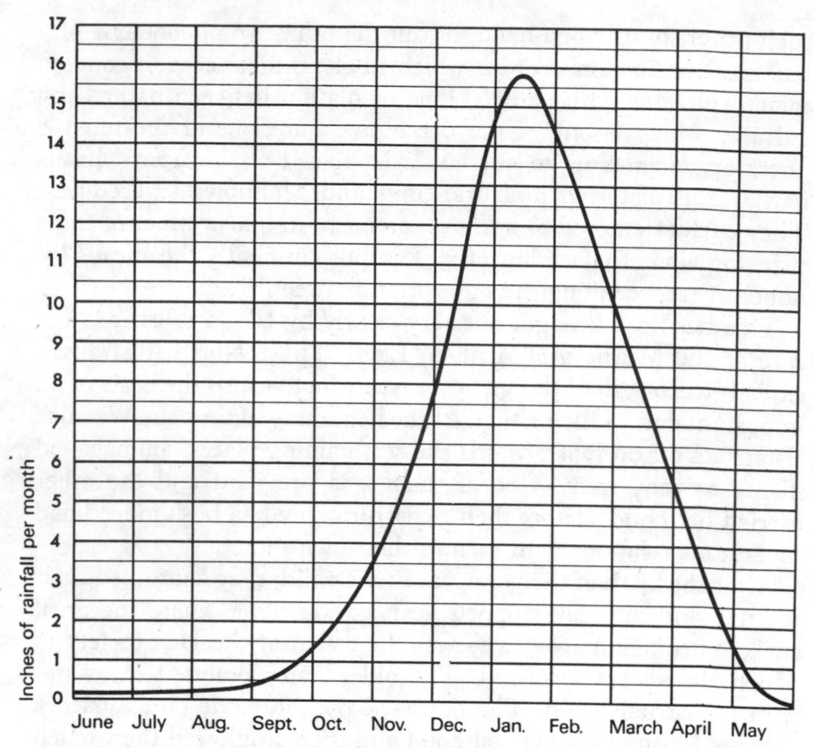

Fig 6 Rain chart for Port Darwin (forty-six-year record) (from Warner, Chart XI, p. 380).

scores of miles, leaves its mark on native thought and activities. The rainy season forces the Murngin to disperse and take refuge in small groups in the areas which have not been submerged. Here they carry on a precarious existence, threatened by famine and inundation. A few days after the floods have receded the vegetation is lush again and animals reappear. Collective life begins once more and abundance reigns. None of this would however have been possible had the floods not swamped and fertilized the plains.

Just as the seasons and winds are divided between the two moieties (the rainy season together with the west and northwest winds are Dua while the dry season and southeast wind are Yiritja), so the protagonists of the great mythical drama, the snake and the Wawilak sisters, are associated with the rainy and the dry season respectively. The former represents the male and initiated element, the latter the female and uninitiated. They must collaborate if there is to be life. As the myth explains: had the Wawilak sisters not committed incest and polluted the water hole of Yurlunggur there would have been neither life nor death, neither copulation nor reproduction on the earth, and there would have been no cycle of seasons.

The mythical system and the modes of representation it employs serve to establish homologies between natural and social conditions or, more accurately, it makes it possible to equate significant contrasts found on different planes: the geographical, meteorological, zoological, botanical, technical, economic, social, ritual, religious and philosophical. The equivalences are roughly the following:

Pure, sacred:	male	superior	fertilizing (rains)	bad season
Impure, profane:	female	inferior	fertilized (land)	good season

One can see at once that there is contradiction embedded in this table which sets out the canon of native logic. In fact, men are superior to women, the initiated to the uninitiated and the sacred to the profane. On the other hand all the terms on the top line are treated as homologous with the rainy season, which is the season of famine, isolation and danger, while the terms on the lower line are homologous with the dry season during which abundance reigns and sacred rites are performed:

> The men's age grade is a snake and purifying element, and the sociological women's group is the unclean group. The male snake-group in the act of swallowing the unclean group 'swallows' the initiates [and so makes them pass] into the ritually pure masculine age grade, and at the same time the whole ritual purifies the whole group or tribe.
>
> The snake is the fertilizing principle in nature according to Murngin symbolism; this explains why it is identified with the men's group rather than with the women; otherwise one would suppose that the male principle, being identified with the positive higher social values, would be associated by the Murngin with the dry season – the time of the year of high social value (Warner, p. 387).

The primacy of the infrastructure is thus in a sense confirmed, for the geography and climate, together with their repercussions on the biological plane, present native thought with a contradictory state of affairs. There are two seasons just as there are two sexes, two societies, two degrees of culture (the 'high' – that of the initiated – and the 'low'; cf. Stanner 1, p. 77 for this distinction). On the natural plane, however, the good season is subordinate to the bad, while on the social plane the relation between the corresponding terms is reversed. It is therefore necessary to decide how to interpret the contradiction. If the good season is said to be male on the grounds that it is superior to the bad season and that men and the initiated are superior to women and the uninitiated (a category to which women also belong) then not only power and efficacy but sterility as well would have to be attributed to the profane and female element. This would be doubly absurd since social power belongs to men and natural fertility to women. The other alternative is equally contradictory but its inconsistency can at least be disguised by the double division of the whole society into the two classes of men and women (now ritually as well as naturally differentiated) and the group of men into the two classes of old and young, initiated and uninitiated, according to the principle that the uninitiated stand in the same relation to the iniated in the society of men as women do to men within the society as a whole. But in consequence men forego embodying the happy side of existence for they cannot both rule and personify it. Irrevocably committed to the role of gloomy owners of a happiness accessible only through an intermediary, they fashion an image of themselves on the model of their sages and old men; and it is striking that two types of people, women on the one hand and old men on the other, constitute, as the means to and the masters of happiness respectively, the two poles of Australian society and that to attain full masculinity young men must temporarily renounce the former and lastingly submit to the latter.

The sexual privileges which old men enjoy, the control they exercise over an esoteric culture and sinister and mysterious initiation rites are undoubtedly general features of Australian societies, and examples could also be found in other parts of the world. I do not wish to claim that these phenomena are attributable to what are obviously local natural conditions. In order to avoid misunderstandings and in particular the charge of reviving an old geographical determinism, this needs to be explained.

The first point is that natural conditions are not just passively accepted. What is more they do not exist in their own right for they are a function of the techniques and way of life of the people who define and give them a meaning by developing them in a particular direction. Nature is not in itself contradictory. It can become so only in terms of some specific human activity which takes part in it; and the characteristics of the environment take on a different meaning according to the particular historical and technical form assumed in it by this or that type of activity. On the other hand, even when raised to that human level which alone can make them intelligible, man's relations with his natural environment remain objects of thought: man never perceives them passively; having reduced them to concepts, he compounds them in order to arrive at a system which is never determined in advance: the same situation can always be systematized in various ways. The mistake of Mannhardt and the Naturalist School was to think that natural phenomena are *what* myths seek to explain, when they are rather the *medium through which* myths try to explain facts which are themselves not of a natural but a logical order.

The sense in which infrastructures are primary is this: first, man is like a player who, as he takes his place at the table, picks up cards which he has not invented, for the cardgame is a datum of history and civilization. Second, each deal is the result of a contingent distribution of the cards, unknown to the players at the time. One must accept the cards which one is given, but each society, like each player, makes its interpretations in terms of several systems. These may be common to them all or individual: rules of the game or rules of tactics. And we are well aware that different players will not play the same game with the same hand even though the rules set limits on the games that can be played with any given one.

To explain the noticeable frequency of certain sociological solutions, not attributable to particular objective conditions, appeal must be made to form and not content. The substance of contradictions is much less important than the fact that they exist, and it would be a remarkable coincidence if a harmonious synthesis of the social and natural order were to be achieved at once. Now, the form contradictions take varies very much less than their empirical content. The poverty of religious thought can never be overestimated. It accounts for the fact that men have so often had recourse to the same means for solving problems whose concrete elements may be very different but which share the feature of all belonging to 'structures of contradiction'.

To return to the Murngin: one can see clearly how the system of totemic symbols permits the unification of heterogeneous semantic fields, at the cost of contradictions which it is the function of ritual to surmount by 'acting' them: the rainy season literally engulfs the dry season as men 'possess' women, and the initiated 'swallow up' the uninitiated, as famine destroys plenty, etc. The example of the Murngin is not however unique. There are suggestive indications of a 'coding' of a natural situation in totemic terms in other parts of the world also. A specialist on the Ojibwa, reflecting on the symbolization of thunder as a bird which is so common in North America, makes the following remark:

> According to meteorological observations, the average number of days with thunder begins with one in April, increases to a total of five in midsummer (July) and then declines to one in October. And if a bird calendar is consulted, the facts show that species wintering in the South begin to appear in April and disappear for the most part not later than October . . . The avian character of the Thunder Birds can be rationalized to some degree with reference to natural facts and their observation (Hallowell, p. 32).

One must refer to meteorological data, as Warner did in the case of Australia, to give a correct account of the personification of natural phenomena, common in the Hawaiian pantheon. The gods Kane-hekili (Male-in-the-form-of-gentle-rain), Ka-poha-Ka-a (Male [= sky]-the-rock-roller) who is the same as Ka̦'uila-nuimakeha (Male- [= sky]-lightning-flash-great-streaking), etc., cannot be distinguished and accurately placed without certain relevant information:

> The downpours, which come in late January, February and March predominantly and with greatest frequency and violence, develop in the following sequences of meteorological phenomena: lowering dark cumulus over sea and uplands, with atmospheric stillness inducing an increasing sense of ominous oppression; 'dry' thunder, sharp and threatening if near, like distant cannon if far away: followed very soon by slow, gentle precipitation, which increases rapidly to a downpour; with continuing heavy thunder, then, in the cloud and rain shrouded uplands, resounding and thudding, slowly passing along the ridges or round the mountain's flank and often then out to sea, where it resounds in dull thuds, and may return in a direction opposite to that along the ridge, a phenomenon produced by the miniature cyclonic action of winds, and by convection (Handy and Pukui, part IV, p. 125 n).

If totemic representations amount to a code which makes it possible to pass from one system to another regardless of whether it is formulated in natural or cultural terms, then it may perhaps be asked why it is that they are accompanied by rules of conduct. At first sight at least totemism, or what is claimed as such, is something more than a mere language. It does not just set up rules of compatibility and incompatibility between signs. It is the basis of an ethic which prescribes or prohibits modes of behaviour. Or at least this consequence seems to follow from the very common association of totemic modes of representation with eating prohibitions on the one hand and rules of exogamy on the other.

The first answer is that this supposed association is the result of a *petitio principi*. If totemism is defined as the joint presence of animal and plant names, prohibitions apply to the corresponding species and the forbidding of marriage between people of the same name and subject to the same prohibition, then clearly a problem arises about the connection of these customs. It has however long been known that any one of these features can be found without the others and any two of them without the third.

That this is so is particularly clear in the case of eating prohibitions, which form a vast and complex set of which the prohibitions referred to as totemic (that is those resulting from a group's affinity with a natural species or class of phenomena or objects) are only a particular case. The Ndembu sorcerer, who is primarily a diviner, must not eat the flesh of bush-buck because of its irregularly spotted hide, for if he did so his divination would stray from the main point. There is a prohibition on the zebra for the same reason, on animals with dark coats (which would cast a shadow over his clairvoyance), on a species of fish with sharp bones because they might prick the diviner's organ of divination, the liver, and on several sorts of spinach with slippery leaves because they might cause his powers of divination to slip away from him (V. W. Turner 2, pp. 47–8).

A Luvale boy may urinate only against the following trees during the time of his initiation: *Pseudo achnostylus deckendti*, *Hymenocardia mollis*, *Afrormosia angolensis*, *Vangueriopsis lanciflora*, *Swartzia madagascarinensis*. These are hard woods symbolizing the penis in erection, their fruits being associated with fertility and life. He is also forbidden to eat the flesh of various animals: *Tilapia melanopleura*, a fish with a red belly, the colour of blood; *Sarcodaces* sp. and *Hydrocyon* sp. which have sharp teeth symbolizing the painful after-effects of circumcision; *Clarias* sp. whose slimy skin symbolizes difficulty in the healing of the scar; the genet whose spotted skin symbolizes leprosy; the hare with his sharp teeth and 'hot' chillies which symbolize painful healing, etc. Female initiates are subject to analogous prohibitions (C. M. N. White, I, 2).

These prohibitions have been mentioned because they are specialized, well-defined and rationalized with precision. They can readily be distinguished from totemic prohibitions within the general category of eating prohibitions and contrasted with them. But Tessman's list of the very large number of prohibitions of the Fang of the Gabon includes examples of intermediate as well as extreme types – which explains why the question of whether the Fang are totemic has been so hotly contested even by those believing in the concept of totemism.

The prohibitions which the Fang call by the general term *beki* may apply to men or to women, to the initiated to the uninitiated, to adolescents or adults, to households in which a child is expected or to those in which it is not. The reasons given for them are moreover of very different kinds. The inside of elephants' tusks may not be eaten because it is a soft and bitter substance. The trunk of the elephant may not be eaten for fear of softening limbs, sheep and goats lest they communicate their panting. Squirrels are forbidden to pregnant women because they make childbirth difficult (cf. above [p. 61]). Mice are specially forbidden to girls because they shamelessly steal manioc while it is being washed and the girls would run the risk of being 'stolen' in the same way. Mice are however also more generally forbidden because they live near homesteads and are regarded as members of the family. Some birds are avoided for such reasons as their ugly cry or their physical appearance. Children may not eat the larvae of dragonfly because it might make them unable to hold their urine.

The idea of a dietetic experiment envisaged by Tessman has recently been taken up by Fischer with respect to the natives of Ponapy who believe that the violation of food taboos results in physiological disorders very like allergies. Fischer shows that allergic disorders often have a psychosomatic origin even among ourselves: in many patients they result from the violation of a taboo of a psychological or moral kind. This apparently natural symptom derives, then, from a cultural diagnosis.

Among the Fang, of whose prohibitions I have mentioned only

a few taken at random from Tessman's imposing list, it is rather a matter of religious analogies: horned animals associated with the moon; chimpanzee, pig, python, etc. because of their symbolic role in particular cults. That the prohibitions result not from intrinsic properties of the species to which they apply but from the place they are given in one or more systems of significance is clearly shown by the fact that the guinea fowl is forbidden to initiates of the female cult Nkang while in male cults the reverse rule holds: the cult animal is permitted to initiates but forbidden to novices (Tessman vol. 2, pp. 184–93).

Food prohibitions may therefore be organized into systems which are extra- or para-totemic. Conversely, many of the systems traditionally regarded as totemic include prohibitions which do not concern food. The only prohibition on food recorded among the Bororo of Brazil attaches to the meat of deer, a non-totemic species; but the animals or plants after which clans and sub-clans are named appear not to be objects of particular prohibitions. The privileges and prohibitions associated with clans are found on a different plane: that of techniques, raw materials and ornaments. Each clan distinguishes itself from others, especially at festivals, by the use of certain feathers, mother-of-pearl and other substances whose form and fashioning as well as nature are strictly laid down for each clan (Lévi-Strauss 2, ch. 19).

The northern Tlingit who inhabit the coast of Alaska also have jealously guarded clan crests and emblems. But the animals depicted or evoked are only prohibited in a mock fashion: the Wolf clan may not rear wolves nor the Crow clan crows and members of the Frog clan are said to be afraid of frogs (McClellan).

The central Algonkin have no food prohibitions applying to their clans' eponymous animals. Clans are primarily differentiated by the way they paint their bodies, their special clothes and the custom of a special ceremonial food for each. Clan prohibitions are never or hardly ever eating ones among the Fox and they are of the most diverse kinds. The Thunder clan is not allowed to draw on the west side of tree trunks nor to take their clothes off to wash. The Fish clan is forbidden to build dams and the Bear clan to climb trees. The Buffalo clan may not skin any cloven-footed animal nor look at these animals while they are dying. Members of the Wolf clan must not bury anyone belonging to their clan and must not strike dogs of any kind. The Bird clan must not do any harm to birds. The members of the Eagle clan are forbidden to put feathers on their heads. The members of the 'Chief' clan should never say anything against a human being, those of the Beaver clan should not swim across rivers and those of the White Wolf should not shout (Michelson 2, pp. 64–5).

Even in the areas where there is the best evidence of eating prohibitions it is striking that they are rarely distributed evenly. A dozen neighbouring cultures (consisting of a hundred tribes) have been described and analysed in the well-circumscribed region of the Cape York Peninsula. They all have one or more forms of totemism, of moiety, section, clan or cult group, but only some of them have eating prohibitions. Clan totemism involves prohibitions among the patrilineal Kauralaig. The Yathaikeno, on the contrary, who are also patrilineal, only forbid initiation totems which are transmitted in the maternal line. The Koko Yao have moiety clan totems which are patrilineally transmitted and permitted, and initiation totems which are matrilineally transmitted and forbidden initiation totems which are matrilineally transmitted and forbidden. The Tjongandji have only patrilineal clan totems which are not subject to any prohibition. The Okerkila are divided into two groups, east and west, one of which has prohibitions while the other does not. The Maithakudi abstain from eating the clan totems, which in their case are matrilineal. The Laierdila have the same rule although they are patrilineal (Sharp) (figure 7).

As Sharp says:

> Eating and killing tabus on edible group totems are invariably associated with maternal cult and matrilineal social totemism. Tabus are more variable in connection with patrilineal cult totemism, being present more commonly for moiety than clan totems (Sharp, p. 70).

The findings within a particular region confirm the general relation between eating prohibitions and matrilineal institutions which Elkin held to exist throughout the continent. As social institutions are the work of men – as a general rule and especially in Australia – what this amounts to is that there is a connection between the male and the consumer and between the female and the thing consumed. I shall return to this later.

Finally there are cases where the idea of eating prohibitions is as it were turned inside out. The prohibition is turned into an obligation and applies not to Ego himself but to someone else; and it no longer relates to the totemic animal thought of as food but to

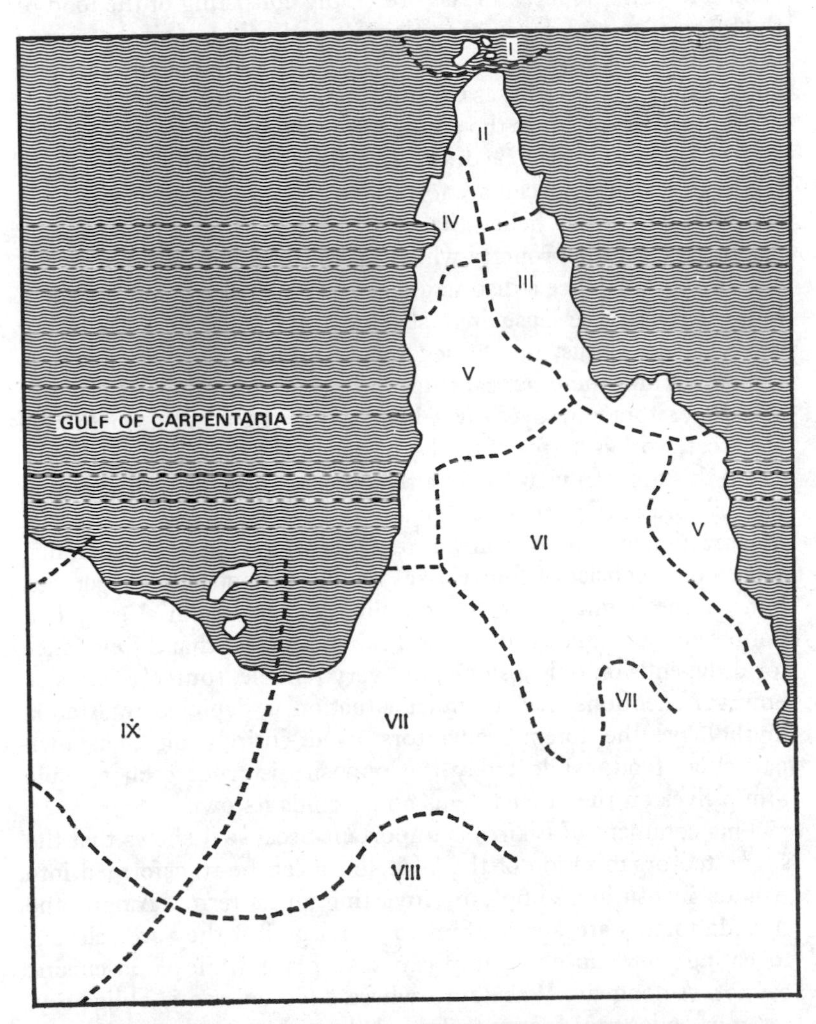

Fig 7 Types of totemic organization in the Cape York Peninsula (following Sharp). I. Kauralaig Type; II. Yaithaikeno Type; III. Koko Yao Type; IV. Tjongandji Type; V. Yir Yoront Type; VI. Olkol Type; VII. Okerkila Type; VIII. Maithakudi Type; IX. Laierdila Type.

the food of this food. This remarkable transformation has been found among some Chippewa Indian groups where the totem may be killed and eaten but not insulted. If a native laughs at or insults the eponymous animal of some other native, the latter informs his clan. The clan prepares a feast preferably consisting of the food of the totemic animal, for instance berries and wild nuts if the animal in question is a bear. The insulter is formally invited and made to gorge himself until he is, as the informants say, 'ready to burst' and is prepared to recognize the power of the totem (Ritzenthaler).

Two conclusions can be drawn from these facts. In the first place the fact that some species are forbidden and others permitted is not attributable to the belief that the former have some intrinsic physical or mystic property which makes them harmful but to the concern to introduce a distinction between 'stressed' and 'unstressed' species (in the sense linguists give to these terms). Prohibiting some species is just one of several ways of singling them out as significant and the practical rules in question can thus be thought of as operators employed by a logic which, being of a qualitative kind, can work in terms of modes of behaviour as well as of images. From this point of view some of the older reports may appear more worthy of attention than has generally been supposed. The social organization of the Wakelbura of Queensland, in east Australia, was said to consist of four classes which were strictly exogamous but, as one might put it, 'endo-culinary'. Durkheim already had doubts about this last feature and Elkin points out that the evidence for it depends on only a single, not very reliable, source. Elkin also however mentions that a similar situation is depicted in Aranda mythology: the totemic ancestors lived entirely on their own particular food, while today the opposite is true: each totemic group lives on the other totems and forbids its own.

This comment of Elkin's is important because it shows that the suggested organization of the Wakelbura can be transformed into Aranda institutions simply by inverting all its terms. Among the Aranda totems are not relevant to marriage but they are relevant to eating: totemic endogamy can take place while endo-cuisine cannot. Among the Wakelburo where endo-cuisine is obligatory, totemic endogamy seems to have been subject to a particularly strict prohibition. The tribe in question has of course long been extinct and the data on it are contradictory. (Compare the account given by Frazer vol. I, p. 423 and that given by Durkheim, p. 215,

n. 2). It is however striking that the symmetry with Aranda institutions remains whichever account is accepted. The difference is only that the relation between marriage rules and eating rules would be supplementary in one case and complementary in the other. Now, the examples of the feminine or masculine Fang cults made it clear that 'the same thing' can be said by means of rules which are formally identical but whose content alone is the reverse. And in the case of Australian societies, when the 'stressed' foods are few or even, as often, consist of a single species, their prohibition provides the most effective method of differentiation. But, if the number of stressed foods should increase (a common phenomenon, as we have seen [p. 88] in the northern tribes who respect their mother's, father's and mother's mother's totems as well as their own) it is easy to see that, without any change in the spirit of the institutions on that account the distinguishing stresses would be reversed and as in photography, the 'positive' would be easier to read than the 'negative' although both convey the same information.

Eating prohibitions and obligations thus seem to be theoretically equivalent means of 'denoting significance' in a logical system some or all of whose elements are edible species. These systems can however themselves be of different types, and this leads to a second conclusion. There is nothing to suggest the existence of totemism among the Bushmen of South Africa in spite of their complicated and exacting prohibitions on food. This is because their system operates on a different plane.

All game killed by means of bows and arrows is forbidden, *soxa*, until the chief has eaten a piece of it. This prohibition does not apply to the liver which the hunters eat on the spot, but which remains *soxa* to women in all circumstances. In addition to these general rules, there are permanent *soxa* for certain functional or social categories. For example, the wife of the man who killed the animal can only eat the superficial covering of meat and fat of the hindquarters, the entrails and the trotters. These pieces constitute the portion reserved for women and children. The adolescent boys have a right to the flesh of the abdominal wall, kidneys, genital organs and udders and the person who killed the animal to the ribs and shoulder blade from one side of it. The chief's part consists of a thick steak from each quarter and each side of the back and a cutlet taken from each side (Fourie, p. 55).

It might seem at first sight as if no system could be less like one of 'totemic' prohibitions. Nevertheless a very simple transformation allows one to pass from one to the other. One need only substitute ethno-anatomy for ethno-zoology. Totemism postulates a logical equivalence between a society of natural species and a world of social groups. The Bushmen postulate the same formal equivalence but in their case it is between the parts making up an individual organism and the functional classes making up the society, that is to say, the society itself is thought of as an organism. Natural and social groupings are homologous in both cases and the selection of a grouping in one order involves the adoption of the corresponding grouping in the other, at least as a predominant form.*

The next chapter will be devoted entirely to an analysis of the same kind (that is, one of a transformation within a group) of the empirical relations which are found between endogamy and exogamy. All that I want to do now is to indicate the connection between this problem and the one which has just been discussed.

In the first place there is an empirical connection between marriage rules and eating prohibitions. Among both the Tikopia of Oceania and the Nuer of Africa a husband abstains from eating animals or plants which his wife may not eat. The reason for this is that ingested food contributes to the formation of the sperm and he would otherwise introduce the forbidden foods into his wife's body during intercourse (Firth I, pp. 319–20, Evans-Pritchard 2, p. 86). In the light of the preceding discussion, it is interesting to observe that the Fang use the reverse argument. One of the many reasons given in support of the prohibition applying to the inside of elephants' tusks is that the penis might become as limp as the gums of the pachyderm (which are apparently particularly so). Out of consideration for her husband, a wife also obeys this prohibition lest she should enfeeble him during intercourse (Tessman, vol. 2, p. 192).

* So-called totemic societies also practise anatomical division but they use it to make secondary distinctions: those between sub-groups of groups or individuals belonging to the group. There is therefore no incompatibility between the two sorts of grouping. It is rather their respective positions in the logical hierarchy which is to be treated as significant. I shall return to this later, cf. p. 174.

If, as G. Dieterlin points out, the Dogon associate totems and parts of the body of a sacrificed ancestor, it is by applying a classificatory system with an inter-tribal application. Consequently the totemic groupings within each tribe, which are made to correspond to parts of the body, are in fact already secondary units.

Now, these comparisons are only particular instances of the very profound analogy which people throughout the world seem to find between copulation and eating. In a very large number of languages they are even called by the same term.* In Yoruba 'to eat' and 'to marry' are expressed by a single verb the general sense of which is 'to win, to acquire', a usage which has its parallel in French, where the verb 'consommer' applies both to marriage and to meals. In the language of the Koko Yao of Cape York Peninsula the word kuta kuta means both incest and cannibalism, which are the most exaggerated forms of sexual union and the consumption of food. For the same reason the eating of the totem and incest are expressed in the same way at Ponapy; among the Mashona and Matabele of Africa the word 'totem' also means 'sister's vulva', which provides indirect confirmation of the equivalence between eating and copulation.

If eating the totem is a kind of cannibalism then one understands that the punishment of real or symbolic cannibalism should be reserved for those who violate the prohibition – voluntarily or otherwise. The symbolic roasting of the guilty in an oven in Samoa is an example. And the equivalence is confirmed again by the similar custom found among the Wotjobaluk of Australia where a man who has committed the crime of absconding with a woman forbidden by the law of exogamy is really eaten by the totemic group. Without going so far afield or invoking other exotic rites, one can quote Tertullian: 'Through love of eating, love of impurity finds passage' (*De Jejune*, I) and St. John Chrysostom: 'The beginning of chastity is fasting' (*Homilia I in Epistolam II ad Thessalonicenses*).

These associations could be multiplied indefinitely. Those I have given as examples show how hopeless it is to attempt to establish a relation of priority between nutritional prohibitions and rules of exogamy. The connection between them is not causal but metaphorical. Sexual and nutritional relations are at once associated even today. Consider for instance slang expressions such as 'faire frire', 'passer à la casserole' etc.† But how is this fact and its universality to be explained? Here again the logical level is reached by semantic impoverishment: the lowest common denominator of the union of

* Cf. Henry, p. 146 for a particularly telling South American example.

† i.e. 'fry' and 'put in the pot', terms used to refer to seduction as well as cooking (trans. note).

the sexes and the union of eater and eaten is that they both effect a *conjunction by complementarity*:

> What is destitute of motion is the food of those endowed with locomotion; (animals) without fangs (are the food) of those with fangs, those without hands of those who possess hands, and the timid of the bold (The Laws of Manu, v, 29).

The equation of male with devourer and female with devoured is the more familiar to us and certainly also the more prevalent in the world but one must not forget that the inverse equivalence is often found at a mythological level in the theme of the *vagina dentata*. Significantly enough this is 'coded' in terms of eating, that is, directly (thus confirming the law of mythical thought that the transformation of a metaphor is achieved in a metonymy). It may also be the case that the theme of the *vagina dentata* corresponds to a point of view, no longer inverted but direct, in the sexual philosophy of the Far East where, as the works of Van Gulik show, for a man the art of love-making consists essentially in avoiding having his vital force absorbed by the women and in turning this risk to his advantage.

This logical subordination of resemblance to contrast is clearly illustrated in the complex attitude of some so-called totemic peoples toward the parts of body of eponymous animals. The Tikuna of the High Solimões, who practise 'hypertotemic' exogamy (the members of the Toucan clan cannot inter-marry either among themselves or with the members of any clan called by a bird name, etc.), freely eat the eponymous animal but they respect and preserve a sacred part of it and use others as distinctive ornaments (Alviano). The totemic animal is thus resolved into an edible part, a part to be respected and an emblematic part. The Elema of Southern New Guinea observe a very strict prohibition on eating their totems. Each clan however retains the exclusive prerogative of using the beak, feathers, tail, etc. of its totem animal for ornamental purposes (Frazer, vol. II, p. 41). There is thus in both cases an opposition between edible and non-edible parts, homologous to that between the categories of *food* and *emblem*. In the case of the Elema it is expressed through a two-fold exclusivism which may be either negative or positive: in relation to the totemic species, each clan *abstains from* its meat but *retains* those parts of it which display the characteristics of its species. The Tikuna are equally exclusive with respect to the distinctive parts of the animals but they adopt a communal attitude towards meat (in terms of which animals distinct in species but edible resemble each other as food). The group of attitudes can be represented in the following way:

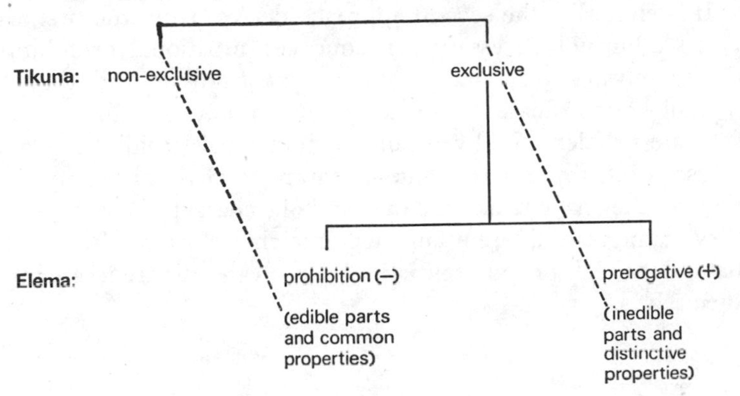

The fur, feathers, beak and teeth can be mine because they are that in which the eponymous animal and I differ from each other: this difference is assumed by man as an emblem and to assert his symbolic relation with the animal. But the parts which are edible and so can be assimilated are the sign of genuine consubstantiality which, contrary to what one might suppose, it is the real aim of the prohibition on eating them to deny. Ethnologists have made the mistake of taking only this second aspect into account and this has led them to conceive the relation between man and animal to be of a single kind: identity, affinity or participation. Matters are in fact infinitely more complex: there is an exchange of similarities and differences between culture and nature, sometimes as amongst animals on the one side and man on the other and sometimes as between animals and men.

The differences between animals, which man can extract from nature and transfer to culture (either by describing them in terms of opposites and contrasts and thus conceptualizing them or by taking over concrete, non-perishable parts: feathers, beaks, teeth – which equally constitutes an 'abstraction') are adopted as emblems by groups of men in order to do away with their own resemblances. And the same animals are rejected as food by the same group of men, in other words the resemblance between man and animal resulting from the fact that the former can assimilate the flesh of the latter is denied, but only in so far as it is perceived that the reverse course would imply recognition on the part of men of their common nature. The meat of *any* animal species must therefore not be assimilated by *any* group of men.

It is clear that the second approach derives from the first, as a possible but not necessary consequence: nutritional prohibitions do not always accompany totemic classifications and they are logically subordinate to them. They do not therefore raise a separate problem. If, by means of nutritional prohibitions, men refuse to attribute a real animal nature to their humanity, it is because they have to assume the symbolic characteristics by which they distinguish different animals (and which furnish them with a natural model of differentiation) to create differences among themselves.

CHAPTER FOUR

TOTEM AND CASTE

Both the exchange of women and the exchange of food are means of securing or of displaying the interlocking of social groups with one another. This being so, we can see why they may be found either together or separately. They are procedures of the same type and are indeed generally thought of as two aspects of the same procedure. They may reinforce each other, both performing the actual function, or one performing it and the other representing it symbolically. Or they may be alternatives, a single one fulfilling the whole function or if that is otherwise discharged, as it can be even in the absence of both procedures, then the symbolic representation of it:

> If . . . a people combines exogamy with totemism, this is because it has chosen to reinforce the social cohesion already established by totemism by superimposing on it yet another system which is connected with the first by its reference to physical and social kinship and is distinguished from, though not opposed to it, by its lack of reference to cosmic kinship. Exogamy can play this same part in types of society which are built on foundations other than totemism; and the geographical distribution of the two institutions coincides only at certain points in the world. (Van Gennep, pp. 351).

However exogamy, as we know, is never entirely absent. This is due to the fact that the perpetuation of the group can only be effected by means of women, and although varying degrees of symbolic content can be introduced by the particular way in which a society organizes them or thinks of their operation, marriage exchanges always have real substance, and they are alone in this. The exchange of food is a different matter. Aranda women really bear children. But Aranda men confine themselves to imagining that their rites result in the increase of totemic species. In the former, although it may be described in conventional terms which impose their own limits on it, what is in question is primarily a way of doing something. In the latter it is only a way of saying something.

Examples of 'accumulation' of some kind have attracted particular attention, no doubt because the repetition of the same scheme on two different planes made them look simpler and more consistent. It is mainly this which has led to the definition of totemism by the parallelism between eating prohibitions and rules of exogamy and to making this supplementary set of customs a special object of study. There are, however, cases in which the relation between marriage and eating customs is one of complementarity and not supplementarity and where they are therefore dialectically related to each other. This form clearly also belongs to the same group. And it is groups in this sense, and not arbitrarily isolated transformations, which are the proper subject of the sciences of man.

In an earlier chapter I quoted a botanist's testimony with regard to the extreme purity of types of seed in the agriculture of so-called primitive peoples, in particular among the Indians of Guatemala. We also know that there is intense fear of agricultural exchanges in this area: a transplanted seedling may take the spirit of the plant with it, with the result that it disappears from its original locality. One may, then, exchange women but refuse to exchange seeds. This is common in Melanesia.

The inhabitants of Dobu, an island to the south-east of New Guinea, are divided into matrilineal lineages called *susu*. Husband and wife, who necessarily come from different *susu*, each bring their own seed yams and cultivate them in separate gardens without ever mixing them. No hope for a person who has not his own seed: a woman who has none will not succeed in marrying and will be reduced to the state of a fisherwoman, thief or beggar. Seed which does not come from the *susu* will not grow, for agriculture is possible only by the use of magic inherited from the maternal uncle: it is ritual which makes the yams swell.

These precautions and scruples rest on the belief that yams are persons: 'Like women, they give birth to children . . .' They go abroad at night and people wait for their return before harvesting. This is the source of the rule that yams may not be dug too early in the morning: they might not yet have returned. It is also the source of the conviction that the fortunate cultivator is a magician who has known how to persuade his neighbours' yams to move and establish themselves in his garden. A man who has a good harvest is reckoned a lucky thief (Fortune 2).

Beliefs of the same type were to be found even in France until recently. In the middle ages there was a penalty of death for 'the sorceress who defiled and injured crops; who, by reciting the psalm *Super aspidem ambulabis*, emptied the fields of their corn to fill her own granary with this goodly produce'. Not so long ago at Cubjac in the Perigord a magical invocation was supposed to assure the person using it of a good crop of turnips: 'May our neighbours' be as big as millet seed, our relations' as big as grains of corn and our own as big as the head of Fauve the ox!' (Rocal, pp. 164–5).

Apart from the modicum of exogamy resulting from the prohibited degrees, European peasant societies practised strict local endogamy. And it is significant that at Dobu extreme endo-agriculture can act as the symbolic compensation for lineage and village exogamy which is practised with repugnance and even fear. In spite of the fact that endogamy within the locality – which consists of between four and twenty villages – is generally assured, marriage even into the next village is looked on as putting a man at the mercy of assassins and sorcerers and he himself always regards his wife as a powerful magician, ready to deceive him with her childhood friends and to destroy him and his (Fortune 2). In a case like this, endo-agriculture reinforces a latent tendency towards endogamy, if indeed it does not express symbolically the hostility to the unwillingly practised rules of a precarious exogamy. The situation is symmetrically the reverse of that prevailing in Australia where food prohibitions and rules of exogamy reinforce one another, as we have seen in a more symbolic and clearly conceptual way in the patrilineal societies (where the food prohibitions are flexible and tend to be formulated in terms of moieties, that is, at a level which is already abstract and lends itself to a binary coding by pairs of oppositions) and in a more literal and concrete fashion in the matrilineal societies (where the prohibitions are rigid and stated in terms of clans which one might often be hesitant to regard as members of systematic sets, given the determining part of demographic and historic factors in their genesis).

Apart from these cases of positive or negative parallelism, there are others in which reciprocity between social groups is expressed only on one plane. Omaha rules of marriage are formulated very differently from those of the Aranda. Instead of the class of the spouse being precisely specified, as it is among the Aranda, any clan not expressly forbidden is permitted. On the plane of food, however, the Omaha have rites very similar to the intichiuma:* the sacred maize is entrusted to particular clans who annually distribute it to the others to vitalize their seeds (Fletcher and La Flesche). The totemic clans of the Nandi of Uganda are not exogamous; but a remarkable development of clan prohibitions, not only on the plane of food but also on those of technical and economic activities, dress and impediments to marriage based on some detail or other of the personal history of the forbidden spouse, compensates for this 'non-functionality' in the sphere of marriage exchanges (Hollis). No system can be constructed from these differences: the distinctions recognized between the groups seem rather to spring from a propensity to accept all statistical fluctuations. In a different form and on a different plane, this is also the method employed by the systems termed 'Crow-Omaha' and by contemporary Western societies to ensure the overall equilibrium of matrimonial exchanges.†

This emergence of methods of articulation more complex than those resulting just from rules of exogamy or food prohibitions, or even of both at once, is particularly striking in the case of the Baganda (who are near the Nandi) because they seem to have accumulated all the forms. The Baganda were divided into forty clans, *kika*, each of which had a common totem, *miziro*, the consumption of which was forbidden by virtue of a rule of food rationing: by depriving itself of the totemic food, each clan leaves more of it available to other clans. This is the modest counterpart of the Australian claim that by refraining from consuming its totem each clan retains the power to increase it.

As in Australia, each clan is characterized by its links with a territory, among the Baganda generally a hill. There is a secondary totem, *kabiro*, as well as the principal totem. Each Baganda clan is thus defined by two totems, food prohibitions and a territory. There are also prerogatives such as eligibility of its members for

* See below, p. 226.

† Rightly or wrongly, Radcliffe-Brown (*3*, pp. 32–3) treats the Nandi kinship system as an Omaha system.

the kingship or other honours, the right to provide royal wives, making and caring for the royal emblems or utensils, ritual obligations to provide other clans with certain kinds of food, and technical specializations: the Mushroom clan, for instance, makes all the bark cloth, and all blacksmiths come from the clan of the Tail-less Cow, etc. Finally, we find some prohibitions, such as that the women of a particular clan cannot be the mothers of male children of the blood royal, and restrictions with regard to the bearing of proper names (Roscoe).

In cases like this it is no longer very clear what type of society is in question. There can, for instance, be no doubt that the totemic clans of the Baganda also function as castes. And yet at first sight it seems that nothing could be more different than these two forms of institution. We have become used to associating totemic groups with the most 'primitive' civilizations and thinking of castes as a feature of highly developed, sometimes even literate, societies. Moreover, a strong tradition connects totemic institutions with the strictest exogamy while an anthropologist asked to define the concept of a caste would almost certainly begin by mentioning the rule of endogamy.

It may therefore seem surprising that between about 1830 and 1850, the first investigators of Australian societies often referred to their marriage classes as 'castes' even though they had some idea of their function (Thomas, pp. 34–5). These intuitions which have the freshness and vivacity of a perception of societies which were still intact, and a vision undistorted by theoretical speculation, are not to be despised. Without going to the root of the problem now, it is clear that there are at least superficial analogies between Australian tribes and societies with castes. Each group has a specialized function indispensable to the collectivity as a whole and complementary to the functions assigned to other groups.

This is particularly clear in the case of tribes whose clans or moieties are bound together by a rule of reciprocity. Among the Kaitish and the Unmatjera, northern neighbours of the Aranda, anyone who gathers wild seeds in the territory of a totemic group named after these seeds must ask the headman's permission before eating them. It is the duty of each totemic group to provide the other groups with the plant or animal for whose 'production' it is specially responsible. Thus a man of the Emu clan out hunting on his own may not touch an emu. But if, on the other hand, he is in company he is permitted and even supposed to kill it and offer it to hunters of other clans. Conversely, when he is alone a man of the Water clan may drink if he is thirsty but when he is with others he must receive the water from a member of the other moiety, preferably from a brother-in-law (Spencer and Gillen, pp. 159-60). Among the Warramunga each totemic group is responsible for the increase and availability to other groups of a particular plant or animal species: 'The members of one moiety . . . take charge . . . of the ceremonies of the other moiety which are destined to secure the increase of their own food supply'. Among the Walpari as well as the Warramunga the secondary totemic prohibitions (applying to the maternal totem) are waived if the food in question is obtained through the agency of a man of the other moiety. More generally and for any totem, there is a distinction between the groups which never eat it (because it is their own totem), those which eat it only if it is procured through the agency of another group (as in the case of the maternal totems), and those which eat it freely in any circumstances. Similarly in the case of the sacred water-holes, women may never approach them, uninitiated men may approach but not drink from them, while some groups drink from them on the condition that the water is given to them by members of other groups who can themselves drink freely from them (Spencer and Gillen, pp. 164, 167). This mutual interdependence is already to be seen in marriage which, as Radcliffe-Brown has shown in the case of Australia (but the same could equally well be said of other clan societies such as the Iroquois), was based on reciprocal gifts of vegetable food (feminine) and animal food (masculine): the conjugal family in these cases was like a miniature society with two castes.

There is thus less difference than would appear between societies which, like some Australian tribes, assign a distinctive magico-economic function to totemic groups and, for instance, the Bororo of Central Brazil, among whom specialists are in charge of the same function of 'liberating' the food production – whether animal or vegetable – for the whole group (Colbacchini). This leads one to doubt whether the opposition between endogamous castes and exogamous totemic groups is really radical. There seem to be connections between these two extreme types, whose nature would appear more clearly if we could show that intermediate forms exist.

I have drawn attention elsewhere to a feature of so-called totemic institutions which in my own view is fundamental to them. The homology they evoke is not between social groups and natural species but between the differences which manifest themselves on the level of groups on the one hand and on that of species on the other. They are thus based on the postulate of a homology between *two systems of differences*, one of which occurs in nature and the other in culture. Indicating relations of homology by vertical lines, a 'pure totemic structure' could thus be represented in the following way:

<table>
<tr><td>NATURE:</td><td>species 1</td><td>≠</td><td>species 2</td><td>≠</td><td>species 3</td><td>≠</td><td>..... species *n*</td></tr>
<tr><td></td><td></td><td>|</td><td></td><td>|</td><td></td><td>|</td><td></td></tr>
<tr><td>CULTURE:</td><td>group 1</td><td>≠</td><td>group 2</td><td>≠</td><td>group 3</td><td>≠</td><td>..... group *n*</td></tr>
</table>

This structure would be fundamentally impaired if homologies between the terms themselves were added to those between their relations or if, going one step further, the entire system of homologies were transferred from relations to terms:

<table>
<tr><td>NATURE:</td><td>species 1</td><td>≠</td><td>species 2</td><td>≠</td><td>species 3</td><td>..... species *n*</td></tr>
<tr><td></td><td>|</td><td></td><td>|</td><td></td><td>|</td><td></td></tr>
<tr><td>CULTURE:</td><td>group 1</td><td>≠</td><td>group 2</td><td>≠</td><td>group 3</td><td>..... group *n*</td></tr>
</table>

In this case the implicit content of the structure would no longer be that clan 1 differs from clan 2 as for instance the eagle differs from the bear but rather that clan 1 is like the eagle and clan 2 like the bear. In other words, the nature of clan 1 and the nature of clan 2 would each be involved separately instead of the formal relation between them.

Now, the transformation whose theoretical possibility has just been considered can sometimes be directly observed. The islanders of the Torres Straits have totemic clans, numbering about thirty at Mabuiag. These exogamous patrilineal clans were grouped into two moieties, one comprising terrestrial and the other marine animals. At Tutu and Saibai this division seems to have corresponded to a territorial division within the village. The structure was already in an advanced state of decay at the time of Haddon's expedition. Nevertheless, the natives had a very strong sense of the physical and psychological affinity between men and their totems and of the corresponding obligation of each group to pursue the appropriate type of behaviour. Thus the Cassowary, Crocodile, Snake, Shark and Hammer-headed Shark clans were said to love fighting and the Shovel-nosed Skate, Ray and Sucker-Fish clans to be peace loving. The Dog clan was held to be unpredictable, dogs being of a changeable disposition. The members of the Crocodile clan were thought to be strong and ruthless and those of the Cassowary clan to have long legs and to run fast (Frazer, vol. II, pp. 3–9, quoting Haddon and Rivers). It would be interesting to know whether these beliefs are survivals from the old organization or whether they developed as the exogamous rules decayed.

The fact is that similar, though not equally developed, beliefs have been observed among the Menomini of the Great Lakes and among the Chippewa further north. Among the latter, people of the Fish clan were reputed to be long-lived, frequently to go bald or to have thin hair, and all bald people were assumed to come from this clan. Peoples of the Bear clan, on the other hand, had long, thick, coarse hair which never went white and they were said to be ill-tempered and fond of fighting. People of the Crane clan had loud ringing voices and provided the tribe with its orators (Kinietz, pp. 76–7).

Let us pause for a moment to consider the theoretical implications of views like these. When nature and culture are thought of as two systems of differences between which there is a formal analogy, it is the systematic character of each domain which is brought to the fore. Social groups are distinguished from one another but they retain their solidarity as parts of the same whole, and the rule of exogamy furnishes the means of resolving this opposition balanced between diversity and unity. But if social groups are considered not so much from the point of view of their reciprocal relations in social life as each on their own account, in relation to something other than sociological reality, then the idea of diversity is likely to prevail over that of unity. Each social group will tend to form a system no longer with other social groups but with particular differentiating properties regarded as hereditary, and these characteristics exclusive to each group will weaken the framework of their solidarity within the society. The more each group tries to define itself by the image which it draws from a natural model, the more difficult will it become for it to maintain its links with other social groups and, in particular to exchange its sisters and daughters with them since it will tend to think of them as being of a particular 'species'. Two images, one social and the other natural, and each articulated separately, will be replaced by a socio-natural image, single but fragmented:*

NATURE:	species 1	species 2	species 3	species n
CULTURE:	group 1	group 2	group 3	group n

It is of course only for purposes of exposition and because they form the subject of this book that I am apparently giving a sort of priority to ideology and superstructures. I do not at all mean to suggest that ideological transformations give rise to social ones. Only the reverse is in fact true. Men's conception of the relations between nature and culture is a function of modifications of their own social relations. But, since my aim here is to outline a theory of superstructures, reasons of method require that they should be singled out for attention and that major phenomena which have no place in this programme should seem to be left in brackets or given second place. We are however merely studying the shadows on the wall of the Cave without forgetting that it is only the attention we give them which lends them a semblance of reality.

This said, to avoid misunderstanding we can summarize what has gone before as an account of the conceptual transformations marking the passage from exogamy to endogamy (or vice versa). Some, at any rate, of the Algonkin tribes, who furnished the last examples, had a hierarchical clan structure which one might suspect would lead to some difficulty in the functioning of exogamous rules formulated in egalitarian terms. But it is in the south-east of the United States, in the tribes of the Muskogi linguistic group, that hybrid institutional forms, half-way between totemic groups and castes, can be seen most clearly; and this also explains the existing uncertainty as to whether they are endogamous or exogamous.

The Chickasaw may perhaps have been exogamous at the clan

* It will perhaps be objected that in the above mentioned work (6), I denied that totemism can be interpreted on the basis of a direct analogy between human groups and natural species. But this criticism was directed against a theory put forward by ethnologists and what is in question here is an – implicit or explicit – native theory which indeed corresponds to institutions that ethnologists would refuse to class as totemic.

level and endogamous so far as their moieties were concerned. The latter in any case had the feature, highly unusual for structures of this type, of displaying an exclusivism verging on mutual hostility. Illness and death were often attributed to the sorcery of people of the opposite moiety. Each moiety performed its rites in jealous isolation; members of the other moiety who witnessed them were punishable by death. The same attitude existed among the Creek: with regard to moieties it is strikingly reminiscent of that prevailing towards totemic groups among the Aranda. Each performed its rites 'among themselves' although only 'the others' were to benefit from them. And this, it is worth remarking in passing, shows that endo-*praxis* and exo-*praxis* are never definable separately and in absolute terms. As Morgan demonstrated against McLennan, they can only be defined as complementary aspects of an ambiguous relation to self and to others.

The moieties, which probably formed opposite sides in competitive games, were considered to differ in temperament and habitat: one was warlike and preferred open country while the other was pacific and lived in forests. They may also have been ordered hierarchically as is suggested by the terms sometimes applied to them : '[people of the] hickory-choppings' [substantial habitations] and '[people of the] worn-out place' [hovels]. However, these hierarchical, psychical and functional differences were primarily manifested at the level of clans or their subdivisions into hamlets. In native accounts of the past, comments like these about each clan or hamlet constantly occur, like a leit-motiv: 'They were very peculiar people . . . they were not like others . . . they had customs and traditions of their own . . .' These peculiarities were of all sorts of different kinds: place of residence, economic activity, dress, food, talents and tastes.

The Raccoon people were said to live on fish and wild fruit, those of the Puma lived in the mountains, avoided water of which they were very frightened and lived principally on game. The Wild Cat clan slept in the daytime and hunted at night, for they had keen eyes; they were indifferent to women. Members of the Bird clan were up before day-break: 'They were like real birds in that they would not bother anybody . . . The people of this clan have different sorts of minds, just as there are different species of birds'. They were said to live well, to be polygamous, disinclined to work, and prolific.

The people of the Red Fox clan were professional thieves, loving independence and living in the heart of forests. The 'wandering Iksa' were nomadic and improvident but nevertheless enjoyed robust health 'for they did not do anything to run themselves down'. They moved slowly, thinking that they were going to live for ever. The men and women paid little attention to their dress or appearance. They were beggars and lazy. The inhabitants of 'the bending-post-oak' house group lived in the woods. They were of a changeable disposition, not very energetic, given to dancing, always anxious and full of care. They were early risers and clumsy. The High Corncrib house group people were respected in spite of their arrogance: they were good gardeners, very industrious but poor hunters, they bartered their maize for game. They were said to be truthful and stubborn, and skilled at forecasting the weather. As for the Redskunk house group: they lived in dugouts underground (Swanton 2, pp. 190–213).

This material was collected at a time when the traditional institutions no longer existed except in old informants' memories and it is plain that it is partly made up of old wives' tales. No society could allow itself to 'act nature' to this extent or it would split up into a whole lot of independent, hostile bands, each denying that the others were human. The data which Swanton collected consist of sociological myths as well as or rather than ethnographic facts. Nevertheless, their wealth, the resemblances they have among themselves, the unity of the underlying scheme, the existence of similar data for neighbouring groups all suggest that even if the real institutions were different, we have here at least a sort of conceptual model of Chickasaw society which has the extremely interesting feature of recalling a society with castes, even though the attributes of the castes and their relations to each other are coded in terms of natural species, that is, after the manner of totemic groups. Further, the relations held to exist between clans and their eponyms are like those found in classical 'totemic' societies: the clan is descended from the animal or alternatively a human ancestor of the clan contracted a marriage with one in mythical times. Now, these societies, which are at the very least conceived of as if they were composed of 'natural' castes – or, in other words, in which culture is thought of as a projection or reflection of nature – are the link between the societies classical authors used to illustrate their conception of totemism (the tribes of the plains and of the south west) and societies such as the Natchez which afford one of the rare examples of genuine castes known in North America.

We have thus established that in the two classical territories of so-called totemism, the institutions defined with reference to this misleading notion can either also be characterized from the point of view of their function, as in Australia or, as in America, make way for forms which are still conceived on the model of totemic groups although they operate more like castes.

Let us now turn to India, also classical territory but of castes. I shall try to show that through their influence institutions traditionally thought of as totemic undergo a transformation exactly the reverse of that in America: instead of castes conceived in terms of a natural model we have here totemic groups conceived in terms of a cultural model.

Most of the totemic names found among certain tribes in Bengal derive from animals or plants. This is the case with some sixty-seven totems recorded among the Oraon of Chota Nagpur with the exception of iron which, as there is little point in proscribing its consumption, is forbidden to come into contact with lips or tongue. This prohibition is thus still formulated in terms that make it approximate to an eating prohibition. Among the Munda of the same region, the majority of the three hundred and forty exogamous clans recorded have animal or plant totems, the consumption of which is forbidden. Totems of a different kind are however already noticeable: full moon, moonlight, rainbow, months of the year, days of the week, copper bracelet, verandah, umbrella, professions or castes such as that of basket-maker and torch-bearer (Risley, vol. II and Appendix). Further west, the forty-three names of the Bhil clans are divided into nineteen plant and seventeen animal names and seven relate to objects: dagger, broken pot, village, thorny stick, bracelet, ankle ring, piece of bread (Koppers, pp. 118-19).

It is towards the south that the reversal in the relation of natural species and objects or manufactured goods becomes particularly conspicuous. Few plants and scarcely any animals figure in the names of the clans of the Devanga, a caste of weavers in the Madras area. On the other hand, the following names are found: buttermilk, cattle-pen, money, dam, house, collyrium, knife, scissors, boat, lamp, cloths, female clothing, ropes for hanging pots, old plough, monastery, funeral pyre, tile. Sixty-seven exogamous clans are recorded among the Kuruba of Mysore. They have animal or plant names or names like the following: cart, cup, silver, flint, roll of woollen thread, bangle, gold, gold ring, pickaxe, coloured border of cloth, stick, blanket, measure, moustache, loom, bamboo tube, etc. (Thurston, vol. II, p. 160 ff., vol. IV, pp. 141–2).

It is possible that this phenomenon is a peripheral rather than a southern one for one is inclined here to recall the mythical role which some south-east Asian tribes ascribe to manufactured objects such as sabre, knife, lance, needle, post, rope, and so on. However this may be, in India the manufactured objects from which clans take their names receive special respect, like totemic plants and animals. Either they constitute the object of a cult at marriages or alternatively the respect paid to them takes a bizarre and specific form. Among the Bhil for example, the clan of the broken pot must collect pieces of a particular kind of pottery and give them burial. At times a certain freedom of invention is perceptible: the Arisana gotram of the Karuba bears the name of turmeric, but as it is held to be inconvenient to be deprived of so essential a condiment, the *Korra* grain replaces it as the forbidden food.

Heterogeneous lists of clan names are known in other parts of the world. Perhaps significantly, they are particularly found in the north of Australia, the part of the continent most subject to outside influences. Individual totems such as a razor blade or money have been noted in Africa:

> When I asked [the Dinka] what I myself should invoke as my clan-divinity, it was half-jokingly suggested that I should invoke Typewriter, Paper, and Lorry, for were these not the things which had always helped my people and which were passed on to Europeans by their ancestors? (Lienhardt, p. 110).

But this heterogeneity is most apparent in India where a high proportion of totemic names are names of manufactured objects, that is, of products or symbols of functional activities which – because they are clearly differentiated in a caste system – can serve to express distinction between social groups within the tribe or the caste itself. It is as if in America the rudiments of castes had been contaminated by totemic classifications, while in India the vestiges of totemic groups had allowed themselves to be won over by symbolism of technological or occupational origin. These 'chassés-croisés' seem less surprising when one realizes that there is a neater and more direct way of translating Australian institutions into the language of castes than that used above.

I have suggested that since each totemic group makes itself responsible for the control of a species of plant or animal for the benefit of the other groups, these specializations of function are, from one point of view, similar to those assumed by occupational castes since the latter also practise a distinctive activity, indispensable to the life and well-being of the whole group. However, in the first place, a caste of potters really makes pots, a caste of launderers really washes clothes, a caste of barbers really shaves people, while the magical powers of Australian totemic groups are of an imaginary kind. And there is a distinction here even if belief in the efficacy of magical powers is shared by their supposed beneficiaries and by those who, in all good faith, claim to possess them. Secondly, the connection between a sorcerer and the natural species he claims to control cannot be conceived in terms of the same logical model as that between a craftsman and his product. For it was only in mythical times that totemic animals were really begotten by the ancestor. Nowadays it is kangaroos which produce kangaroos, and the sorcerer contents himself with assisting them.

Now, if Australian (and other) institutions are considered from a wider point of view, it becomes possible to distinguish a field in which the parallel with a caste system is very much clearer. We need only turn our attention to social organization instead of religious beliefs and practices. For the early observers of Australian societies were in a sense right to speak of marriage classes as 'castes': an Australian section produces its women for other sections in the same way as an occupational caste produces goods and services which other castes cannot obtain otherwise than through its agency . . . It would therefore be superficial to regard them as opposites simply because one is exogamous and the other endogamous. Occupational castes and totemic groups are really both 'exo-practising', the former in the exchange of goods and services and the latter so far as marriage is concerned.

A coefficient of 'endo-*praxis*' is however always discernible in either case. Castes are ostensibly endogamous apart from the restrictions on marriage which, as I have shown elsewhere (I, ch.

25), tend to multiply in compensation. The Australian groups are exogamous but their exogamy most commonly takes the form of restricted exchange which is an imitation of endogamy within exogamy itself, for in restricted exchange groups consider themselves as closed to the outside and their internal exchanges double up on each other. It can therefore be contrasted with generalized exchange which is more open to the outside and allows the incorporation of new groups without upsetting the structure. These relations can be shown by means of a diagram:

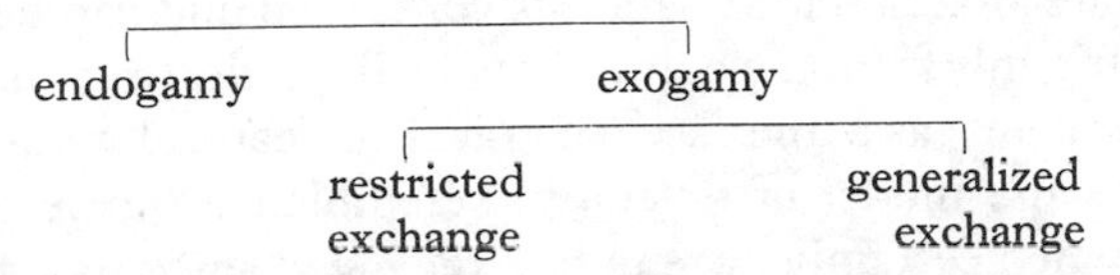

It will be seen that restricted exchange, the 'closed' form of exogamy is logically closer to endogamy than the 'open' form, generalized exchange.

There is a further point. A fundamental difference exists between the women who are exchanged and the goods and services which are also exchanged. Women are biological individuals, that is, natural products naturally procreated by other biological individuals. Goods and services on the other hand are manufactured objects (or operations performed by means of techniques and manufactured objects), that is, social products culturally manufactured by technical agents. The symmetry between occupational castes and totemic groups is an inverted symmetry. The principle on which they are differentiated is taken from culture in one case and from nature in the other.

Nevertheless, this symmetry is present only on an ideological plane. It has no concrete basis. So far as culture is concerned professional specialities are truly different and complementary. The same could not be said, with respect to nature, of the specialization of exogamous groupings in the production of women of different species. For even granting that occupations do constitute distinct 'social species', this does not alter the fact that the women of different sections or sub-sections all belong to the same natural species.

This is the trap reality sets for the imagination and men try to escape it by seeking real diversity in the natural order, which is (if they pay no attention to the division of labour and occupational specialization) the only objective model on which they can draw for establishing relations of complementarity and co-operation among themselves. In other words, men conceive these relations on the model of their conception of the relations between natural species (and at the same time of their own social relations). There are in fact only two true models of concrete diversity: one on the plane of nature, namely that of the diversity of species, and the other on the cultural plane provided by the diversity of functions. The model illustrated by marriage exchanges lying between these two true models, has an ambiguous and equivocal character. Women are alike so far as nature is concerned and can be regarded as different only from the cultural angle. But if the first point of view is predominant (as is the case when it is the natural model which is chosen as the model of diversity) resemblance outweighs difference. Women certainly have to be exchanged since they have been decreed to be different. But this exchange presupposes that basically they are held to be alike. Conversely, when the other viewpoint is taken and a cultural model of diversity adopted, difference, which corresponds to the cultural aspect, outweighs resemblance. Women are only recognized as alike within the limits of their respective social groups and consequently cannot be exchanged between one caste and another. Castes decree women to be naturally heterogeneous; totemic groups decree them to be culturally heterogeneous. And the final reason for this difference between the two systems is that castes exploit cultural heterogeneity in earnest while totemic groups only create the illusion of exploiting natural heterogeneity.

All this can be expressed in a different way. Castes, which are defined on the basis of a cultural model, really exchange cultural objects. But they have to pay a price for the symmetry they postulate between nature and culture: in that the castes are themselves composed of biological beings, they are constrained to conceive their natural product according to a natural world, since this product consists of women whom they both produce and are produced by. It follows that women are made diverse on the model of natural species and cannot be exchanged any more than species can cross with one another. Totemic groupings make the reverse sacrifice. They are defined on the basis of a natural model and exchange natural objects – the women they produce and are produced by naturally. The symmetry postulated between nature and culture involves in that case the assimilation of natural species on the cultural plane. In the same way that women who are homogeneous so far as nature is concerned are declared to be heterogeneous from the point of view of culture, so natural species, which are heterogeneous so far as nature is concerned are proclaimed to be homogeneous from the point of view of culture: culture asserts them all to be subject to the same type of beliefs and practices since in the eyes of culture, they have the common feature that man has the power to control and increase them. Consequently, men by cultural means exchange women who perpetuate these same men by natural means and they claim to perpetuate species by cultural means and exchange them *sub specie naturae*: in the form of foodstuffs which are substitutable for each other since they all provide nourishment and since, as with women also, a man can satisfy himself by means of some foods and go without others in so far as any women or any foods are equally suitable to achieve the ends of procreation or subsistence.

We thus arrive at the common properties of which occupational castes and totemic groups provide contrary illustrations. Castes are heterogeneous in function and can therefore be homogeneous in structure: since the diversity of function is real, complementarity is already established on the level of reality and the operation of marriage exchanges – between the same social units – would be a case of 'accumulation' of functions (why this is of no practical value has been shown above [cf. p. 109]). Conversely, totemic groups are homogeneous so far as their function is concerned, for it makes no real yield and amounts to no more than a repetition of the same illusion for all the groups. They therefore have to be heterogeneous in structure, each being destined for the production of women of a different social species.

In totemism, consequently, purported reciprocity is constructed out of modes of behaviour homogeneous with each other and simply juxtaposed. Each group similarly imagines itself to have magical power over a species, but as this illusion has no foundation it is in fact no more than an empty form and as such identical to the other forms. The true reciprocity results from the articulation of two processes: the natural one which comes about by means of women, who procreate both men and women, and the cultural one which men bring about by characterizing these women socially when nature has brought them into existence.

In the caste system reciprocity is manifested by specialization of function and it is practised on the cultural plane. The valencies of homogeneity are therefore freed; from being formal, the analogy postulated between human groups and natural species becomes substantial (as the example of the Chickasaw and the quotation from the Laws of Manu [cf. p. 106], shows) and true reciprocity being otherwise secured, endogamy is made available.

There are, however, limits to this symmetry. Totemic groups certainly give an imitation of gift-giving which has a function. But, apart from the fact that it remains imaginary, it is not cultural either since it must be classed, not among the arts of civilization, but as a fake usurpation of natural capacities which man as a biological species lacks. Certainly also the equivalent of food prohibitions are found in caste systems but, significantly enough, they are principally expressed in the reverse form of 'endo-cuisine' and moreover they occur on the level of the preparation, rather than the production of food, in other words, on the cultural plane. They are precise and detailed but mainly with respect to culinary operations and utensils.

Finally, women are naturally interchangeable (from the point of view of their anatomical structure and the physiological functions) and in their case culture finds the field open for the great game of differentiation (whether this is thought of in a positive or a negative way and used therefore as a basis for exogamy on the one hand or endogamy on the other). Foods however are not altogether able to be substituted for each other. The game reaches its limits more quickly in this second domain for one is much less inclined to class all foods as totemic since, as we have seen, it is harder to do without turmeric than *korra*. Now, this applies even more to occupational functions. Because they really are different and complementary, they allow the establishment of reciprocity in its truest form. On the other hand, they exclude negative reciprocity and so set bounds to the logical harmony of caste systems. Each caste remains partly 'endo-functional'; it cannot forbid rendering also to itself the differentiating services it is called on first of all to provide for the other castes, since these have been ruled to be irreplaceable. Or who would shave the barber?

Introducing (socially) instituted diversity into a single natural species, the human species, is not therefore the same as projecting the diversity (naturally) existing between animal and plant species on to the social plane. Societies with totemic groups and exogamous sections in vain believe that they manage to play the same game with species which are different, and women who are identical. They do not notice that since women are identical, it falls to the social will to make them different, while species being different, no one can make them identical, in the sense of all subjects in the same way to human will. Men produce other men, they do not produce ostriches.

Nevertheless it remains true that we can on a very general plane perceive an equivalence between the two main systems of differences to which men have had recourse for conceptualizing their social relations. Simplifying a great deal, it may be said that castes picture themselves as natural species while totemic groups picture natural species as castes. And this must be refined: castes naturalize a true culture falsely, totemic groups culturalize a false nature truly.

In both views it must be granted that the system of social functions corresponds to the system of natural species, the world of living creatures to the world of objects, and we must therefore recognize the system of natural species and that of manufactured objects as two mediating sets which man employs to overcome the opposition between nature and culture and think of them as a whole. But there is also another means.

Several hunting tribes in North American say that at the beginning of time buffaloes were ferocious beasts and 'all bone'. They were not only inedible to man but also cannibal. Men were thus once the food of the animal which later came to be their prime food but which was at that time the reverse of a food since it was animal food in its inedible form: bone. How is so complete a change to be explained?

It came to pass, according to the myth, that a buffalo fell in love with a girl and wanted to marry her. This girl was the only member of her sex in a community of men, for a man had conceived her after being pricked by a thorny plant. The woman thus appears to be the product of a negative union, between nature hostile to man (the bush of thorns) and human antinature (the pregnant man). In spite of their affection for their daughter and their fear of the buffalo, men thought it wise to agree to the marriage and they collected together presents, each of which was to stand for a part of the buffalo's body : a war-bonnet was to become the backbone, a quiver of otter-skin the skin on its chest, a woven blanket the paunch, a pointed quiver the stomach, moccasins the kidneys, a bow the ribs, etc. Nearly forty correspondences are enumerated in this way (cf. Dorsey and Kroeber, no. 81, for a version of this myth).

The marriage exchange thus functions as a mechanism serving to mediate between nature and culture, which were originally regarded as separate. By substituting a cultural architectonic for a supernatural primitive one, the alliance creates a second nature over which man has a hold, that is a mediatized nature. After these occurrences buffaloes became 'all flesh' instead of 'all bone' and edible instead of cannibal.

The same sequence is sometimes reversed as in the Navaho myth which ends in the transformation of a woman into a cannibal she-bear: exactly the converse of a cannibal buffalo being transformed into a husband. The metamorphosis is extended in a scattered pattern which follows the model of the differences between wild species: the vagina of the ogress turned into a hedgehog, her breasts into pinyon nuts and acorns, her paunch into other seeds ('alkali': *sporobolus cryptandrus*, *airoides*, Torr.), the trachea turned into a medicinal plant and the kidneys into mushrooms, etc. (Haile-Wheelwright, p. 83).

These myths are an admirable expression of the way in which marriage exchanges can furnish a model directly applicable to the mediation between nature and culture among peoples where totemic classifications and functional specialization, if present at all, have only a very limited yield. This confirms what I suggested above, namely, first that the 'system of women' is, as it were, a middle term between the system of (natural) living creatures and the system of (manufactured) objects and secondly that each system is apprehended as a transformation within a single group.

The system of living creatures is the only one of the three systems which has an objective existence outside man and that of functions the only one which has a completely social existence, that is, within man. But the completeness of each on one plane explains why neither is readily handled on the other: a food in general use cannot be wholly 'totemized' at least not without a kind of cheating* and, equally, castes cannot avoid being

* We read the following about the 'clan divinities' of the Dinka—which the older authors would have had no hesitation in calling totems: '. . . few are of any dietetic importance, and where they are the respect paid to them may yet permit

endofunctional while they serve to construct a grandiose scheme of reciprocity. Reciprocity is not therefore absolute in either case. It is, as it were, blurred and distorted at the periphery. Logically speaking, the reciprocity of marriage exchanges represents an equally impure form since it lies mid-way between a natural and a cultural model. But it is this hybrid character which allows it to function perfectly. Associated with one or the other form, or with both, or present on its own, as the case may be, the reciprocity of marriage exchanges alone can claim universality.

The first conclusion which emerges from this analysis is that totemism, which has been rendered amply formal in 'primitive language', could at the cost of a very simple transformation equally well be expressed in the language of the regime of castes which is quite the reverse of primitive. This is already sufficient to show that we are here dealing not with an autonomous institution, which can be defined by its distinctive properties and is typical of certain regions of the world and certain forms of civilization but with a *modus operandi* which can be discerned even behind social structures traditionally defined in a way diametrically opposed to totemism.

Secondly, we are in a better position to resolve the difficulty arising from the fact that so-called totemic institutions include not only the conceptual systems we have chosen to consider but also rules of action. For I have tried to show that food prohibitions are not a distinctive feature of totemism ; they are also found associated with other systems which they similarly serve to 'stress' and conversely systems of names deriving from the natural kingdoms are not always accompanied by food prohibitions: they can be 'stressed' in diverse fashions.

Further, exogamy and food prohibitions are not objects distinct from the nature of society, which should be studied separately or between which causal relations could be discovered. As language shows almost anywhere, they are two aspects or two modes serving to give concrete expression to a *praxis* which as a social activity can be turned outwards or inwards and which always has these two orientations even although they manifest themselves on different

them to be eaten'. Thus the clan of the Giraffe consider that they can eat the meat of this animal provided only that they do not shed its blood (Lienhardt, pp. 114–15).

planes and by means of different codes. If the relation between totemic institutions and castes can be regarded as superficially identical to one between exogamy and endogamy (we have seen that things are in fact more complex), between species and function, and finally between a natural and cultural model, it is because a similar scheme emerges in all the empirically observable and apparently heterogeneous cases and it is this which furnishes scientific investigation with its true subject of study. There is an analogy between sexual relations and eating in all societies, but either the man or the woman may occupy the position of eater or eaten according to the case and the level of thought. This can but indicate the common requirement that terms should be differentiated from each other and each identified unequivocally.

Here again I do not mean to suggest that social life, the relations between man and nature, are a projection or even result, of a conceptual game taking place in the mind. 'Ideas', Balzac wrote, 'form a complete system within us, comparable to one of the natural kingdoms, a sort of bloom whose iconography will be traced by a man of genius who will pass perhaps as mad.'* But more madness than genius would be required for such an enterprise. If, as I have said, the conceptual scheme governs and defines practices, it is because these, which the ethnologist studies as discrete realities placed in time and space and distinctive in their particular modes of life and forms of civilization, are not to be confused with *praxis* which – and here at least I agree with Sartre (p. 181) – constitutes the fundamental totality for the sciences of man. Marxism, if not Marx himself, has too commonly reasoned as though practices followed directly from *praxis*. Without questioning the undoubted primacy of infrastructures, I believe that there is always a mediator between *praxis* and practices, namely the conceptual scheme by the operation of which matter and form, neither with any independent existence, are realized as structures, that is as entities which are both empirical and intelligible. It is to this theory of superstructures, scarcely touched on by Marx, that I hope to make a contribution. The development of the study of infrastructures proper is a task which must be left to history – with the aid of demography, technology, historical geography and ethnography.

* H. de Balzac, 'Louis Lambert' in: *Oeuvres complètes*, Bibl. de la Pléiade, Vol X, p. 396.

It is not principally the ethnologist's concern, for ethnology is first of all psychology.

All that I claim to have shown so far is, therefore, that the dialectic of superstructures, like that of language, consists in setting up *constitutive units* (which, for this purpose, have to be defined unequivocally, that is by contrasting them in pairs) so as to be able by means of them to elaborate a system which plays the part of a synthesizing operator between ideas and facts, thereby turning the latter into *signs*. The mind thus passes from empirical diversity to conceptual simplicity and then from conceptual simplicity to meaningful synthesis.

The most appropriate conclusion to this chapter is an illustration of this idea by a native theory. The Yoruba myth, a veritable *Totem and Taboo* before the fact, takes the complex edifice of denomination and prohibition to pieces bit by bit.

What is in question is the explanation of the following rules. On the third day after a child is born, a priest is called in to give the child 'its *Orisha* and its *ewaws*'. The *Orisha* is the creature or thing which it worships, and the child may not marry anyone who has the same *Orisha*. This creature or thing becomes the principal *ewaw* of the person in question who passes it on to his descendants for four generations. His son takes as his second *ewaw* his father's wife's animal *ewaw*. The son of this son in turn takes his father's wife's third or vegetable *ewaw*. And the son of the son of this son takes the same relative's fourth *ewaw*, i.e. a rat, bird or snake.

In native thought these complicated rules are based on an original division of people into six groups: that of the fisherman; that of 'omens': fish, snake and bird; that of the hunter; that of quadrupeds; that of the farmer; that of plants. Each group comprises both men and women, giving twelve categories altogether.

To begin with unions were incestuous within each group, brother marrying sister. The same Yoruba term is used for marriage, meal, ownership, merit, gain and earnings or winnings. Marrying and eating are one and the same thing. Using A and B to represent a brother and sister of the first group, C and D a brother and sister of the second group and so on, the initially incestuous position can be summarized in the table:

1	2	3	4	5	6
AB	CD	EF	GH	IJ	KL

Human beings however soon got tired of this monotonous 'diet', so the son of the couple AB took the female product of CD and so on for EF and GH etc.:

ABD CDB EFH GHF IJL KLJ

Even then they were not satisfied and so the fisherman made war on the hunter, the hunter on the farmer and the farmer on the fisherman, and each appropriated the other's product. The result was that from then on the fisherman ate flesh, the hunter the products of the soil and the farmer fish:

ABDF CDBH EFHJ GHFL IJLB KLJD

By way of reprisal, the fisherman demanded the products of the soil, the farmer flesh and the hunter fish:

ABDFJ CDBHL EFHJB GHFLD LJLBF KLJDH

Things could not go on like this, so a great palaver was called and the families agreed that they would give their daughters in marriage to one another; and charged the priests to prevent confusion and disorder by the rule that a wife continues to worship her own *Orisha* after marriage but her children do not inherit it. The *Orisha* represented by the second letter in each series (viz. BD FHJL) thus drop out in the next generation and the systems of *ewaws* becomes:

ADFJ CBHL EHJB GFLD ILBF KJDH

In future each person's *ewaws* were to consist of one *Orisha*, one 'omen', one animal and one plant. Each *ewaw* would continue in the family line for four generations, after which the priest would renew it. So A C E G I K now drop out and a male *Orisha* is needed to complete the *ewaws*. A person whose index is ADFJ (group 1) can marry a child of group 2 whose *ewaws* are all different. A and C are therefore permutable and similarly E and G, I and K:

DFJC BHLA HJBG FLDE LBFK JDHI

In the next generation the letters D B H F L J drop out. Group 1 needs fish and takes B; group 2 also needs fish and takes D; group 3 needs meat and takes F; group 4 also needs meat and takes H; group 5 needs a plant and takes J; group 6 needs a plant and takes I:

FJCB HLAD JBGF LDEH BFKJ DHIL

The letters F H J L B D now drop out in turn. Being short of meat groups 1 and 2 marry H and F respectively; short of plants, groups 3 and 4 marry L and J; short of fish, groups 5 and 6 marry D and B:

JCBH LADF BGFL DEHJ FKJD HILB

J L B D F H drop out and the male *Orishas* come to the fore again:

CBHL ADFJ GFLD EHJB KJDH ILBF

As there are said to be two hundred and one *Orishas* of which about half are male, and also a considerable number of omens, animals and plants which are used for designating impediments to marriage, the number of possible combinations is very high (Dennett, pp. 176–80).

No doubt, what we have here is just a theory in the form of a fable. The author who recorded it mentions various facts which seem, if not to contradict it, at least to suggest that things did not function with this perfect regularity in his day. But, as theories go, the Yoruba seem to have been able to throw more light than ethnologists on the spirit of institutions and rules which in their society, as in many others, are of an intellecutal and deliberate character.* Sensible images undoubtedly come in, but they do so as symbols: they are counters in a game of combinations which consists in permuting them according to rules without ever losing sight of the empirical significants for which, provisionally, they stand.

* The example of the Ashanti among whom a boy inherits his father's, and a girl her mother's, food prohibitions, equally suggests that the spirit of such systems is 'logical' rather than 'genealogical'.

CHAPTER FIVE

CATEGORIES, ELEMENTS, SPECIES, NUMBERS

In inquiring into the nature of mythical thought Boas came to the conclusion in 1914 that the 'essential problem' was to know why 'human tales are preferably attached to animals, celestial bodies, and other personified phenomena of nature'. (Boas 5, p. 490). This problem is in fact the last remnant of the speculations about totemism but it seems possible to solve it.

I have already tried to show that the heterogeneous beliefs and customs arbitrarily collected together under the heading of totemism do not rest on the idea of a relationship of substance between one or more social groups and one or more natural domains. They are allied to other beliefs and practices, directly or indirectly linked to classificatory schemes which allow the natural and social universe to be grasped as an organized whole. The only distinctions which could be introduced between all these schemes derive from preferences, which are never exclusive, for this or that level of classification.

All the levels of classification in fact have a common characteristic: whichever, in the society under consideration, is put first it must authorize – or even imply – possible recourse to other levels, formally analogous to the favoured one and differing from it only in their relative position within a whole system of reference which operates by means of a pair of contrasts: between general and particular on the one hand, and nature and culture on the other.

The mistake which the upholders of totemism made was arbitrarily to isolate one level of classification, namely that constituted by reference to natural species, and to give it the status of an institution, when like all levels of classification it is in fact only one among others and there is no reason to regard it as more important than, say, the level operating by means of abstract categories or that using nominal classes. What is significant is not so much the presence – or absence – of this or that level of classification as the existence of a classification with, as it were, an adjustable thread which gives the group adopting it the means of 'focusing' on all planes, from the most abstract to the most concrete, the most cultural to the most natural, without changing its intellectual instrument.

In the work referred to above, Boas was doubtful whether the predilection which is so frequent for classification based on a natural model could be adequately explained by the 'distinctness and individualization of species of animals ... [which] set them off more clearly as characters of a tale than the undifferentiated members of mankind' (loc. cit.). Boas did, however, touch on an important truth here. To have recognized it he need only, contrary to a commonly held position, have been prepared, instead of reducing the story or myth to a mere narrative, to try to discover the scheme of discontinuous oppositions governing its organization behind the mythical 'discourse'. Furthermore, the natural 'distinctiveness' of biological species does not furnish thought with a definitive and readily apprehended model but rather with a means of access to other distinctive systems which have their own repercussions on it. All things considered, if it is the case that zoological and botanical typologies are employed more often and more readily than other typologies, this can only be by reason of their intermediate position as logically equidistant from the extreme forms of classification: categorical and singular. There is a balance between the point of view of extension and that of comprehension in the notion of a species: considered in isolation, a species is a collection of individuals; in relation to other species, however, it is a system of definitions. Moreover each of these individuals, the theoretically unlimited collection of which makes up the species, is indefinable in extension since it forms an organism which is a system of functions. The notion of species thus possesses an internal dynamic: being a collection poised between two systems, the species is the operator which allows (and even makes obligatory) the passage from the unity of a multiplicity to the diversity of a unity.

As I have tried to show elsewhere (6, p. 133 ff.), Bergson discerned the importance of the part which, in view of its logical structure, the notion of species was to play in the critique of totemism. But there is every reason to fear that, had he been forced to make his analysis more specific, he would have restricted it to the subjective and practical aspect of the relation between man and the natural world, of the kind exemplified by someone asking what there is for lunch today and being wholly satisfied with the answer 'veal'. In fact the importance of the notion of species is to be explained not so much by a propensity on the part of the practising agent to dissolve it into a genus for biological and utilitarian reasons (which would amount to extending to man the famous dictum that it is grass in general which attracts the herbivore)* as by its presumptive objectivity: the diversity of species furnishes man with the most intuitive picture at his disposal and constitutes the most direct manifestation he can perceive of the ultimate discontinuity of reality. It is the sensible expression of an objective coding.

It is a striking fact that modern biology turns to schemata resembling those used in Communication Theory to explain the diversity of species. We cannot here embark on problems outside the ethnologist's province. But if it were true, as biologists hold, that the anatomical, physiological, and ethnological diversity of some two million living species may be analysed in terms of variations of the chromosomes which are reducible to a periodicity in the distribution of four distinct groups on the molecular chain, then we could perhaps grasp the deeper reason for the special significance man has seen in the notion of species. We should understand how this idea can furnish a mode of sensory apprehension of a combination objectively given in nature, and that the activity of the mind, and social life itself, do no more than borrow it to apply it to the creation of new taxonomies. This would serve to resolve the apparent mystery of the fascination which the notion of species has always possessed for men, of which the obscure

* Which indeed is as false in the case of animals as of man. The attempts to establish national parks in Africa to preserve species threatened with extinction comes up against the difficulty that even if the pasturage is of sufficient area, the animals only use it as a home-base and go far beyond the limits of the reserve in search of grasses richer in protein than the pastures allotted to them for the simplistic reason that they are sufficiently extensive (Grzimek, p. 20). It is thus not grass but the difference between species of grass which interests the herbivore . . .

fascination which totemism has had for ethnologists would just constitute a particular case.

The natural sciences for a long time regarded themselves as concerned with 'kingdoms', that is, independent and sovereign domains each definable by its own characteristics and peopled by creatures or objects standing in special relations to one another. This view, which is now out-moded but still the 'commonsense' one, could not but obliterate the logical power and the dynamism of the notion of species, since in this light species appeared as inert and separate classes, confined within the limits of their respective 'kingdoms'. The societies which we call primitive do not have any conception of a sharp division between the various levels of classification. They represent them as stages or moments in a continuous transition.

The Hanunóo of the Southern Philippines divide the universe into what can and what cannot be named. What can be named is distinguished into things on the one hand and persons or animals on the other. When a Hanunóo utters the word 'plant' he excludes the possibility that the thing of which he is speaking should be a rock or a manufactured object. The class of 'herbaceous plant' in turn excludes other classes of plants such as 'woody plant', etc. Among herbaceous plants, the term 'pepper plant' is differential in relation to 'rice plant', etc. 'Houseyard pepper' excludes 'wild pepper', and 'houseyard chile pepper' excludes 'houseyard green pepper'; finally, 'cat-penis' specifies the individual in question as not being a member of the five other varieties or *taxa* which the native culture distinguishes within the group of houseyard peppers (Conklin, 4, p. 131).

This mode of operation, which can be represented by a series of dichotomies, has been described in the following way:

> While not to be confused, nor categorically equated, with the botanical concept of species, the Hanunóo plant type does exhibit one similar feature: barring mistaken identification, plant type names are mutually exclusive . . . Each of the 1,625 Hanunóo plant types* has a full specific name differing in at least one component from all others. . . . Full plant names are made up of from one to five, free, full-word lexical units. The most common form is a binomial combination . . . Similarities between Hanunóo and botanical classification decrease rapidly as we approach the

* Of which 500 to 600 are only edible (l.c., p. 141) and 406 of purely medicinal use (l.c., p. 188). These 1,625 types, grouped into 890 categories by indigenous thought, correspond to 650 genera and about 1,100 species in scientific botany . . . (l.c., pp. 122–3).

higher-level, more inclusive categories (Conklin I, pp. 115–17 and p. 162).

In fact the classes which correspond to Linnaean categories (pepper plant: *Capsicum sp.*, houseyard pepper: *Capsicum annum L.*, wild pepper: *Capsicum frutescens L.*) do not belong either to the same level or to the same side of the system of dichotomies. And above all the domain of scientific botany is cut off neither from the popular botany practised by the gardener or housewife nor from philosophers' and logicians' categories. It is mid-way between them and makes it possible to pass from one to another and to conceptualize each level with the help of a code borrowed from another (cf. diagram [p. 141]).

The Subanun, another Philippine tribe, classify diseases on the same principle. They begin by distinguishing skin diseases from wounds. They subdivide skin diseases into 'inflammations', 'sores' and 'ringworm'. Each of these three forms is further specified by means of several binary oppositions: simple/multiple, hidden/exposed, severe/mild, shallow/deep, distal/proximal (Frake, p. 129).

The documentation adduced in Chapters 1 and 2 in conjunction with these examples shows how commonly zoological and botanical classifications do not constitute separate domains but form an integral part of an all-embracing dynamic taxonomy the unity of which is assured by the perfect homogeneity of its structure, consisting as it does of successive dichotomies. One consequence of this feature is that it is always possible to pass from *species* to *category*. Again there is no inconsistency between the *system* (in evidence at the top) and the *lexicon* whose role becomes progressively more dominant as one descends the ladder of dichotomies. The problem of the relation between *continuous* and *discontinuous* receives a solution in terms of origin since the universe is represented as a continuum made up of successive oppositions.

This continuity is already apparent in the scheme which governs the liturgy of seasonal rites among the Pawnee Indians: the posts of the lodge where the celebration takes place are chosen, according to their orientation, from four species of trees painted in different colours, which themselves correspond to directions symbolizing the seasons which together make up the year:

SPACE						TIME
poplar	white	south-west	south	summer	year	
box-elder	red	south-east				
elm	black	north-east	north	winter		
willow	yellow	north-west				

The same explicit passage from species or group of species to a system of properties or categories can be illustrated by Melanesian examples. We have already seen that at Mawatta, an island of the Torres Straits, clans with animal names are grouped according to species into land or sea, warlike or pacific. Among the Kiwai an opposition between the sago people and the yam people is expressed by means of two emblems: that of the nude woman and that of the bull-roarer, also called 'the mother of yams', and it also corresponds to the alternation of the seasons and of the prevailing winds. In the Trobriand Islands there is a correspondence, in the case of each clan, between a bird, an animal, a fish, and a plant. The binary system of the Solomons appeals either to two birds (wild cock and hornbill) or to two insects (pharma and mantis) or to two divinities who are, however, the incarnation of antithetical modes of behaviour (Mr Wise and Mr Clumsy) (Frazer, vol. II, *passim*).

We can thus see that, depending on the code chosen, the logical rigour of the oppositions can be unequally manifested without thereby implying any difference of kind. The classificatory systems of the Sioux provide a good example, for they constitute so many variations on a common theme. Only the semantic level adopted to signify the system changes.

All the tribes have circular camps which an imaginary diameter divides into two moieties. But in several of them this apparent dualism conceals a principle of tripartition, the symbolic substance of which varies from one tribe to another. Among the Winnebago there are twice as many clans in one moiety as in the other (eight and four respectively). The ten Omaha clans are distributed equally between the two moieties, but one has two chiefs and the other only one. There are seven clans in each Osage moiety but one moiety is divided into two sub-moieties while the other is homogeneous. In all three cases and in whichever way the opposition is realized it

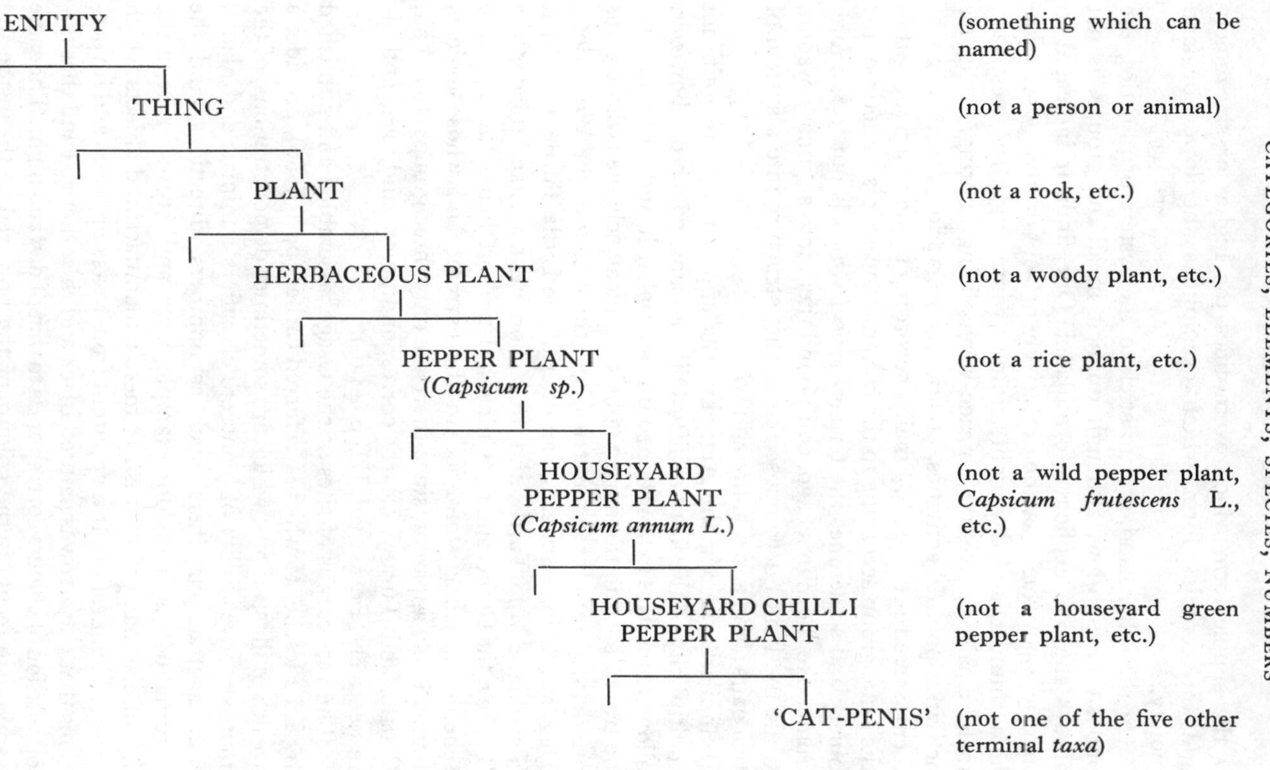
ENTITY
(something which can be named)
THING
(not a person or animal)
PLANT
(not a rock, etc.)
HERBACEOUS PLANT
(not a woody plant, etc.)
PEPPER PLANT
(*Capsicum sp.*)
(not a rice plant, etc.)
HOUSEYARD PEPPER PLANT
(*Capsicum annum L.*)
(not a wild pepper plant, *Capsicum frutescens* L., etc.)
HOUSEYARD CHILLI PEPPER PLANT
(not a houseyard green pepper plant, etc.)
'CAT-PENIS'
(not one of the five other terminal *taxa*)
(Conklin 4, p. 131)

is the simple form which exemplifies the higher or sky moiety and the complex form which exemplifies the lower or land moiety.

On the other hand, and to stick to the system of moieties, the opposition high/low, although implicit in all the groups, is not always the one explicitly formulated. One finds it indicated in diverse ways which may be exclusively present or juxtaposed: sky/land, thunder/land, day/night, summer/winter, right/left, west/east, male/female, peace/war, peace-war/policing-hunting, religious activities/political activities, creation/conservation, stability/movement, sacred/profane . . . Finally, according to the group (or within the same group according to the circumstances) it is sometimes the binary and sometimes the ternary aspect which is put to the fore. Some, like the Winnebago, compound them into a quinary system, while the Ponca decompose the dualist structure into a system of two pairs: land and sea, fire and wind.

Similarly, among the Algonkin the apparently non-significant multiplicity of the forty or fifty Ojibwa clans, which do, however, allow themselves to be grouped into animal, fish, and bird clans, can be traced back to the more explicit Mohican scheme (whose clans are divided into three phratries, one consisting of the Wolf, Bear, Dog, and Oppossum clans, another of the Little Turtle, the Great Turtle, the Mud Turtle, and the Yellow Eel clans, and third of the Turkey, the Crane, and the Chicken clans) and then to the Delaware scheme, which is simplified in the extreme and whose logic is immediately apparent, since there are only three groups, the Wolf, Turtle, and Turkey, clearly corresponding to land, sea, and air respectively (Frazer, vol. III, p. 44 ff.).

The vast corpus of rites of the Osage, assembled and published by La Flesche, to which I referred earlier (pp. 59–60), provides a wealth of illustrations, which are sometimes demonstrations, of the mutual convertibility of 'concrete classifiers': animals and plants, and 'abstract classifiers' such as numbers, directions, and the cardinal points. Thus, for example, bows and arrows figure in the list of clan names but it is not merely manufactured objects which are here in question. It is apparent from texts of prayers and invocations that one arrow is painted black and the other red and that this opposition of colours corresponds to that of day and night. The same symbolism recurs in the colours of the bow, red on the inside and black on the outside: shooting with the red and black bow, using alternatively a red and a black arrow, is an expression of Time, itself measured by the alternation of day and night (cf. La Flesche, 2, p. 9, and 3, pp. 207, 233, 364–5).

The concrete classifiers not only serve to convey ideas; they can also, in their sensory form, show that a logical problem has been solved or a contradiction surmounted. Among the Osage, when a pair of moccasins are made, their owner must perform a complex rite. This special attention accorded an article of clothing might seem surprising did the texts not reveal in the moccasin something other than its utilitarian function: the moccasin, a cultural object, is opposed to 'evil' grass which the walker tramples and crushes. It thus corresponds to a warrior who tramples his enemies underfoot. Now, in the sociocosmological scheme of the Osage, the martial function connotes the land moiety, to which grass also belongs. The particular symbolism of the moccasin is thus inconsistent with the general symbolism, since the moccasin is 'anti-land' in the former and congruent with land in the latter. The minutia of the ritual is clarified by the evidence of what one would like to call the logical instability of a manufactured article: an instability which a highly ritualized manufacturing technique precisely serves to palliate (cf. l.c. 3, pp. 61–7).

In Osage thought, the most important opposition, which is also the simplest and has the greatest logical power, is that between the two moieties: *Tsi'-zhu*: sky, and *Hon'-ga*; subdivided into *Hon'-ga*, properly speaking: dry land, and Wa-zha'-zhe: water. Starting from here a complex grammar is developed by means of a system of correspondences with more concrete or more abstract domains but within which the original scheme, acting as a catalyst, initiates the crystallization of other schemes of two, three, four, or more variables. First the cardinal points, since, in the initiating hut, sky and land are opposed as north and south, and dry land and water as east and west respectively.

Secondly, the opposition of odd and even gives rise to a mystic numerology. As I indicated in Chapter 4, the number six belongs to the sky moiety, the number seven to the land moiety, and their sum, thirteen, corresponds, on the cosmological plane, to the number of rays of the rising sun (which is a *demi-sun*) and, on the social plane, to the notable actions which may be counted to his credit by an accomplished warrior (who is a *demi-man*, since the function of war is the prerogative of one of the two moieties which together constitute the tribe).*

Thus the quality and the unity of the two great divisions of the tribe might be symbolized as a man or an animal, but the Hon'-ga great division must always represent the right side of the man or animal and the Tsi'-zhu the great division of the left. This idea of the duality and unity of nature was not only reflected in the tribal organization but, in former times, instilled in the minds of the people by certain personal habits, as for instance members of the Hon'-ga great division when putting on their moccasins put the moccasin on the right foot first, while members of the Tsi'-zhu great division put the moccasin on the left foot first (La Flesche 3, p. 115).

I want here to digress for a moment to point out that this meticulous rigour in the practical application of a logical system is not an isolated phenomenon. At Hawaii the death of a chief was marked by violent manifestations of mourning. The participants wore their loin cloths around their neck instead of loins. This vestimentary inversion of high and low was accompanied by (and no doubt also signified) sexual licence. The importance of the opposition between high and low was expressed in a large number of prohibitions. A receptacle containing food must not be covered by any object which may have been walked on or sat on; it was forbidden to sit on a pillow or to use it as a footrest, to lay your head on a seat cushion, to sit above anything containing food, or, for menstruating women, to use as pads anything but material from old skirts worn below the waist:

The old time Hawaiians used to talk often, when I was a small child, of the terrible custom the Whites had of using a sheet sometimes to lie upon and sometimes to lie under – they (the Whites) did not seem to know that what belonged above (*ma luna*) should remain above and what belonged below (*ma lalo*) should stay below . . .

In a *hula* school conducted by my cousin Ilala-ole-o-Ka'ahumanu, one of the pupils thoughtlessly draped her skirt over her shoulder. The *hula* master spoke sharply to her, saying 'What belongs above should stay above, and what belongs below should stay below' (*Ko luna, no luna no ia; Ko lalo no lalo no ia*). (Handy and Pukui, Part VI, p. 165, and Part VII, pp. 316, 317).

Recent studies (Needham 3, Beidelman) show the refinement with which the African tribes of Kenya and Tanganyika exploit the, to them, fundamental opposition between right and left (usually

* The responsibility for this analysis, which is not given in the texts, is my own.

apparently the right and left hands rather than feet, but we have already noticed the particular attention which the Osage pays to the lower extremities). A Kaguru man uses his left hand for making love and a woman her right hand (that is, the hands which are impure for each sex respectively). The first payment which has to be made to a healer, before treatment can begin, is made with the right hand, the last with the left, etc. The nomadic Fulani of the Sahel zone of the Niger, the Bororo of Africa, seem, like the Kaguru, to associate the right side with men and – in the temporal order – with what comes first, the left side with women and what comes after.* Symmetrically, the masculine hierarchy goes from south to north and the feminine from north to south, so that, in the camp, the woman places her calabashes in order of decreasing size, with the largest to the south, while a man fastens his calves in the reverse order (Dupire).

To return to the Osage: the number thirteen, as we have seen, is first of all the sum of the two social groups, right and left, north and south, winter and summer; thereafter it is specified concretely and developed logically. In the image of the rising sun, in which the beholder venerates the source of all life (thus facing east, which means that the south is on his right and the north on his left),† the number thirteen can symbolize the union of two terms: six and seven, sky and land, etc. But when it relates to a star the solar symbolism is particularly attached to the sky moiety. Hence there come to be other concrete specifications of the number thirteen, in this case reserved to sub-groups of the other moiety: thirteen footprints of the black bear to represent the notable actions of the land clans and thirteen willow trees to represent those of the water clans (La Flesche 3, p. 147).

Thirteen is thus the expression of a double human totality: collective, since the tribe is made up of two asymmetrical moieties (quantitatively: one is single, the other divided; and qualitatively: one in

* Cf. Diamond for an analogous spatio-temporal system in the same region.

† The officiant is painted red 'to express his craving that through the sun his life may be made fruitful and that he may be blessed with a long line of descendants'. When his whole body has been painted red, 'a dark line is drawn on his face running upward from one cheek to the forehead, then across to the opposite side and downward to the middle of the other cheek. This line represents the dark horizon line of the earth and is called a "snare" or an enclosure into which all life is drawn and held captive'. (La Flesche 3, p. 73).

charge of peace, the other of war) and individual but equally asymmetrical (the right and the left). As a totality, this union of even and odd, of collective and individual, social and organic, is geared to the ternary cosmological scheme: there is a 'thirteen' of sky, a 'thirteen' of land, a 'thirteen' of water. Finally, added to this coding by elements, there is a coding by species where the two groups composed respectively of seven and six 'animals' are duplicated by the appearance of antagonists, thus (as might be foreseen) bringing the number of units of the system at the most concrete level to twenty-six. The seven animals and their antagonists are shown in the following table:

ANIMALS	ANTAGONISTS
lynx	young male deer, with curved horns
grey wold	young male deer, with grey horns
male puma	full grown male deer, with dark horns
male black bear	hummock full of little bugs (insects?)
buffalo bull	high bank
elk	a plant whose blossoms always look up to the sun (*Silphium laciniatum*)
deer*	no antagonist: his strength lies in flight

The system of six animals is less neat. It includes two varieties of owl, each opposed to a male raccoon, one young and one adult, the golden eagle opposed to the turkey, finally, apparently, the river mussel (the shell of which is used to make the mother of pearl pendants which symbolize the sun), buffalo hair (?), and a little pipe (?) (La Flesche 3, pp. 54–61).

A logical structure – initially a simple opposition – thus fans out in two directions: one abstract, in the form of a numerology, and the other concrete, first of elements and then of species. On each level semantic short-circuits permit direct connections with the level furthest away. The level of species, which is also the most particularized of those we have considered, does not, however, constitute a sort of limit or stopping point of the system: the latter does

* Timidity of the deer is due to its having no gall-bladder. Its role is twofold: alimentary, its meat being regarded as the most regular source of animal food, comparable from this point of view to the vegetable food provided by four essential plants: *Nelumbo lutea, Apios apios, Sagitarria latifolia, Falcata comosa.* The deer and these four plants are necessary to the very existence of the tribe and the primary role of the warrior is to defend that land where they are found (l.c., pp. 129–30). The deer also has a cultural role: its body is the source of the sinews which women use for sewing and men for fastening feathers to their arrows (l.c., p. 322).

not fall into inertia but continues to progress through new detotalizations and retotalizations which can take place on several planes.

Each clan possesses a 'symbol of life' – a totem or divinity – whose name it adopts: puma, black bear, golden eagle, young deer, etc. The clans are thus defined, in relation to each other, by means of differentiating features. Nevertheless, the ritual texts found each distinctive choice on a system of invariant characteristics, assumed to be common to all species: each affirms of itself what the puma, for instance, declares on its own account:

> 'Behold the soles of my feet, that are black in colour.
> I have made the skin of the soles of my feet to be as my charcoal.
> When the little ones [men] also make the skin of the soles of my feet to be as their charcoal,
> They shall always have charcoal that will easily sink into their skin as they travel the path of life.
> Behold the tip of my nose, that is black in color, etc.
> Behold the tips of my ears, that are black in color, etc.
> Behold the tip of my tail, that is black in color, etc.'
>
> (La Flesche 2, pp. 106–7)

Each animal is thus decomposed into parts, according to a law of correspondence (muzzle = beak, etc.) and the equivalent parts are regrouped among themselves and then all together in terms of the same relevant characteristic: the presence of 'charcoaled' parts, on account of the protective role which the Osage attribute to fire and its product, charcoal, and finally, and by way of consequence, to the colour black. The 'black thing', charcoal, is the object of a special rite which warriors have to perform before going into battle. If they neglect to blacken their faces, they will lose the right to recount their notable actions and to claim military honours (La Flesche 3, p. 327 seq.). We therefore already have a system on two axes, one devoted to diversities and the other to similarities:

CHARCOAL ANIMAL

Natural species	black paws	black muzzle	black tail	etc.
puma				
bear				
eagle				
deer				
swan				
etc.				

The analytic procedure which makes it possible to pass from categories to elements and from elements to species is thus extended by a sort of imaginary dismembering of each species, which progressively re-establishes the totality on another plane.

This double movement of detotalization and retotalization also takes place on a diachronic plane, as is shown by the admirable chants of the Bear and the Beaver (representing land and water respectively). They are meditating on the coming winter and preparing themselves for it in accordance with their particular habits (here endowed with symbolic significance), so that the coming of spring and their restored strength can appear as the pledge of the long life promised to men: When 'six moons had passed . . . [the bear] made a close examination of his body, looking carefully over all its parts'. He enumerated the signs of his emaciation (that is, a diminished body which, however, as he has remained alive, testifies the more to the power of life: shrunken flesh, shrivelled toes, wrinkled ankles, flabby abdomen, protruding ribs, flaccid arms, sagging chin, lines on the corner of the eyes, bald forehead, scant hair). He next made footprints, symbols of warlike deeds, six on one side, seven on the other, and 'then the bear went forth with quickened footsteps, and came to a land upon which the air quivered with the warmth of the sun' (La Flesche 3, pp. 148–64).

The synchronic structure of the tribe, expressed in the division into three elemental groups, themselves divided into clans bearing totemic names, is indeed, as we have seen,* no more than a projection into the order of simultaneity of a temporal process which the myths describe in terms of succession: when the first men appeared on the earth (according to this version, from the sky; in another version (Dorsey I) they came from the subterranean world), they began to march in the order of their arrival: first the water people, then the land people, and last the sky people (La Flesche 2, pp. 59–60); but when they found the earth covered with water they appealed first to the water-spider, then to the whirligig, next to the white leech, and finally to the black leech to guide them to habitable spots (id., pp. 162–5).

It may be seen, therefore, that in none of these cases can the animal, the 'totem' or its species be grasped as a biological entity: through its double character of organism – that is, of system – and of emanation from a species – which is a term in a system – the animal

* Cf. above, pp. 68–9.

François Clouet. Portrait of Elizabeth of Austria

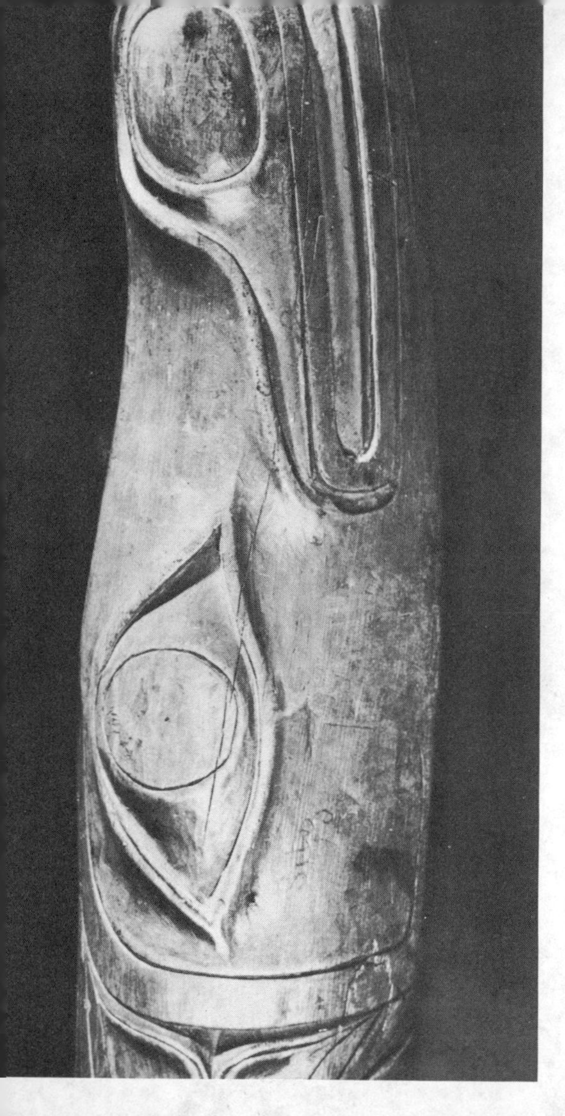

2 Club used for killing fish

3 The opposite of totemism : Naturalized Man. Sketch by Le Brun

4 Humanized Nature. Sketch by Grandville

5 Alphabet of Birds

CARICATURES.

M. MOUTON

6 Society of Animals

7 Australian Churinga

8 Aranda water-colours

appears as a conceptual tool with multiple possibilities for detotalizing or retotalizing any domain, synchronic or diachronic, concrete or abstract, natural or cultural.

Thus it is never, properly speaking, the eagle which the Osage invoke. For, according to the time and circumstances, it is eagles of different species which are in question: the golden eagle, the spotted eagle, the bald eagle, etc., or eagles of different colours: red, white, spotted, etc.; or finally eagles at different stages of their life: young, old, etc. This three-dimensional matrix, a genuine system *by means of* a creature, and not the creature itself, constitutes the object of thought and furnishes the conceptual tool.* Were the image not so trivial one would be tempted to compare this tool to a utensil with crossed metal blades which is used for cutting potatoes into slices or chips: a 'preconceived' grid is applied to all the empirical situations with which it has sufficient affinities for the elements obtained always to preserve certain general properties. The number of pieces is not always the same nor is the form of each absolutely identical but those which come from the centre remain in the centre, those which come from the periphery on the periphery . . .

As medial classifier (and therefore the one with the greatest yield and the most frequently employed) the species level can widen its net upwards, that is, in the direction of elements, categories, and numbers, or contract downwards, in the direction of proper names. This last aspect will be considered in detail in the next chapter. The network to which this twofold movement gives rise is itself cross-cut at every level, for there are a great many different manners in which these levels and their ramifications can be signified: nomenclature, differences of clothing, bodily paintings or tattoos, ways of being or behaviour, privileges and prohibitions. Each system is therefore defined with reference to two axes, one horizontal and one vertical, which correspond up to a point with Saussure's distinction between syntagmatic and associative relations. But 'totemic' thought, unlike speech, has this in common with mythical and poetical thought that, as Jakobson has established for the latter, the principle of equivalence acts on both planes. The social group can code the message without any alteration in its content by means of different

* 'We do not believe', as an Osage explained 'that our ancestors were really animals, birds, etc., as told in traditions. These things are only *wa-wi-ku-ska*'-*ye* (symbols) of something higher' (J. O. Dorsey, I, p. 396).

lexical elements: as a categoric opposition: high/low, or as an elemental one: sky/earth, or again as a specific one: eagle/bear. And equally it has the choice of several syntactic procedures to assure the transmission of the message: nomenclature, emblems, modes of behaviour, prohibitions, etc., used either alone or together.*

Were the task not so immense, a classification of these classifications could be undertaken. Systems would be distinguished according to the number of categories they employ – ranging from two to several dozen – and according to the number and choice of elements and dimensions. They would then be distinguished into macro- and micro-classifications, the former being characterized by the admission of a large number of animal and plant species to the status of totems (the Aranda recognize more than four hundred) and the latter by having totems all, as it were, inscribed within the limits of the same species. The Banyoro and Bahima in Africa provide an

* Considered separately, in their component parts and their respective relations with their surroundings, a suburban villa and a stronghold are syntagmatic sets: their elements are related to each other by contiguity: container and content, cause and effect, end and mean, etc. What, as a bricoleur, Mr Wemmick of *Great Expectations* undertook and realized (cf. above, p. 17) was the establishment of paradigmatic relations between the elements of these two chains: he can choose between villa and castle to signify his abode, between pond and moat to signify the piece of water, between flight of steps and drawbridge to signify the entrance, between salad and food reserves to signify his lettuces. How has this come about?

It is clear that to begin with his castle is a small-scale model, not of a real castle but of a castle signified by camouflages and fittings which have the function of symbols. He has not indeed acquired a real castle through these transformations, but he has well and truly lost a real villa, since his fantasy binds him to a whole number of servitudes. Instead of living as a bourgeois, his domestic life becomes a succession of ritual actions, the minute repetition of which serves to promote, as the sole reality, the paradigmatic relations between two equally unreal syntagmatic chains: that of the castle which has never existed and that of the villa which has been sacrificed. The first aspect of bricolage is thus to construct a system of paradigms with the fragments of syntagmatic chains.

But the reverse is equally true. His old father's deafness lends Mr Wemmick's castle a real value: a stronghold is normally provided with cannons; and his father is so deaf that only the noise of a cannon can penetrate to him. The initial syntagmatic chain, that of the suburban villa, is objectively broken by the paternal infirmity. Father and son, its sole inhabitants, lived juxtaposed without it being possible to establish any relation whatever between them. The villa need only become a castle for the cannon, fired daily at nine o'clock, to institute an effectual form of communication. A new syntagmatic chain thus results from the system of paradigmatic relations. A practical problem is solved: that of communication between the inhabitants of the villa, but thanks to a total reorganization of the real and the imaginary, whereby metaphors take over the mission of metonyms, and vice versa.

instance of this. Clans are named after particular types or parts of cows: striped cow, brown cow, cow in full milk, etc., cow's tongue, tripe, heart, kidneys, etc. The systems may equally be distinguished by the number of their dimensions. Some are purely animal, some purely plant, others appeal to manufactured articles, and yet others juxtapose a variable number of dimensions. They can be simple (one name or one totem per clan) or multiple as in the case of the Melanesian tribes who define each clan by a plurality of totems: a bird, a tree, a mammal, and a fish. Finally, the systems can be homogeneous like that of the Kavirondo where the totemic lists are composed of elements of the same type: crocodile, hyena, leopard, baboon, vulture, crow, python, mongoose, frog, etc. Or they can be heterogeneous, as the totemic lists of the Bateso illustrate: sheep, sugar cane, boiled bones of meat, mushroom, antelope (common to several clans), sight of the forbidden antelope, shaved skull, or again, those of certain north-east Australian tribes: sexual passion, adolescence, various diseases, named places, swimming, copulation, the making of a spear, vomiting, various colours, various physical states, heat, cold, corpse, ghost, various accessories of ritual, various manufactured objects, sleep, diarrhoea, dysentery, etc.*

Such a classification of classifications is perfectly conceivable but so many documents would have to be gone through and dimensions of such variety taken into account to realize it, that even if we confined ourselves to the societies for which the data are sufficiently full, accurate, and comparable among themselves, it could not be done without the aid of machines. Let us therefore content ourselves with mentioning this programme, reserved for the ethnology of a future century, and return to the most simple properties of what I am, for convenience, calling the totemic operator. A description with the help of a diagram, and considering only a small portion of the cell (for we are making it begin at the species level and arbitrarily restricting the number of species, and also the number of parts of the body, to three each), is sufficient to give an indication of its complexity (figure 8).

It can be seen that the species admits first empirical realizations: Seal species, Bear species, Eagle species. Each includes a series of

* 'It appears that a totem may be any enduring element of the physical or mental environment, either unique conceptual entities, or, more frequently, classes or species of things, activities, states, or qualities which are constantly recurring and are thus considered to be perdurable' (Sharp, p. 69).

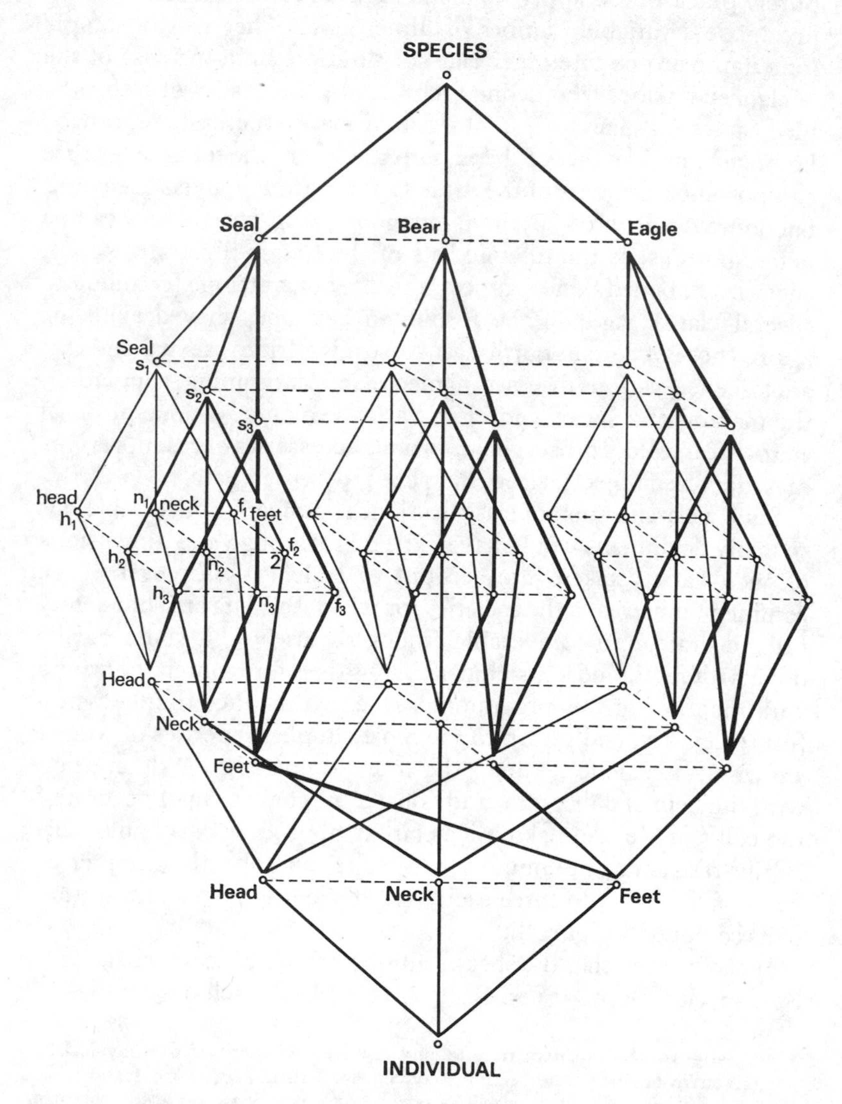

Fig 8 The totemic operator.

individuals (also reduced to three in the diagram): seals, bears, eagles. Each animal can be analysed into parts: head, neck, feet, etc. These can be regrouped first within each species (seals' heads, seals' necks, seals' feet) and then together by types of parts: all heads, all necks . . . A final regrouping restores the model of the individual in his regained entirety.

The whole set thus constitutes a sort of conceptual apparatus which filters unity through multiplicity, multiplicity through unity, diversity through identity, and identity through diversity. Endowed with a theoretically unlimited extension on its median level it contracts (or expands) into pure comprehension at its two extreme vertices, but in symmetically reverse forms, and not without undergoing a sort of torsion.

The model which I have used here as an illustration clearly only represents a minute fraction of the ideal model; since the number of natural species is in the order of two million, the conceivable number of individuals is unlimited, and the organs or parts of the body which are distinguished and named rises to almost four hundred in some indigenous vocabularies (Marsh and Laughlin). And there are probably no human societies which have not made a very extensive inventory of their zoological and botanical environment and described it in specific terms. Is it possible to estimate an order of magnitude, or limits? In going through ethnozoological and ethnobotanical works, one notices that, with rare exception, the species and varieties recorded seem to be in the order of several hundred, around three hundred to six hundred. No work of this kind is exhaustive, however, being limited by the time spent in collecting the material, the number and competence of the informants, and finally the fieldworker's own competence, the extent of his knowledge, and the variety of his preoccupations. One can therefore hardly go wrong in putting the real figure considerably higher, and the best works confirm this:

> The Hanunóo classify their local plant world, at the lowest (terminal) level of contrast, into more than 1800 mutually exclusive folk taxa, while botanists divide the same flora – in terms of species – into less than 1300 scientific taxa (Conklin 4, p. 129).

This quotation from an ethographer specializing in taxonomy curiously echoes a comment of Tylor's on the subject of Rabbinical philosophy:

> . . . which apportions to each of the 2100 species, of plants for instance, a presiding angel in heaven, and assigns this as the motive of the Levitical prohibition of mixtures among animals and plants (Tylor, vol. II, p. 246).

In the present state of knowledge, the figure of two thousand appears to correspond well, in order of magnitude, to a sort of threshold corresponding roughly to the capacity of memory and power of definition of ethnozoologies or ethnobotanies reliant on oral tradition. It would be interesting to know if this threshold has any significant properties from the point of view of Information Theory.

A recent student of initiation rites among the Senufo has brought to light the role of fifty-eight figurines which are shown to novices in a determinate order, and form, as it were, the canvas of the instruction imparted to them. These figurines represent animals or persons, or symbolize types of activities. Each therefore corresponds to a species or to a class:

> The elders present a certain number of objects to the neophytes . . . This inventory, sometimes very lengthy, constitutes a sort of lexicon of symbols and the different possible modes of using them are indicated. In the most developed *poro* the men learn in this way to handle the ideographical supports of a way of thought which manages to assume a truly philosophical character (Bochet, p. 76).

In other words, in systems of this type there is a constant passage in both directions between ideas and images, grammar and lexicon. This phenomenon, to which I have drawn attention several times already, raises a difficulty, namely, whether it is legitimate to postulate, as it might be objected I have implicitly done, that these systems are motivated at all levels. Or, more precisely: are what we have here genuine systems, where images and ideas, lexicon and grammar are always united by strict and invariable relations, or must we acknowledge that there is a certain measure of contingence and arbitrariness at the most concrete level – that of images and lexicon – which casts doubt on the systematic nature of the whole? This problem arises whenever one claims to have discovered a logic of clan names. As I showed in an earlier chapter, one almost always comes up against a difficulty which may at first seem insurmountable. The societies which claim to form a coherent and articulated system (whether the 'stress' of the system is on names, modes of behaviour, or prohibitions) are also collectivities of living beings. Even if, consciously or unconsciously they apply rules of marriage whose effect is to keep the social structure and rate of reproduction constant, these mechanisms never function perfectly; and they are also endangered by wars, epidemics, and famines. It is thus plain that history and demographic development always upset the plans conceived by the wise. In such societies there is a constantly repeated battle between synchrony and diachrony from which it seems that diachrony must emerge victorious every time.

What this means in relation to the problem just raised is that the nearer we get to concrete groups the more we must expect to find arbitrary distinctions and denominations which are explicable primarily in terms of occurrences and events and defy any logical arrangement. 'Everything is a potential totem', it is said of tribes of North-west Australia which already number such things as 'white fellow' and 'sailor' among their totems in spite of the recent date of their first contact with civilization (Hernandez).

Certain tribes of Groote Eylandt, in the east of Arnhem Land, are divided into two moieties comprising six clans. Each clan possesses one or more miscellaneous totems: winds, ship, water, animals and plant species, stones. The 'wind' totems are probably connected with the annual visits of the Makassans and the same is true of the 'ship' totem, as a myth referring to the manufacture of ships by the Makassans in the island of Bickerton demonstrates. Other totems are borrowings from natives of the interior. Some are in the process of being abandoned while others are recent introductions.

Consequently, the author of these remarks concludes, it would be imprudent to regard the choice and distribution of totems as an attempt to fit various features of the environment into the dualist scheme: 'the list . . . is in fact a product of historical accretion rather than any attempt to systematize the natural environment according to some philosophical scheme.' There are totemic songs inspired by two known ships, the *Cora* and the *Wanderer*, and even, since there was an air-base established on one clan's territory during the War, by the Catalina flying boats. Facts of this kind lead us to think that some totems may have had their origin in historical events, all the more so because in the language of the tribes in question the same word is used to refer to totems, myths, and any species of beautiful, unusual, or curious object, such as a particularly attractive beauty-spot or a pretty little phial of medicine. The aesthetic inspiration and individual invention, no less than the events, speak in favour of contingence (Worsley).

I referred to the role of the aesthetic imagination in the elaboration of classificatory systems several times in the first chapter of this book. It is a role already recognized by theorists on taxonomy, which, in Simpson's words, 'is also an art' (p. 227). There is nothing disquieting about this aspect of the problem; quite the contrary. But what of historical factors?

Linguists have been well aware of this problem for a long time and Saussure resolved it very clearly. Saussure, who laid down the principle (for which the evidence seems to us today much less conclusive) of the arbitrary character of linguistic signs, himself concedes that this arbitrariness admits of degrees and that the sign may be relatively motivated. So much is this the case that languages can be classified in terms of the relative motivation of their signs: the Latin *inimicus* is more strongly motivated than the French *ennemi* (which is less readily identified as the reverse of *ami*); and signs are also differently motivated within a single language: the French *dix-neuf* is motivated, while the French *vingt* is not. For the word *dix-neuf* 'suggests it own terms and other terms associated with it'. If the irrational principle of the arbitrariness of the sign were applied without restriction, it 'would lead to the worst sort of complication . . . But the mind contrives to introduce a principle of order and regularity into certain parts of the mass of signs, and this is the role of relative motivation'. In this sense we might say that some languages are more *lexicological* and others more *grammatical*:

> Not because 'lexical' and 'arbitrary' on the one hand and 'grammar' and 'relative motivation' on the other, are always synonymous, but because they have a common principle. The two extremes are like poles between which the whole system moves, two opposing currents which share the movement of language: the tendency to use the lexicological instrument (the unmotivated sign) and the preference given to the grammatical instrument (structural rules) (Saussure, pp. 133–4).

For Saussure, therefore, language moves from arbitrariness to motivation. The systems we have been considering so far on the other hand go from motivation to arbitrariness: conceptual schemes (at the limit, simple binary opposition) are constantly broken open to introduce elements taken from elsewhere; and there is no doubt that these additions often entail modification of the system. Moreover, they do not always succeed in getting incorporated in it and the systematic appearance is then disturbed or temporarily put in abeyance.

The example of the nine hundred survivors of some thirty Australian tribes which were haphazardly regrouped in a Government Settlement provides a tragic illustration of this constant struggle between history and system. The Settlement contained (in 1934) about forty wooden cottages, supervised dormitories segregated by sex, a school, a hospital, a prison, shops; and the missionaries (unlike the natives) could enjoy themselves to their hearts' content: in the course of a few months, visits were made by Non-Conformists, Presbyterians, the Salvation Army, Church of England, and Roman Catholics ...

I mention these facts not for polemical reasons but because they make the maintenance of traditional beliefs and customs seem so highly improbable. The natives' first response to the regrouping was, however, the adoption of a common terminology and of rules of correspondence for harmonizing the tribal structures, which were basically ones of moieties and sections in the whole of the relevant region. A native, asked what his section was, could therefore give the reply: 'I am so-and-so in my own lingo – that is Wungo here.'

The distribution of totemic species between moieties does not seem to have been uniform, which is hardly surprising. But the regularities and the systematic way in which the informants solved each problem is all the more striking. Except in one region, opossum belongs to the Wuturu moiety. Fresh water is Yanguru along the coast but in the west it belongs to the Wuturu moiety. The natives say: 'nearly always cold skin with Wuturu and feathers with Yanguru', so that Wuturu had water, lizard, frog, etc., and Yanguru emu, duck, and other birds. But where the frog was in the opposite moiety to the opossum another principle of opposition was brought to the rescue: both kinds of animal hop and this resemblance is ascribed to the fact that the frog is the opossum's 'father', and in a matrilineal society father and son belong to opposite moieties :

When informants worked out lists of totem contained in each moiety, they invariably reasoned along these lines: trees and the birds which made their nests in them were in the same moiety; trees which grew alongside creeks or in water-holes and swamps were in the same moiety as water, fishes, water-fowl, lily-roots. 'Eaglehawk, plain turkey, everything that flies all work together. Carpet snake [*Python variegatus*] and ground goanna [*Varanus Gould*?] all work together – they travel together in olden time' (Kelly, p. 465).

The same species sometimes figures in both moieties. This is so in the case of the *Python variegatus* (carpet-snake); but the natives distinguish four varieties according to their skin markings and these varieties are divided between the moieties in pairs. The same holds for the varieties of turtle. The grey kangaroo is Wuturu and the red Yanguru but they would not fight with each other in battle. Another native group say that certain natural species belong to fire and others to water: opossum, bee, and sand goanna (*Varanus eremius*?) are said to 'own fire', *Python variegatus* (carpet-snake), *Leipoa ocellata* (scrub turkey), lizard, and porcupine 'own water'. It was claimed that long ago the ancestors of the group in question had fire, and the people living in the scrub had water. They joined up and shared water and fire. Finally, each totem was specially related to a species of tree, and a branch of the relevant clan tree is placed in the grave of a deceased member of the clan. The emu is said to own box tree (*Bursaria sp.*?), porcupine and eagle-hawk own certain varieties of acacia (*brigalow*), opossum another acacia (*Kidji*), the carpet-snake owns sandal wood, and the sand goanna bottle-tree (*Sterculia*?). In the western groups the dead were buried facing east or west according to the moiety (l.c., pp. 461–6).

So, although the social organization is reduced to chaos by the new conditions of life imposed on the natives and the lay and religious pressures to which they have been subjected, the theoretical attitude continues to flourish. When it is no longer possible to retain the traditional interpretations, others are worked out which, like the first, are inspired by motivations (in Saussure's sense) and by schemes. Social structures previously simply juxtaposed in space are made to correspond at the same time as the animal and plant classifications of each tribe. According to their tribal origin, the informants conceived the dual scheme on the model of opposition of resemblance, and they formalized it in terms of kinship (father and son) or directions (east and west) or elements (land and sea, water and fire, air and land), or again in terms of the differences or resemblances between natural species. They took these various procedures into account also and sought to formulate rules of equivalence. If the process of deterioration were halted, there is no doubt that this syncretism could serve as the starting point of a new society, for working out an entire system with all its aspects adjusted.

This example shows how the logical dynamism, which is a property of the system, succeeds in overcoming what, even for Saussure, does not constitute an antinomy. Apart from the fact that systems of classification, like languages, may differ with respect to arbitrariness and motivation without the latter ceasing to be operative,* the dichotomizing character which we have found in them explains how the arbitrary aspects (or those which appear to us arbitrary, for one can never be sure that a choice which is arbitrary for the observer may not be motivated from the point of view of indigenous thought) come to be grafted on to the rational aspects without altering their nature. I have represented systems of classification as 'trees'; and the growth of a tree is a good illustration of the transformation just mentioned. A tree is, as it were, strongly motivated so far as its lower parts are concerned: it must have a trunk and the trunk must be nearly vertical. The lower branches already allow more arbitrariness: their number, although it may be expected to be limited, is never fixed in advance, nor is the orientation of each and its angle in relation to the trunk. But these aspects nevertheless remain bound by reciprocal relations, since the larger branches, given their own weight and the foliage-laden branches they hold up, must balance the pressures which they apply at the common point of support. The part played by motivation, however, diminishes, and that of arbitrariness increases progressively as we turn our attention higher: the terminal branches can no longer compromise the tree's stability nor alter its characteristic shape. Their multiplicity and insignificance has freed them from the initial constraints and their general distribution can be explained either as a series of repetitions, on an ever-diminishing scale, of a plan which is also written into the genes in

* As the Lovedu of South Africa say: 'The ideal is to return home, for "The only place one never returns to is the womb" ' (Krige, p. 323).

their cells or as the result of statistical fluctuations. The structure, intelligible at the start, in branching out reaches a sort of inertia or logical indifference. Without contradicting its primary nature, it can thereafter undergo the effect of multiple and varied incidents which occur too late to prevent an attentive observer from identifying it and classing it in a genus.

CHAPTER SIX

UNIVERSALIZATION AND PARTICULARIZATION

The antinomy which some believe they have detected between history and system* would seem to be present in the cases considered only if we were not aware of the dynamic relation between the two aspects. There is room between them for a diachronic and non-arbitrary construction providing a transition from one to the other. Starting from a binary opposition, which affords the simplest possible example of a system, this construction proceeds by the aggregation, at each of the two poles, of new terms, chosen because they stand in relations of opposition, correlation, or analogy to it. It does not, however, follow from this that the relations in question have to be homogeneous. Each 'local' logic exists in its own right. It consists in the intelligibility of the relation between two immediately associated terms and this is not necessarily of the same type for every link in the semantic chain. The position is somewhat comparable to that of inexperienced players in a game of dominoes who consider only the value of the adjacent halves in joining the pieces but manage to continue the game none the less for their lack of previous knowledge of its composition.

The logic of the system need not, therefore, coincide at every

* But this disillusioned reflection on the part of one of the champions of purely historical ethnology is enough to convince one that these two notions are of value only as limiting cases: 'The present state of Zande clans and that of their totemic affiliations can only be understood in the light of the political development of Zande society, even though it can be for us only a glimmering light. Hundreds of thousands of people of different ethnic origin all jumbled up – the ethnologist in Africa may sometimes sigh for some neat little Polynesian or Melanesian island community!' (Evans-Pritchard, 2, p. 121).

point with the set of local logics inserted in it. This general logic can be of a different order. It is then definable by the number and nature of the axes employed, by the rules of transformation making it possible to pass from one to another, and finally by the relative inertia of the system, that is, its greater or less receptiveness to unmotivated factors.

The so-called totemic classifications, the beliefs and practices connected with them, are only one aspect or mode of this general systematic activity. From this point of view I have so far done little more than develop and deepen some comments of Van Gennep's:

> Every ordered society necessarily classes not only its human members, but also the objects and creatures of nature, sometimes according to their external form, sometimes according to their dominant psychic characteristic, sometimes according to their utility as food, in agriculture or in industry, or for the producer or consumer . . . Nothing entitles us to regard any one system of classification, say the zoological system of totemism or the cosmographic system or the occupational system (castes) as prior to the others (Van Gennep, pp. 345–6).

A footnote makes it clear that Van Gennep was fully conscious of the boldness and novelty of this passage:

> It will be seen that I do not accept Durkheim's view (*Formes*, p. 318) that the cosmic classification of living creatures (including man) and material objects is a consequence of totemism. In my own view, the special form of cosmic classification found in totemism is not even a nuance of it but one of its primitive and essential components. For peoples without totemism also possess a system of classification which in this case too is one of the primordial elements of their general system of social organization and as such reacts on their lay and magico-religious institutions. Examples are the oriental systems, Chinese and Persian dualism, Assyro-Babylonian cosmographism, the so-called magical system of sympathetic correspondences, etc.

Van Gennep's demonstration is inadequate, however, in spite of these sound views, for he continued to believe in totemism as an institutional reality. He no longer tried to make it into a classificatory system from which all others derived, but he still attempted to preserve a distinctiveness for it comparable to that of a species objectively identifiable within a genus:

> The notion of totemic kinship is thus composed of three elements: physiological kinship . . . social kinship . . . and cosmic, classificatory kinship which links all the men of a single group to creatures or objects theoretically belonging to the group. What characterizes totemism . . .

is . . . the particular combination of these three elements, just as a certain combination of copper, sulphur, and oxygen makes copper sulphate (l.c.).

Although so near the truth, Van Gennep thus remained a prisoner of the traditional classification in whose framework he was content to confine his argument. In neither his own nor his predecessors' writings can one find any foundation for the rash comparison he brings in support of his thesis. That copper sulphate is a chemical substance, in spite of the fact that none of its constituent elements are exclusive to it, is due to the fact that their combination results in a set of differential properties: form, colour, flavour, effect on other substances and on biological beings, all properties which are not found together in anything else. But the same is not true of totemism, however it may be defined. It is not a substance in an ethnological kingdom, but consists rather of rough qualities of varying elements, whose thresholds are arbitrarily selected by each theorist and whose presence, absence, or degree involves no specific effects. The most that can be discerned in the cases traditionally diagnosed as 'totemic' is a relative inflation of the classificatory scheme at the species level, without any real change in its nature or structure. Moreover, we are never sure that this inflation is an objective property of the scheme and not just the result of the particular conditions under which the observation was conducted. The work of the late Marcel Griaule, of G. Dieterlein, G. Calame-Griaule, and D. Zahan among the Dogon and the Bambara has shown in the course of its development over twenty years how the observers have gradually had to connect the 'totemic' categories, originally isolated in conformity with the fiat of traditional ethnology, with facts of a different order, so that they have now come to look like no more than one of the points of view from which a system of several dimensions may be comprehended.

All that can therefore be conceded to the upholders of totemism is the special position devolving on the notion of a species considered as a logical operator. But this discovery considerably antedates the earliest speculations about totemism, having been formulated first by Rousseau (Lévi-Strauss 6, pp. 142–6) and then, with reference to issues considered in this work, by Comte. Comte sometimes employed the notion of taboo but, although he could have been acquainted with Long's book, the idea of totemism seems to have remained unknown to him. It is all the more significant that in his discussion of the passage from fetishism to polytheism (where he would probably have put totemism), Comte makes it a consequence of the emergence of the notion of species:

> When, for example, the similar vegetation of the different trees in a forest of oaks had finally to lead to the representation, in theological conceptions, of what their phenomena presented in common, this abstract being was no longer the fetish belonging to any tree; it became the God of the forest. So the intellectual passage from fetishism to polytheism is essentially reducible to the inevitable preponderance of specific over general ideas (52e leçon, vol. V, p. 54).

Tylor, the founder of modern ethnology, appreciated the use that could be made of Comte's idea, which, he remarks, is even more applicable to this special category of deities, the deified species:

> The uniformity of each kind not only suggested a common parentage, but also the notion that creatures so wanting in individuality, with qualities so measured out as it were by line and rule, might not be independent arbitrary agents, but mere copies from a common model, or mere instruments used by controlling deities (Tylor, vol. II, p. 243).

The logical power of the specific operator can also be illustrated in other ways. For this allows domains very different from each other to be integrated into the classificatory scheme, thus affording classifications a means of going beyond their limits: either extending to domains outside the initial set – by universalization, or alternatively by particularization – taking the classificatory approach past its natural bounds, that is, to individuation.

The first point can be dealt with briefly. A few examples are sufficient. So little is the species 'grid' confined to sociological categories that (notably in America) it sometimes serves to order a domain as restricted as that of diseases and remedies. The Indians of the south-east United States attribute pathological phenomena to a conflict between men, animals, and plants. Vexed with men, animals sent them diseases. Plants, who were friends of men, retorted by supplying remedies. The important point is that each species possesses a specific disease or remedy. Thus, according to the Chickasaw, stomach disorders and pains in the legs come from snakes, vomiting from dogs, aches in the jaw from deer, pains in the abdomen from bears, dysentery from skunks, nose-bleeding from squirrels, jaundice from otters, disturbances of the lower part of the abdomen and the bladder from moles, cramp from eagles, eye diseases and somnolence from owls, pain in the joints from rattle-snakes, etc. (Swanton, 2).

Similar beliefs are found among the Pima of Arizona. They attribute throat diseases to the badger, swellings, headaches and fever to the bear, diseases of the throat and lungs to the deer, children's diseases to the dog and coyote, stomach trouble to the gopher or prairie-rat, ulcers to the jack-rabbit, constipation to the mouse, nose-bleed to the ground-squirrel, haemorrhages to the hawk and eagle, syphilitic sores to the vulture, children's fevers to the Gila monster, rheumatism to the horned toad,* 'white fever to the lizard, kidney and stomach troubles to the rattle-snake, ulcers and paralysis to the turtle, internal pains to the butterfly, etc. (Russell).† Among the Hopi, who are a day's march from the Pima, an analogous classification is based on the organization into religious orders, each of which can inflict a punishment in the form of a particular disease: abdominal swelling, sore ears, horn-like swelling on the top of the head, deafness, eczema on the upper part of the body, twisting and twitching of the face and neck, soreness in the bronchial tubes, bad knee (Voth 2, p. 109 n.). The problem of classifications could undoubtedly be tackled from this angle and some curious resemblances, symptomatic of logical connections which could be of considerable importance, might be found between distant groups (the association of the squirrel and nose-bleeding, for instance, seems to recur in a large number of North American peoples).

The specific categories and the myths connected with them can also serve to organize space, and the classificatory system is then extended on a territorial and geographical basis. A classic example is the totemic geography of the Aranda, but there are other people equally exacting and subtle in this respect. In Aluridja territory a rocky site measuring five miles round the base was recently discovered and described in which every accident of relief corresponds to a phase of ritual in such a way that this natural rock illustrates the structure of their myths and the order of the ceremonies for the natives. Its north side is the side of the moiety of the sun and of the

* It may be noted, in support of the considerations adduced earlier (pp. 64–5) that it is probably the same behaviour on the part of this animal which suggests entirely different associations to the American Indians and the Chinese. The Chinese ascribe aphrodisiac virtues to the flesh of the phrynosoma or to the wine in which it has been macerated because the male holds on to the female so hard during copulation that he does not let go even when caught.

† For closely related ideas among the Papago, cf. Densmore.

ritual cycle Kerungera, its south side that of the moiety of the shade and the ritual Arangulta. Thirty-eight points on the base of the plateau are named and annotated (Harney).

North America also furnishes examples of mythical geography and totemic topography, from Alaska to California as well as in the south-west and north-east of the continent. In this respect the Penobscot of Maine exemplify a general tendency on the part of the northern Algonkin to interpret all the physiographic aspects of the tribal territory in terms of the peregrinations of the civilizing hero Gluskabe and other mythical personage or incidents. An elongated rock is the hero's canoe, a streak of white rock represents the entrails of the moose he killed, Kineo mountain is the overturned cooking pot in which he cooked the meat, etc. (Speck 2, p. 7).

Again, in the Sudan, a mytho-geographical system has been discovered which covers the entire Niger valley, and thus extends over more than the territory of any single group, and in which is translated down to the minutest detail a conception of the relations between different cultural and linguistic groups which is at once diachronic and synchronic.

This last example shows that the systems of classification not only permit the 'furnishing', as it were, of social time (by means of myths) and of tribal space (with the help of a conceptualized topography). The filling in of the territorial framework is accompanied by enlargement. In the same way that, on the logical plane, the specific operator effects the transition to the concrete and individual on the one hand and the abstract and systems of categories on the other, so, on the sociological plane, totemic classifications make it possible both to define the status of persons within a group and to expand the group beyond its traditional confines.

Primitive societies have, and not without justification, been said to treat the limits of their tribal group as the frontiers of humanity and to regard everyone outside them as foreigners, that is, as dirty, coarse sub-men or even non-men: dangerous beasts or ghosts. This is often true, but what is overlooked when this is said is that one of the essential functions of totemic classifications is to break down this closing in of the group into itself and to promote an idea something like that of a humanity without frontiers. There is evidence of this phenomenon in all the classical areas of so-called totemic organization. In a region in West Australia the clans and their totems 'are grouped together into a number of what may be called inter-tribal totemic divisions' (Radcliffe-Brown 1, p. 214). This is equally true of other parts of the same continent:

I have ascertained that in 167 cases (56%) out of 300 names of common totemic animals, the Western Aranda and the Loritja use the same or similar terms; and comparison of totemic plant names used by the Western Aranda and Loritja shows that the same terms are found in both languages to refer to 147 of the 220 species of plants which I recorded (67%) (C. Strehlow, pp. 66–7).

Analogous observations have been made in America among the Sioux and the Algonkin. The Menomini Indians, who belong to the latter, entertain a:

... general belief in the common relationship of not only the individuals of a certain totem within the tribe, but of all persons of a similarly named totem of another tribe belonging to the same linguistic family; and in the belief of the Menomini this extended also to tribes other than those of the same linguistic family (Hoffman, p. 43).

Similarly, among the Chippewa:

All members with the same totem regarded themselves as related even though of different villages or different tribes ... When two strangers met and found themselves to be of the same totem they immediately began to trace their genealogy, ... and the one became the cousin, the uncle, or the grandfather of the other, although the grandfather might often be the younger of the two. The ties of the totem were considered so strong that if a quarrel should happen between a person with the same totem as a bystander and a cousin or other near relative of the latter but with a different mark, the bystander would side with the person with the same totem whom perhaps he had never seen before (Kinietz, pp. 69–70).

This totemic universalization not only breaks down tribal frontiers and creates the rudiments of an international society. It also sometimes goes beyond the limits of humanity in a biological, and no longer merely sociological, sense, when totemic names are applicable to totemic animals. This occurs among the Australian tribes of the Cape York Peninsula in the case of dogs* – also referred to as 'brothers' or 'sons' according to the group (Sharp, p. 70; Thomson) – and among the Ioway and Winnebago Indians in the case of dogs and horses (Skinner 3, p. 198).

* Among the Wik Munkan a dog is called Yatut 'extracting bones of ... the totem fish' if his master is of the Bone-fish clan, Owun 'illicit or stolen meeting' if his master is of the Ghost clan (Thomson, pp. 161–2).

I have given a brief indication of how the meshes of the net can stretch indefinitely in accordance with the dimensions and generality of the field. It remains to be shown how they can also shrink to filter and imprison reality but this time at the lower limit of the system by extending its action beyond the threshold which one would be inclined to assign to all classification, that beyond which it is no longer possible to class, but only to name. These extreme operations are in fact less widely separated than they might appear and, when seen in the perspective of the systems we are studying, they may even be superposed. Space is a society of named places, just as people are landmarks within the group. Places and individuals alike are designated by proper names, which can be substituted for each other in many circumstances common to many societies. The Yurok of California provide one example among others of this personified geography, where trails are conceived of as animated beings, each house is named, and the names of places replace personal names in current usage (Waterman).

An Aranda myth well expresses this feeling of correspondence between geographical and biological individuation: the earliest divine beings are shapeless, without limbs, and welded together until the coming of the god Mangarkunjerkunja (the fly-catcher lizard), who proceeded to separate them and fashion them individually. At the same time (and is this not indeed the same thing?) he taught them the arts of civilization and the system of sections and sub-sections. The eight sub-sections were originally divided into two main groups: four land ones and four water ones. It was the god who 'territorialized' them by allotting each site to a pair of sub-sections. Now, this individuation of territory corresponded to biological individuation in another way as well, in that the totemic mode of fertilizing the mother explains the anatomic differences observable among children. Those with fine features were conceived by the operation of a *ratapa*, embryo-spirit; those with large features by magical projection of a rhomb into a woman's body; children with fair hair were direct reincarnations of totemic ancestors (C. Strehlow). The Australian tribes of the Drysdale River, in Northern Kimberley, divide all kinship relations, which together compose the social 'body', into five categories named after a part of the body or a muscle. Since a stranger must not be questioned, he announces his kinship by moving the relevant muscle (Hernandez, pp. 228–9). In this case, too, therefore, the total system of social relations, itself bound up with a system of the universe, can be projected on to the anatomical plane. In Toradja there are fifteen terms to name the cardinal points which correspond to the parts of body of a cosmic divinity (Woensdregt). Other examples could be cited, from ancient Germanic kinship terminology as well as from the cosmological and anatomical correspondences of the Pueblo and Navajo Indians and the Sudanese Negroes.

It would certainly be instructive to make a detailed study of the mechanics of this homological particularization in a sufficient number of cases. Its general relation with the forms of classification we have encountered so far can be seen clearly in the following derivation:

If
(group *a*) : (group *b*) : : (bear species) : (eagle species)
then
(member *x* of *a*) : (member *y* of *b*) : : (limb *l* of bear): (limb *m* of eagle)

These formulae have the advantage of throwing into relief a problem traditionally discussed in Western philosophy, though the question of whether or not, or in what form, it arises in exotic societies has received little attention: I mean the problem of organicism. The equations above would be inconceivable were it not for the postulate of a fairly general correspondence between the 'members' of society and if not the members themselves, then at least the attributes of natural species: parts of the body, characteristics details, ways of being or behaviour. The available evidence on this subject suggests that a great many languages equate parts of the body, regardless of the diversity of orders and families, or sometimes even of kingdoms, and that this system of equivalence is susceptible of very considerable extensions (Harrington).* Morphological classifiers therefore function in addition to and alongside the specific classifiers. The theoretical account of these remains to be given, but we have seen that they operate on two planes: that of anatomical detotalization and that of organic retotalization.

These are equally interdependent, as we have shown in the case

* In America the following equivalences are found: horns (quadrupeds) = eyestalks (Molluscs) = antennae (arthropoda); penis (vertebrates) = siphon (molluscs); blood (animals) = juice (plants); slobber (babies' ≠ saliva of adults) = excretion; byssus of mussel = tie, string, etc. (Harrington).

of the other levels. We showed a moment ago that the Aranda attribute empirically established morphological differences to hypothetic differences in modes of totemic conception. But the examples of the Omaha and Osage furnish evidence of a correlative tendency which consists in introducing symbolically expressed specific differences into empirical and individual morphology. The children of each clan wear their hair cut in a characteristic style evoking a distinctive feature or aspect of the animal or natural phenomenon which serves as an eponym (La Flesche 4, pp. 87–9).

This modelling of the appearance according to specific, elemental, or categorical schemes has psychological as well as physical consequences. A society which defines its segments in terms of high and low, sky and land, day and night, can incorporate social or moral attitudes, such as conciliation and aggression, peace and war, justice and policing, good and bad, order and disorder, etc., into the same structure of opposition. In consequence, it does not confine itself to abstract contemplation of a system of correspondence but rather furnishes the individual members of these segments with a pretext and sometimes even a provocation to distinguish themselves by their behaviour. Radin (I, p. 187), referring to the Winnebago, very rightly insists on the reciprocal influence of religious and mythical conceptions of animals on the one hand and the political functions of social units on the other.

The Sauk Indians provide a particularly instructive example by reason of their individuating rule for determining membership of a moiety. The moieties were not exogamous and their role, which was purely ceremonial, was principally manifested at feasts. It is important, from our point of view, to notice that these were connected with rites for the giving of names. Membership of moieties was determined by a rule of alternation: the first born was affiliated to the moiety of which his father was not a member, the next child to the moiety of which his father was a member, and so on. Now, at least in theory, these affiliations determined behaviour which one might call 'dispositional': members of the Oskûsh moiety ('the Blacks') had to complete all their enterprises, those of the Kishko moiety ('the Whites') might give up or turn back. In theory, if not in practice, an opposition in terms of categories thus directly influenced everyone's temperament and vocation, and the institutional scheme which made it possible for this to happen testifies to the link between

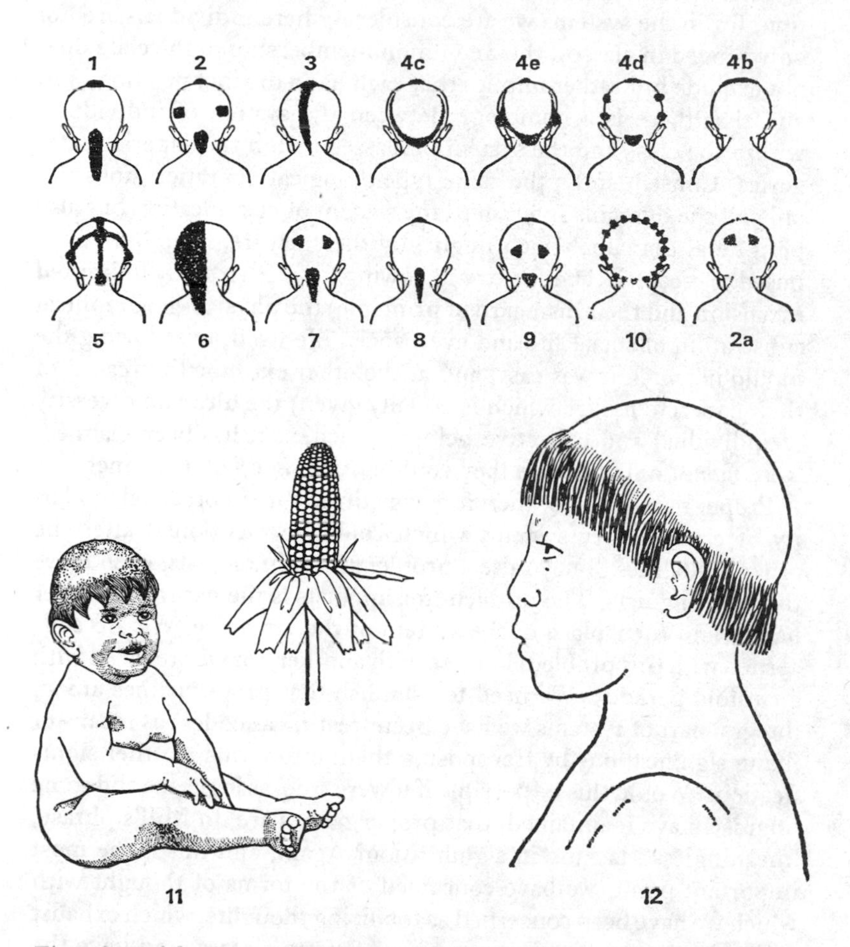

Fig 9 Cut of Osage and Omaha boys' hair according to clan. 1. Head and tail of elk; 2. Head, tail and horns of buffalo; 2a, Horns of buffalo; 3. Line of buffalo's back as seen against the sky; 4b. Head of bear; 4c. Head, tail and body of small birds; 4d. Shell of the turtle with the head, feet and tail of the animal; 4e. Head, wings and tail of the eagle; 5. Four points of the compass; 6. Shaggy side of the wolf; 7. Horns and tail of the buffalo; 8. Head and tail of the deer; 9. Head, tail and knobs of the growing horn of the buffalo calf; 10. Reptile teeth; 11. Petals of the cone flower; 12. Rock with algae floating round (following La Flesche 4, pp. 87, 89).

the psychological aspect of personal destiny and its social aspect, which is the result of the giving of a name to each individual.

Thus we reach the final level of classification: that of individuation, for in the systems we are considering here individuals are not only ranged in classes; their common membership of the class does not exclude but rather implies that each has a distinct position in it, and that there is a homology between the system of individuals within the class and the system of classes within the superior categories. Consequently, the same type of logical operation links not only all the domains internal to the system of classification but also peripheral domains which might, by their nature, have been supposed to escape it: at one extreme (owing to their virtually unlimited extension and their disregard of principle) the physico-geographical substratum of social life and even social life itself, overflowing the mould in which it was cast; and at the other extreme (by reason of their concrete nature which is equally given) the ultimate diversity of individual and collective beings, which, so it has been claimed, were *named* only because they could not be *signified* (Gardiner).

Proper names do not therefore constitute a mere practical modality of classificatory systems which could be mentioned after the other modalities. They raise a problem for ethnologists, even more than for linguists. The problem for linguists is the nature of proper names and their place in the system of the language. We are concerned with this problem but also with another, for we are faced with a twofold paradox. We need to establish that proper names are an integral part of systems we have been treating as codes: as means of fixing significations by transposing them into terms of other significations. Would this be possible if it were true, as logicians and some linguists have maintained, that proper names are, in Mill's phrase, 'meaningless', lacking in signification? Again, and this is the most important point, we have conceived of the forms of thought with which we have been concerned as totalizing thoughts, which exhaust reality by means of a finite number of given classes, and have the fundamental property of being *transformable* into each other. How could this quantified thought, to which, on the practical plane, we attributed the great discoveries of the neolithic revolution, have been both theoretically satisfying and effectively applied to the concrete, if the latter contained a residue of unintelligibility – to which, in the last analysis, concreteness itself is reducible – which is essentially recalcitrant to signification? The principle of all or nothing not only has heuristic value to thought founded on the operation of dichotomies, but is also an expression of a property of what exists: either everything, or nothing, makes sense.*

Let us now return to the ethnographic facts at the point at which we left them. Almost all the societies I have mentioned construct their proper names from clan appellations. The proper names of the Sauk, who furnished our last example, are said always to be related to the clan animal: either because they mention the name of the animal itself, or because they suggest one of its habits, attributes, or characteristic qualities (real or mythical), or because they refer to some animal or object with which it is associated. Sixty-six names of the Bear clan, eleven of the Bison clan, thirty-three of the Wolf clan, twenty-three of the Turkey clan, forty-two of the Fish clan, thirty-seven of the Great Sea clan, forty-eight of the Thunder clan, fourteen of the Fox clan, and thirty-four of the Deer clan have been recorded (Skinner 2).

The list of Osage proper names which belong to clans or subclans, although fragmentary, is long enough to occupy forty-two quarto pages in La Flesche 4 (pp. 122–64). The rule of formation is the same as among the Sauk. Thus for the Black Bear clan we have: Flashing-eyes (of the bear), Tracks-on-the-prairies, Ground-cleared-of-grass, Black-bear-woman, Fat-on-the-skin of the black bear, etc. Among the Tlongit of Alaska 'all names . . . are felt to belong to a particular sib, and some have even been designated as belonging to a particular "house" or "lineage" ' (Laguna, p. 185). These examples can be multiplied, for similar ones are found in almost all the Algonkin and Sioux tribes and in those of the north-west coast, that is to say, in the three classical domains of 'totemism' in North America.

South America provides illustrations of the same phenomenon, notably among the Tupi Kawahib, whose clans possess proper names derived from the eponym (Lévi-Strauss 3). The proper names of the Bororo also seem to belong to particular clans or even to powerful lineages. Those who have to depend on the good will of other clans for having a name are said to be 'poor' (Cruz).

The connection between proper names and totemic appellations is found in Melanesia:

* Everything, except the existence of what exists, which is not one of its properties (cf. below, p. 255).

> The totemic system [of the Iatmul] is enormously elaborated into a series of personal names, so that every individual bears names of totemic ancestors – spirits, birds, stars, pots, adzes, etc., etc. – of his or her clan, and one individual may have thirty or more such names. Every clan has hundreds of these polysyllabic ancestral names which refer in their Etymology to secret myths (Bateson, p. 127).

The position seems to have been the same throughout Australia. 'By knowing a native's name, if one knew the Aranda language well enough, it would seem one would also know his or her totem by deduction' (Pink, p. 176). Another observation, relating to the Murngin of Arnhem Land, echoes this one: 'The names of the living are all taken from some part of the totemic complex and refer directly or indirectly to the totem' (Warner, p. 390). The proper names of the Wik Munkan also derive from their respective totems. For instance, for men whose totem is the fish barramundi (Osteoglossum), which they spear: the-barramundi-swims-in-water-and-sees-a-man, the barramundi-moves-its-tail-as-it-swims-around-its-eggs, the-b.-breathes, the-b.-has-its-eyes-open, the-b.-breaks-a-spear, the-b.-eats-mullet, etc. And for women whose totem is the crab: the-crab-has-eggs, tide-takes-crabs-out-to-sea, the-crab-stops-down-hole-and-is-dug-out, etc. (McConnel, p. 184). The tribes of the Drysdale River region have proper names derived from clan appellations, as the author quoted above underlines: 'Proper names . . . always bear relation to one's totem' (Hernandez).

It is clear that these individual appellations belong to the same system as the collective appellations discussed above and that, through the intermediary of the latter, one can, with the help of transformations, pass from the horizon of individuation to that of more general categories. Every clan or sub-clan possesses a quota of names which only its own members can bear and, just as an individual is part of the group, so an individual name is 'part' of the collective appellation, either in the sense that it may cover the whole animal, and the individual names correspond to its parts or limbs, or that the collective appellation may depend on an idea of the animal conceived at the highest level of generality and the individual appellations correspond to one of its predications in time or space: Barking-dog, Angry-bison, or there may be a combination of both procedures: Flashing-eyes-of-the-bear. The animal may be subject or predicate in the relation so expressed: The-*fish*-moves-its-tail, Tide-takes-*crabs*, etc. Whichever procedure is employed (and they are most often found juxtaposed) the proper name refers to a partial aspect of the animal or plant entity just as it corresponds to a partial aspect of the individual being – in general, and in particular, in those societies in which an individual receives a new name at every important point of his life. Neighbouring societies, moreover, employ the same constructions for forming in some cases personal names (borne by individual members of a clan group) and in others collective names (borne by bands, lineages, or groups of lineages, that is, sub-groups of a single clan).

Two parallel detotalizations are thus involved: of species into parts of the body and attitudes, and of social segments into individuals and roles. But just as the detotalization of the concept of a species into particular species, of each species into its individual members, and of each of these individuals into organs and parts of the body could, as I tried to show with the help of a figurative model, issue into a retotalization of the concrete parts into abstract parts and of the abstract parts into a conceptualized individual, so here the detotalization takes place in the form of retotalization. Kroeber's observations about proper names among the Miwok of California serve to provide a final example and at the same time open up a new perspective:

> There are no subdivisions of any sort within the moieties. Associated with each, however, is a long list of animals, plants and objects; in fact, the native concept is that everything in the world belongs to one or the other side. Each member of a moiety stands in relation to one of the objects characteristic of his moiety – a relation that must be considered totemic – in one way only: through his name. This name given him in infancy by a grandfather or other relative, and retained through life, refers to one of the totem animals or objects characteristic of his moiety.
>
> Nor is this all: in the great majority of cases the totem is not mentioned in the name, which is formed from some verbal or adjectival stem, and describes an action or condition that might apply equally well to other totems. Thus on the verb *hausu-us* are based the names *Hausu* and *Hauchu*, which connote, respectively, the yawning of an awakening bear and the gaping of a salmon drawn out of the water. There is nothing in either name that indicates the animals in question – which even belong to opposite moieties. The old men who bestowed them no doubt announced the totemic reference of the names; the bearers, and their family, kin, and more intimate associates, knew the implication; but a Miwok from another district would have been uncertain whether a bear, a salmon, or one of a dozen other animals was meant (Kroeber 2, pp. 453–4).

This feature does not appear to be peculiar to the Miwok. Lists of clan names among the Sioux tribes contain plenty of analogous examples and what Kroeber says also coincides with a characteristic of the Hopi Indians' system of naming. Thus the name Cakwyamtiwa, the literal meaning of which is 'Blue (or green)-having-come-out' can refer to the matured flower of the tobacco plant or to that of the *Delphinium scaposum* or again to the germination of plants in general, depending on the clan of the donor of the name. Similarly, the name Lomahongioma, 'Stand up' or 'rise gracefully' can refer to the stem of the reed or to the erect wings of the butterfly, etc. (Voth 3, pp. 68–9).

The prevalence of the phenomenon raises a psychological problem, relevant to the theory of proper names, which I shall come back to later. I want now just to emphasize that the relative indeterminacy of the system corresponds, virtually at least, to the phase of retotalization: proper names are formed by detotalizing species and by deducting a partial aspect of them. But by stressing exclusively the fact of the deduction and leaving the species which is the subject of it indeterminate, there is a suggestion that all the deductions (and so all the acts of naming) have something in common. A unity divined at the heart of diversity is claimed in advance. From this point of view, too, the dynamics of individual names derives from the classificatory systems we have been analysing. It consists of approaches of the same type, and similarly oriented.

Further, it is striking that systems of prohibitions with the same characteristics are to be found on the plane of individual appellations as well as on that of collective names. In some cases the plant or animal serving as a social group's eponym may not be used as food by that group; in other cases, however, it is the linguistic use of the plant or animal serving as an individual's eponym which is prohibited. It is possible to some extent to pass from one plane to the other. Proper names of the type to which we have so far confined ourselves are usually formed by an imaginary dissection of the body of the animal, inspired by the gestures of the huntsman or the cook; but they can also be formed by linguistic dissection. In the tribes of the Drysdale River region in North Australia, the woman's name Poenben is formed from the English 'spoon', an implement associated, as one might expect, with the totem 'white-fellow' (Hernandez, p. 218).

In Australia, as well as in America, we find prohibitions on the use of the names of the dead which 'contaminate' any words with a phonetic resemblance to these names. The Tiwi of the Melville and Bathurst islands taboo not only the proper name 'Mulankina' but also the word 'mulikina' which means: full, filled, enough (Hart). This usage finds a parallel in that of the Yurok of California: 'When *Tegis* died, the common word *tsis*, "woodpecker scalps", was not uttered in the hearing of his relatives or by them' (Kroeber 2, p. 48).* The Dobu islanders forbid the use of proper names between individuals temporarily or permanently connected by a 'species' tie through being companions on a voyage, eating together, or sharing the favours of the same woman, as the case may be (Bateson).

Such facts have a double claim on our interest. In the first place, they afford an indisputable analogy with food prohibitions, which have been wrongly associated with totemism alone. In the same way that at Mota a woman is 'contaminated' by a plant or animal, as a result of which she gives birth to a child subject to the corresponding eating prohibition, and at Ulawa it is the dying man who 'contaminates' by his incarnation in an animal or plant species which his descendants are then forbidden to consume, so, by homophony, a name 'contaminates' other words, the use of which then comes to be forbidden. Secondly, this homophony defines a class of words, to which the prohibition applies because they belong to the same 'species', and which thus acquires an *ad hoc* reality comparable to that of animal or plant species. These 'species' of words 'stressed' by the same prohibition bring together both proper names and common names. And this is a further reason for suspecting that the difference between the two types of words is not as great as we were near to admitting at first.

The customs and procedures which I have just mentioned are not found in all exotic societies nor even in all those which designate their segments by animal and plant names. The Iroquois, who are an instance of the latter, seem to have a system of proper names entirely distinct from the system of clan appellations. Their names most commonly consist of a verb with an incorporated noun or a noun followed by an adjective: In-the-Centre-of-the-Sky, He-raises-the-Sky, Beyond-the-Sky, etc.; Hanging-Flower, Beautiful-Flower, Beyond-the-Flowers; He-announces-Defeat (or Victory),

* There are other examples in Elmendorf and Kroeber 1960, which was not available to me at the time of writing this section.

He carries-the-News, etc.; She-works-in-the-House, She-has-two-Husbands, etc.; The-Place-where-Two-Rivers-meet, The-Crossing-of-the-Roads, etc. There is thus no reference at all to the eponymous animal but only, and whatever the clan, to technical or economic activities, to peace and war, to natural phenomena and celestial bodies. The example of the Mohawk of the Grand River, where the clan organization decayed more rapidly than in the other groups, suggests how all these names could originally have been arbitrarily created. Thus we find: Ice-floating-down-the-River for a child born when ice was thawing on the river, or She-is-in-want for the son of a poor woman (Goldenweiser, pp. 366–8).*

The situation is not, however, fundamentally different from that among the Miwok and Hopi, described above, whose names, although in theory evocative of the clan plant or animal, do not make explicit reference to either and contain a hidden meaning. Even if this meaning is not indispensable, it is no less true that among the Iroquois also, proper names, of which there are several hundred or thousand, are jealously guarded clan possessions. It is indeed this which made it possible for Goldenweiser to show that the clans of the Little and Great Turtle, of the Little and Great Snipe, etc., were formed by duplication: they hold the same names in common. The names instanced by Goldenweiser are no doubt not the result of a detotalization of the clan animal. But they do suggest a detotalization of those aspects of social life and the physical world which the system of clan appellations has not already caught in the meshes of its net. The principal difference between the Iroquois system of proper names and the systems of the Miwok, Hopi, Omaha, and Osage (to mention only a few examples) may therefore be that the latter tribes extend an analysis already begun in the sphere of clan appellations to the plane of proper names while the Iroquois employ proper names for undertaking an analysis devoted to new objects but of the same formal type as the other.

The case of various African tribes is more troublesome. The Baganda have names (more than two thousand of which have been collected) each of which belongs to a clan. As among the Bororo of Brazil, some clans are rich in names and others poor. These names are not confined to human beings. They are also given to hills, rivers, rocks, forests, wells, landing places, bushes, and single trees. But,

* An analytic classification of about 1,500 Iroquois proper names can be found in Cooke.

in contrast to the cases considered above, these names form only one category among others (Nsimbi, pp. 212–13), and a very different procedure for the formation of names becomes even more evident in other tribes of the same region:

> Most usually Nyoro personal names may be regarded as expressing what may perhaps best be described as the 'state of mind' of the parent or parents who give the name (Beattie, p. 100).

The phenomenon has been studied closely in another Uganda tribe, the Lugbara, where the child is given its name by its mother, sometimes assisted by her mother-in-law (her husband's mother). Three-quarters of the 850 names collected from a single sub-clan refer to the behaviour or character of one or other of the parents: 'In-laziness' because the parents were idle, 'In-the-beer-pot' because the father was a drunkard, 'Give-not' because the mother fed her husband badly, etc. The other first names refer to recent or imminent death (of other children of the same parents, the parents themselves, or other members of the same group) or to attributes of the child. It has been pointed out that most of these names are uncomplimentary to the child's father or even mother, although it is she who invents the name. They allude to the negligence, immorality, or social or material destitution of one or both of the parents. How can a woman describe herself, in choosing a name for her child, as an evil sorceress, an unfaithful wife, or as kinless, poverty-stricken, and starving?

The Lugbara say that names of this type are not generally chosen by the mother but by the grandmother (father's mother). The latent antagonism between lineages allied through marriage, which explains that the mother avenges herself for the hostility of which she is a victim among her family-in-law by giving their son a name humiliating to his father, also explains that the grandmother, linked to her grandchildren by a very strong emotional tie, symmetrically expresses her antagonism towards the wife of her son (Middleton). This explanation, however, does not seem very satisfactory, since, as the author who records it remarks, the grandmother also comes from an outside lineage and was herself in the same position as her daughter-in-law in the past. Beattie's explanation of a similar custom among the Banyoro seems sounder and more coherent. Among the Banyoro also 'personal names are concerned with the themes of death, sorrow, poverty, neighbourly spite.' But 'the person giving the name is almost always thought of as being acted upon, not as acting; the victim of the envy and hatred of others'. This moral passivity, which projects upon the child an image of the self created by others, finds expression on the linguistic plane: '. . . the two verbs "to lose" and "to forget" . . . are used in Lunyoro with the thing forgotten as the subject, the forgetter as the object . . . The loser or forgetter does not act upon things, they act upon him . . .' (Beattie, p. 104 and n. 5).

Different as this method of forming personal names is from the one considered above, the two are found side by side among the Banyoro and the Lugbara. Special names are reserved for children whose birth was marked by some notable circumstance.

Among the Lugbara we find, for instance: Ejua for a male twin and Ejurua for a female twin; Ondia for a boy and Ondirua for a girl, if their mother was previously thought to be barren; 'Bilene' ('for the grave') for a child who is the first of several children to survive (Middleton, pp. 34–5). These names exist before the individuals who bear them and they are assigned to them on account of the position which is objectively theirs but in which other individuals may equally find themselves, and which the group regards as charged with significance. They differ in every respect from names which are freely invented by a determinate individual for another equally determinate individual and express a transitory state of mind. Are we to say that the former denote classes and the latter individuals? Both are, however, equally proper names and the cultures in question are so well aware of this that they consider them substitutable for each other: should the occasion arise, a Lugbara mother can choose between the two methods of naming.

There are, moreover, intermediate types. A feature in which they resemble the second kind was provisionally disregarded in classifying Hopi names in the first category. Although they have to relate to an objective order (in this case that of clan appellations) the relation is not with the clan of the bearer of the name (as it is, for example, among the Yuma) but with that of its donor.* The name I

* This rule is reminiscent of that of the Australian tribes of Cherburg, Queensland. Every individual has three names. The first is associated with the bearer's totemic place and the other two with the father's totem, although totemic affiliations are transmitted in the maternal line. Thus a woman whose personal totem is opossum has the name Butilbaru, which designates a particular dried-up-creek-bed, and two names derived from her father's totem – in this case, emu – which means 'emu moves his head this way and that' and 'old emu walking

bear refers to an aspect not of the plant or animal which serves as my clan eponym but of that which serves as my sponsor's clan eponym. This objectivity subjectivized by another, of which I am the vehicle, is no doubt concealed by the indeterminate nature of the names which, as we have seen, do not refer explicitly to eponyms. But it is also reinforced in two ways: by the fact that one needs to refer back to the concrete social circumstances in which the name was conceived and attributed in order to understand it; and by the donor's relative freedom to follow his own inclinations in creating the name provided only that he respects the initial restriction that it must be possible to interpret the name in terms of his own clan appellation. *Mutatis mutandis*, this was also the position among the Miwok where the (equivocal and invented) name has to relate to beings or things attached to the moiety of the person named.

What we have here are thus two extreme types of proper name between which there are a whole series of intermediate cases. At one extreme, the name is an identifying mark which, by the application of a rule, establishes that the individual who *is named* is a member of a preordained class (a social group in a system of groups, a status by birth in a system of statuses). At the other extreme, the name is a free creation on the part of the individual who *gives the name* and expresses a transitory and subjective state of his own by means of the person he names. But can one be said to be really naming in either case? The choice seems only to be between identifying someone else by assigning him to a class or, under cover of giving him a name, identifying oneself through him. One therefore never names: one classes someone else if the name is given to him in virtue of his characteristics and one classes oneself if, in the belief that one need not follow a rule, one names someone else 'freely', that is, in virtue of characteristics of one's own. And most commonly one does both at once.

Suppose I buy a pedigree dog. If I determine to preserve his value and prestige and to transmit them to his descendants, then I shall have scrupulously to observe certain rules in the choice of his name, these rules being mandatory in the society of pedigree dog owners to which I aspire to belong. Usually the dog will in any case already

up and down'. The son of an opossum father is called 'Karingo' (the name of a little spring), Myndibambu: 'the opossum when his chest is slit up' and Mynwhagala: 'opossum up the tree, now down', etc. (Kelly, p. 468).

have been given a name on the initiative and responsibility of the kennels where he was born, and when I acquire him he will already have been registered with the authorized dog-breeders' association. The name will begin with an initial which by convention corresponds to the animal's year of birth and it will sometimes be completed by a prefix or affix connoting its breeding, much in the manner of a patronymic name. I am, of course, at liberty to address my dog differently. It still remains the case that this miniature poodle to which, for the purpose of calling him, his master has given the name 'Bow-wow', bears the name of 'Top-Hill Silver Spray' in the registers of the British Kennel Club, this name being composed of two terms, the first connoting a particular kennel and the second representing an available name. Only the choice of a term of address is therefore left to the owner's initiative. The term of reference is stereotyped and since it connotes both a date of birth and membership of a group it is, as we shall see later, identical with the product of the combination of what ethnologists call a clan name and an ordinal name.

I may, on the other hand, regard myself as free to name my dog according to my own tastes. But if I select 'Médor' I shall be classed as commonplace; if I select 'Monsieur' or 'Lucien', as eccentric and provocative; and if I select 'Pelléas' as an aesthete.

Moreover, the name selected must also be a member of the class of dog-names which is conceivable in the civilization to which I belong and one which is available, if not absolutely, then at least relatively, that is, not chosen already by my neighbour. My dog's name will therefore be the product of the intersection of three domains: it is a member of a class, a member of the sub-class of the names vacant within the class, and a member of the class formed by my own wishes and tastes.

It is clear that the problem of the relation between proper names and common names is not that of the relation of naming and signifying. One always signifies, either oneself or someone else. It is only here that there is a choice, rather like that open to a painter between representational and non-representational art, which amounts to no more than a choice between assigning a class to an identifiable object or, by putting it outside a class, making the object a means of classing himself by expressing himself through it.

From this point of view, systems of appellations also have their 'abstracts'. Thus the Seminole Indians form adults' names by employing several series of a few elements, combined without regard for their meaning. There is a 'moral' series: wise, crazy, cautious, malicious, etc.; a 'morphological' series: square, round, spherical, elongated, etc.; a 'zoological' series: wolf, eagle, beaver, puma, etc. By means of these, by taking a term from each series and juxtaposing them, they form the name 'crazy-spherical-puma' (Sturtevant, p. 508).

The ethnographic study of personal names has constantly encountered difficulties of a kind well analysed by Thomson in the Australian example of the Wik Munkan, who inhabit the western side of the Cape York Peninsula. On the one hand, proper names are derived from totems and depend on sacred and esoteric knowledge; but, on the other, they are connected with social personality and are the occasion of customs, rites, and prohibitions. On both accounts they are inextricably associated with a more complex system of appellations, which includes the kinship terms normally used as terms of address, and therefore profanely, and sacred names which themselves include proper names and totemic appellations. But even granting this distinction between sacred and profane, it remains the case that proper names (sacred) and kinship terms (profane) used as terms of address are individual terms, while totemic appellations (sacred) and kinship terms (profane) used as terms of reference are group terms. For this reason, the sacred and profane aspects are bound up together.

Another difficulty arises from the multiplicity of prohibitions affecting the use of proper names. The Wik Munkan forbid any mention of a name or names for three years after the death of their bearer, that is, until his mummified body has been burnt. There are certain names, such as those of his sister or his wife's brother, which a man may never mention. An inquirer committing the blunder of asking them is supplied with a substitute name which means literally 'no name', 'without name' or 'the second born'.

There is a final difficulty, due to the large number of categories of names. Among the Wik Munkan, the following must be distinguished: kinship terms, *nämp kämpan*; names indicating status or condition; nicknames, *nämp yann*, literally; 'name nothing'. such as 'crawler' (for someone partly paralysed) or 'the left-handed'; and finally true proper names, *nämp*. Only kinship terms are normally used as terms of address except in periods of mourning when names corresponding to the nature of the mourning are employed, the meaning of which is: widower or widow, or alternatively, 'afflicted by the loss of a relative', the relative being specified as a (elder or younger) brother or sister, child, nephew or niece (parallel or cross), or grandparent. Later on we shall encounter a parallel usage among the tribes of the interior of Borneo.

The procedure for forming proper names is of particular interest. Each individual has three personal names: an 'umbilical' name, *nämp kort'n*, a big name, *nämp pi'in*, and a little name, *nämp mäny*. Big and little names are all derived from totems or attributes of totems and they are therefore owned by clans. Big names relate to the head or top half of the totemic animal, little names to its legs, tail, or the lower half of its body. Thus a man of the Bonefish clan will have *Pämpikän*, 'the man strikes' (the head), as his big name and *Yänk* 'leg' (= the narrow base of the tail) as his little name, while a woman of the same clan will be called *Pamkotjätta* and *Tippunt* (fat) 'of the belly'.

The umbilical names are the only ones which can come from a clan, or even sex, other than the bearer's. As soon as a child is born, before the placenta is delivered, an authorized person shakes the umbilical cord and at the same time a number of names are called, first names of men of the paternal lineage, then women's names, and finally names of men of the maternal lineage. The name spoken at the moment the placenta is delivered becomes the child's name. The cord is no doubt often manipulated to produce the desired name (Thomson). We thus have here, as in the cases instanced above, a method of forming names which reconciles requirements of an objective order with the play (which is partly free within the limits of this order) of inter-personal relations.

This apparently (but falsely) 'probabilistic' technique with respect to birth corresponds to ones recorded in other Australian tribes on the occasion of death to determine, not the name of the new born, but that of the supposed murderer. The Bard, Ungarinyin, and Warramunga put the corpse between the branches of a tree or on a raised platform. They lay out a circle of stones or row of sticks on the ground directly beneath. Each unit represents a member of the group and the guilty man will be indicated by the exudations of the corpse flowing towards his stick or stone. In North Western Australia the body is interred and as many pebbles put on the tomb as the group contains members or suspects. The pebble found to be bloodstained indicates the murderer. Or again the dead man's hairs are tugged one by one and each time the name of a suspect is mentioned: the first hair to come out identifies the murderer (Elkin 4, pp. 305–6).

It is clear that all these procedures are formally of the same type and that they have a striking characteristic which they share with the other systems of proper names of societies with finite classes. It was shown above that in such systems (which no doubt illustrate a general state of affairs) names always signify membership of an actual or virtual class, which must be either that of the person named or of the person giving the name, and that all the differences between names attributed in accordance with a rule and invented names can be reduced to this slight distinction. It is worth adding that this distinction does not correspond, except perhaps superficially, to that drawn by Gardiner between 'disembodied' and 'embodied' names, the former being chosen from a compulsory and limited list (like that of the Saints of the Calendar) and so borne simultaneously and successively by a large number of individuals, and the latter given to a single individual like Vercingetorix and Jugurtha. The former seem in fact to be of too complex a nature to be definable by the only characteristic retained by Gardiner. They class the parents who selected their children's names in a milieu, in a period, and in a style; and they class their bearers in various ways: in the first place, because a John is a member of the class of Johns, and secondly, because every christian name has a conscious or unconscious cultural connotation which parades the image others form of its bearer, and may have a subtle influence in shaping his personality in a positive or negative way.*

Now, all this could also be shown in the case of 'embodied' names did we not lack the ethnographic background. The name Vercingetorix only appears to be confined to the victor at Gergovia because we know so little about the Gauls. Gardiner's distinction does not, therefore, concern two types of names but two situations in which the observer faces either the system of names of his own society or that of a society foreign to him.

* '... children's names were chosen by their parents ... and scholars have frequently honoured colleagues by naming discoveries after them. But the choice involved has often not been an entirely arbitrary one. Parents are guided by social and religious traditions, scholars by a rule of priority. Everyone reveals the nature of his preoccupations and the limits of his horizon by his choice' (Bröndal, p. 230).

This said, it is easier to extract the principle underlying the Wik Munkan system of names. They construct people's names in a way analogous to that in which we ourselves construct species names. To identify an individual, they first combine two class indicators, a major and a minor (the 'big' and 'little' names respectively). This set already produces the dual effect of attesting the bearer's membership of a totemic group, by evoking meanings well-known to be its exclusive property, and of circumscribing the position of the individual within the group. The combination of the big and little names is not itself individuating. It delimits a sub-set of which the bearer of the name, along with others provisionally defined by the same combination, is a member. It is therefore the 'umbilical' name which completes individuation, but the principle on which it is based is quite different. For one thing it can be either a 'big' or a 'little' name (of the same or another clan), either a masculine or a feminine name (irrespective of the bearer's sex). Then again, its attribution is a function not of a system but of an event: the coincidence of a physiological effect (theoretically independent of man's will) and a point in an enumeration.

Let us now compare this trinome with those of scientific botany and zoology. Consider in botany: *Pscilocybe mexicana Heim*, or in zoology: *Lutrogale perspicilata maxwelli*. The first two terms of each trinome assigns what is under consideration to a class and sub-class belonging to a preordained set. But the third term, which is the discoverer's name, completes the system by recalling an event. It is a series, not a group, term.

There is no doubt a difference: in scientific trinomes the discoverer's name adds nothing to the identification, which is already completed by the first two terms; it is merely a tribute to their author. This is not, however, quite accurate. The statistical term has a logical, as well as a moral, function. It brings into evidence the system of distinctions employed by the author in question or one of his colleagues and so enables the specialist to effect the transformations necessary to resolve problems of synonymy: to know, for instance, that *Juniperus occidentalis* Hook and *Juniperus utahensis* Engelm., which might be thought to be different without the discoverer's or sponsor's name, are in fact the same thing. The function of the statistical term in scientific taxonomies is consequently exactly the reverse of that which it fulfills among the Wik Munkan. It makes it possible to associate, not dissociate; instead of attesting the perfection of a unique way of making distinctions, it brings into evidence a plurality of possible ones.

The case of the Wik Munkan is only of particular demonstrative value because of the strangeness of the technique conceived by the natives, which throws a harsh light on the structure of the system. But this structure is readily found in the societies from which all our examples were taken. Among the Algonkin, for instance, a complete personal name consists of three terms:* a name derived from the clan appellation, an ordinal name (expressing the order of birth in the family), and a military title, that is, in this case, one 'mechanical' and two 'statistical' terms of different power. There are more military titles than ordinal names and the probability of the same combination being repeated in the case of two distinct people is all the smaller because, although the former derive from a group which is obligatory as a group, the choice exercised among all the possible names by the giver of the name will be dictated, among other considerations, by the need to avoid duplications. This is a good opportunity to make the point that the 'mechanical' or 'statistical' character is not intrinsic: it is defined in relation to the person of the donor and that of the bearer. The name derived from the clan appellation identifies the bearer without question as a member of a given clan but the way it is chosen from a list is governed by complex historical conditions: names currently vacant, the donor's personality and intentions. Conversely, 'statistical' terms unequivocally define an individual position in the system of natal statuses or in the military hierarchy; but actual occupation of these positions is an outcome of demographical, psychological, and historical circumstances, that is to say, the future bearer is not determined objectively.

This impossibility of defining proper names otherwise than as a means of allotting positions in a system admitting of several dimensions is also brought out by another example, drawn from contemporary societies. For the social group taken as a whole, the second term, in names like John Smith and John Robinson, denotes the class and the first the individual. John Smith belongs, first, to the class Smith and in this class he occupies an unequivocal position as John. Within the class Smith, he is John Smith as distinct from

* Two terms among the Lacandons of Mexico, who speak the Mayan language. They form names by the employment of a binome composed of an animal name and an ordinal name (Tozzer, pp. 42–3 and 46–7).

Peter Smith, Andrew Smith, etc. So little is it a case of a 'proper' name that, within a more restricted group, the logical relation between the terms is reversed. Suppose there is a family whose members all address each other by their christian names in the usual way and where a brother and brother-in-law both happen to have the same christian name, John. The ambiguity will be dispelled by the discriminative apposition of the patronym to the christian name. Thus when one member of the family says to another, 'John Smith phoned', he no longer in fact refers to the same binome: the patronym has become a nickname. For the members of the family in question there is, first, a class of Johns, within which 'Smith' and 'Robinson' secure individuation. The functions of the binomial terms are reversed according to whether they are seen in the context of the administration or of a particular social group.

Given that the same term can, depending only on its position in a context, play the part either of a class indicator or of an individual determinant, it is fruitless to enquire, as many ethnologists have done, whether the appellations in use in this or that society really constitute proper names. Skinner admits this in the case of the Sauk but doubts it in the case of their neighbours the Menomini, whose names seem rather to be honorific titles, limited in number and to which an individual accedes for his lifetime without power to transmit them to his descendants (Skinner 2, p. 17). Similarly, among the Iroquois:

> Clearly the individual name . . . is only to a very limited extent comparable to our personal name. It must rather be conceived of as a sort of ceremonial designation, and also as a more intimate expression of one's membership in a clan than is involved in the association with a clan name (Goldenweiser, p. 367).

As for Wik Munkan proper names:

> Although I have called them 'personal names' they are really group names and signify membership of, and solidarity with, a totemic group (Thomson, p. 159).

These reservations are due to the fact that the list of names which are the property and prerogative of each clan is often restricted and that two people cannot bear the same name simultaneously. The Iroquois have 'guardians' to whom they entrust the task of remembering the repertoire of clan names and who always know which names are available. When a child is born the 'guardian' is summoned to say which names are 'free'. Among the Yurok of California, a child can remain without a name for six or seven years, until a relative's name becomes vacant through the death of its bearer. On the other hand, the taboo on the dead man's name comes to an end after a year if a young member of the lineage puts it back into circulation.

Some names seem still more perplexing: these, like the ones given in Africa to twins or to the first child to survive after a series of still-births, assign some individuals a place in a rigid and restricted taxonomic system. The Nuer reserve the names of birds which fly low, such as guinea fowl, francolin, etc., for twins. In effect, they regard twins as creatures of supernatural origin like birds (Evans-Pritchard 2, discussion in Lévi-Strauss 6). The Kwakiutl of British Columbia express an analogous belief in their association of twins with fish. Thus the names Salmon-Head and Salmon-Tail are reserved for children whose birth immediately precedes or succeeds that of twins. Twins themselves are believed to be descended either from olachan (if they have small hands) or from *Oncorhynchus kisutch* (Silver-Salmon) or from *Oncorhynchus nerka* (Sockeye-Salmon). The diagnosis is made by an old man who is himself a twin. In the first case he names the male twin Making-Satiated and the female twin Making-Satiated-Woman; in the second case the names are Only-One and Abalone-Woman respectively; and in the third Head-Worker and Head-Dancer (Boas 4, part I, pp. 684–93).

Among the Dogon of the Sudan there is a very strict method of allotting proper names: each individual's position is plotted on the basis of a genealogical and mythical model where each name is linked with a sex, a lineage, and an order of birth and with the qualitative structure of the group of siblings to which the individual belongs: himself a twin, first- or second-born before or after twins, boy born after one or two girls, or vice versa, boy born between two girls or vice versa, etc. (Dieterlen 3).

Finally, one is often hesitant to regard as proper names the ordinal names found among most of the Algonkin and Sioux, among the Mixe (Radin 2), the Maya (Tozzer) and in the south of Asia (Benedict), etc. Let us confine ourselves to one example, that of the Dakota, among whom the system is particularly developed, with the following names corresponding to the order of birth of the first seven girls and the first six boys:

	GIRLS	BOYS
1.	Wino'ne	Tcaske'
2.	Ha'pe	Hepo'
3.	Ha'psti	Hepi'
4.	Wiha'ki	Watca'to
5.	Hapo'nA	Hake'
6.	HapstinA	Tatco'
7.	Wihake'da	—

(Wallis, p. 39).

Terms which replace proper names at different stages of initiation can be put in the same category. The Australian tribes in the north Dampier Land have a series of nine names given to novices before the extraction of teeth, then before circumcision, before the ritual bleeding, etc. The Tiwi of the Melville and Bathurst islands off North Australia give novices special names according to their grade. There are seven men's names covering the period from the fifteenth to the twenty-sixth year and seven women's names going from the tenth to the twenty-first year (Hart, pp. 286–7).

However, the problems which arise in these cases are no different from that raised by the custom with which we are acquainted in our society whereby an eldest son is given his paternal grandfather's christian name. 'Grandfather's name' can also be regarded as a title which is both obligatory and exclusive. There is an imperceptible transition from names to titles, which is connected not with any intrinsic property of the terms in question but with their structural role in a classificatory system from which it would be vain to claim to separate them.

CHAPTER SEVEN

THE INDIVIDUAL AS A SPECIES

The naming system of the Penan, who are nomads of the interior of Borneo, enables us to give a more precise account of the relation between the terms to which we should be inclined to reserve the title of proper name and others which seem at first sight to be of a different kind. Depending on his age and family situation, a Penan may be designated by three sorts of terms: a personal name, a teknonym ('father of so-and-so', 'mother of so-and-so') and, finally, what one feels like calling a necronym, which expresses the kinship relation of a deceased relative to the subject: 'father dead', 'niece dead', etc. The western Penan have no less than twenty-six distinct necronyms, corresponding to the degree of kinship, relative age of the deceased, sex and the order of birth of children up to the ninth.

The rules governing the use of these names are of surprising complexity. Simplifying a great deal, we can say that a child is known by its proper name until one of his ascendants dies. If it is a grandfather who dies, the child is then called Tupou. If his father's brother dies he becomes Ilun and remains so until another relative dies. He then receives a new name. A Penan may thus pass through a series of six or seven or more necronyms before he marries and has children.

At the birth of their first child a father and mother adopt a Teknonym expressing their relation to the child whose name forms part of it. Thus: Tama Awing, Tinen Awing, 'father (or mother) of Awing'. Should the child die, the teknonym is replaced by a necronym: 'Eldest child dead.' When the next child is born a new teknonym takes the place of the necronym, and so on.

The position is further complicated by the special rules relating to siblings. A child is called by his own name if all his brothers and sisters are alive. If one of them dies he takes on a necronym 'elder (or younger) sibling dead', but the necronym is abandoned at the birth of a new brother or sister and he uses his own name again (Needham *I, 4*).

There are many obscurities in this description and it is difficult to see how the various rules affect each other in spite of the fact that they appear to be functionally related. The system as a whole is definable by three types of periodicity: in relation to his ascendants, an individual passes from necronym to necronym; in relation to his siblings he passes from autonym (the term it is convenient to use for proper names in a system of this kind) to necronym; and in relation to his children he passes from teknonym to necronym. But what is the logical relation between these three types of terms and again between these three types of periodicity? Teknonyms and necronyms refer to a kinship tie and are therefore 'relational' terms. Autonyms do not have this characteristic and can be opposed to them from this point of view: an autonym only determines a 'self' by contrast to other 'selves'. This opposition between 'self' and 'other', implicit in the autonym allows in return a distinction between the teknonym and the necronym. The former contains a proper name (which is not that of the subject and it can be defined as expressing a *relation to an 'other' self*. The necronym contains no proper name at all and consists in the statement of a kinship relation, which is that of an unnamed 'other' with a 'self', equally unnamed. It can therefore be defined as an *'other' relation*. And finally, this relation is negative since the necronym mentions it only to declare it extinct.

Autonym and necronym emerge clearly from this analysis in a relationship of inverted symmetry:

	AUTONYM	NECRONYM
relation present (+) or absent (−):	−	+
opposition between self (+) and other (−):	+	−

A first conclusion becomes apparent at the same time: the autonym, which we have no hesitation in considering as a proper name, and the necronym, which has the features of a simple class indicator, belong in fact to the same group. One passes from one to the other by means of a transformation.

Let us now turn to the teknonym. What is its relation with the other two types of term, in particular with the necronym? It is tempting to say that the teknonym connotes the entry into life of another self, while the necronym refers to the departure of an other self into death, but this is too simple for it does not explain why the teknonym mentions the self of an other (autonym being incorporated in it) while the necronym may be reduced to a negation of the *other* relation without reference to a self. There is, therefore, no formal symmetry between the two types.

In the study which I have used as the point of departure for this analysis, Needham makes the interesting comment:

> Something very slightly similar to death-names is seen in the older English usage of 'widow' as a title . . ., the contemporary French and Belgian use of 'veuve', and similar usages in many other countries of Europe. But these are so far from death names in nearly every respect that they can provide no pointers to understanding (Needham I, p. 426).

This is giving up too soon. To have perceived the implications of his observation, Needham need only have noticed, in the examples he quotes, the connection between the right to a necronym and the prior possession of a name in every way comparable to a teknonym. In traditional French usage 'veuve' (widow) incorporates a proper name but the masculine 'veuf' (widower) or 'orphelin' (orphan) does not. Why this exclusivism? The patronym belongs to the children in their own right; it is, we say, a classifier of lineages in our societies. Children's relation to a patronym is therefore not affected by the death of parents. This is all the more true in the case of men, whose relation to their patronym remains immutable whether they be unmarried or widowed.

It is otherwise with women. If a woman's husband dies she becomes 'widow so-and-so'; but this is only because during her husband's lifetime, she was 'the wife of so-and-so', in other words, had already relinquished her autonym in favour of a term expressing her relation to an *other* self. And this is precisely how we defined the teknonym. In this case, of course, 'teknonym' would not be the appropriate word. We could coin the term andronym (Greek ἀνήρ, husband) to preserve the parallel but there is little point in this as the identity of structure is immediately apparent without recourse to neologism. In French usage the right to a necronym thus depends on the possession of a name analogous to a teknonym: because my self is defined by my relation to an other self my identity can be preserved at this other's death only by retaining this relation, unchanged in form but governed from now on by a negative sign. 'Widow Smith' is the wife of a Smith who is not extinct but who now exists only in his relation to that other who defines herself through him.

It will be objected that in this example both terms are constructed in the same way, by adding a kinship relation to a patronymic determinant, while, as I have pointed out, the necronym among the Penan contains no proper name. Before resolving this difficulty, let us consider the series of siblings where autonym and necronym alternate. Why autonym and not a term analogous to teknonym, say a 'fratronym' of the type 'brother (or sister) of so-and-so'? The answer is easy: the personal name of the child who has just been born (whose brothers and sisters are thereby relieved of their necronyms) is brought into play elsewhere. It is used to form the parents' teknonym and they have in some way appropriated it for inclusion in the particular system by which they are defined. The name of the last-born is thus separated off from the series of siblings and, as the other siblings can be defined neither through it nor through that of their dead brother or sister (since one is no longer in the 'key of death', as it were, but in the 'key of life'), they fall back on the only course left open to them: the resumption of their own name which is also their proper name. But, it must be emphasized, this is only in default of 'other' relations which have either become unavailable because they are turned to a different use or not relevant because the sign governing the system has changed.

The clarification of this point leaves us with only two problems: the use of teknonyms by parents, and the absence of proper names in necronyms, a problem we came across just now. At first sight the former seems to raise a question of content and the second one of form. But they are in fact a single problem amenable to one and the same solution. *The names of the dead are never mentioned*, and this suffices to explain the structure of the necronym. So far as the teknonym is concerned, the inference is clear: the reason why parents may no longer be called by their name when a child is born is that they are 'dead' and that procreation is conceived not as the addition of a new being to those who exist already but as the substitution of the one for the others.

The Tiwi custom of forbidding the use of proper names during initiation and child-birth is also to be understood in this way:

> The birth of a child is, to a native, a most mysterious affair and the woman is regarded as being intimately in touch with the spirit world. Hence her name as part of herself is invested with a ghostly character and this is expressed by the tribe in treating her husband as if she did not exist, as if she were dead in fact and for the time being no longer his wife. She is in touch with the spirits and the result will be a child for her husband (Hart, pp. 288–9).

A remark of Needham's suggests a similar interpretation in the case of the Penan. The teknonym, he says, is not honorific and not to have a child is not a matter of shame.

> If you have no child, informants say, . . . it is not your fault. You are sorry because there is no one to replace you, no one to remember your name . . . But you are not ashamed. Why should you be? (l.c., p. 417).

The couvade can be explained in the same way for it would be a mistake to suppose that a man is taking the place of the woman in labour. The husband and wife sometimes have to take the same precautions because they are identified with the child who is subject to great dangers during the first weeks or months of its life. Sometimes, frequently for instance in South America, the husband has to take even greater precautions than his wife because, according to native theories of conception and gestation it is particularly his person which is identified with that of the child. In neither event does the father play the part of the mother. He plays the part of the child. Anthropologists are rarely mistaken on the first point; but they yet more rarely grasp the second.

Three conclusions can be drawn from this analysis. In the first place, proper names, far from constituting a category apart, form a group with other terms which differ from them even though they are united with them by structural relations. The Penan themselves think of these terms as class indicators: they speak of 'entering into' a necronym, not of taking or receiving it.

Secondly, proper names occupy a subordinate position in this complex system. It is really only children who overtly bear their names, either because they are too young to be structurally qualified by the family and social system or because the means of qualification have, for the time being, been suspended in favour of their parents. Proper names thus undergo a truly logical devaluation. They are the mark of being 'unclassed' as candidates for a class, of being temporarily obliged to define themselves either as unclassed (as in the case of siblings resuming the use of their autonyms) or alternatively by their relation to an unclassed person (like parents when they assume a teknonym). When, however, death causes a breach in the social fabric, the individual is, as it were drawn in. Thanks to the necronym, which has an absolute logical priority over other forms, his proper name, a mere place in the queue, is replaced by a position in the system, which from the most general point of view, can therefore be considered as formed of discrete quantified classes. The proper name is the reverse of the necronym, of which the teknonym in turn presents an inverted image. The case of the Penan is to all appearances the opposite of that of the Algonkin, Iroquois and Yurok. Among the former a person must await a relative's death to be rid of the name he bears, while often among the latter he must await it to succeed to his name. But in fact there is as great a logical devaluation of names in the latter case as there is in the former:

> The individual name is never used in either direct address or indirect reference to relatives, the relationship term doing service in all such cases. Even when addressing a non-relative, the individual name is very seldom used, the form of address consisting in a relationship term, according to the relative age of the speaker and the person addressed. Only when non-relatives are referred to in conversation is it customary to use the individual name, which even then will not be used if the context plainly indicates the person referred to (Goldenweiser, p. 367).

So, among the Iroquois too, and in spite of the differences pointed out, a person is left unclassed only when there is no alternative.*

* To avoid using proper names, the Yurok of California have conceived a system of appellations composed of a root corresponding to a place of residence – a village or house – and a suffix, which differs for men and women, describing their marital status. The men's names refer to the wife's place of birth and the women's to the husband's place of birth. The suffix of the name indicates whether it is a case of a patrilocal marriage by purchase, a matrilocal one or a free union, whether the marriage has been dissolved through the death of husband or wife or by divorce, etc. Other affixes, entering into the names of children and the unmarried, refer to the place of birth of their living or deceased mother, or their deceased father. Thus the only names employed are of one of the following types: Married to a woman of ——; Married to a man of ——; Has a 'simi' husband in the house of birth of ——; Is 'half' married to a woman of ——; Widower belonging to ——; Divorced from a woman (or man) of ——; Woman of ——

All sorts of beliefs have been invoked to explain the very common prohibition on pronouncing the names of the dead. These beliefs are real and well authenticated but the question is whether they should be regarded as the origin of the custom, as one of the factors which have contributed to reinforce it or perhaps even as one of its consequences. If the explanations I have given are correct, the prohibition on the names of the dead is a structural property of certain systems of naming. Proper names are either already class operators of alternatively they provide a temporary solution for those awaiting classification. They always represent classes at their most modest. In the limiting case, as among the Penan, they are no more than the means, temporarily unclassed, of forming classes or again, as it were, bills drawn on the logical solvency of the system, that is on its discounted capacity to supply the creditor with a class in due course. Only newcomers, that is, the children who are born, raise a problem: there they are. Any system which treats individuation as classification (and I have tried to show that this is always so) risks having its structure called in question every time a new member is admitted.

There are two types of solution to this problem, and intermediate forms between them. If the system in question consists of *classes of positions*, it has only to command a reserve of unoccupied positions sufficient to accommodate all the children born. The available positions being always more numerous than the population, synchrony is protected against the vagaries of diachrony, at least in theory. This is the Iroquois solution. The Yurok are less farsighted. Among them, children have to wait their turn; but as they are nevertheless assured of being classified after a few years, they can remain temporarily undifferentiated while awaiting a position in a class, which the structure of the system guarantees them.

Everything is different when the system consists of *classes of relations*. It is then no longer the case that one individual ceases to exist and another replaces him in a position labelled by means of a proper name which outlasts any particular person. For the relation itself to become a class term, proper names, which present the terms related as so many distinct entitles, have to be eliminated. The ultimate units of the system are no longer single member classes with a train of successive living occupants, but classed relations between

who allows a man to live with her, has a lover or illegitimate children; His father was of ——; Their late mother was ——; Unmarried person of ——; etc. (Waterman, pp. 214–18; Kroeber in: Elmendorf and Kroeber, pp. 372–4, n. 1) the dead or even those who are so in effect (parents are described as dead by contrast with the life they have created) and the living, whether really living or in effect so (new born children who have a proper name so that their parents may be defined in relation to them until the real death of an ascendant allows them in turn to be defined in relation to him). In these systems, the classes are thus composed of different types of dynamic relations associating entries and departures, while among the Iroquois and other societies of the same sort, they are founded on a collection of static positions which may be vacant or occupied.*

The prohibition on the names of the dead does not therefore raise a separate problem for anthropology. A dead person loses his name for the same reason that – among the Penan – a living person loses his; when the living Penan enters the system he assumes a necronym, that is to say, he becomes one of the terms in a relationship, of which the other – since he is dead – no longer exists save in that relation which defines a living person with reference to him. Finally, for the same reason as the dead lose their names a mother and father lose theirs also when they assume a teknonym, resolving in this way (until the death of one of their children) the difficulty created for the system by the procreation of a supernumerary member. The latter must wait 'outside the door' as a named person until someone's departure allows him to make his entrance. Then two beings of whom one did not previously belong within the system and the

* Consequently, systems of relations, unlike systems of positions whose discontinuous nature is evident, tend rather to be continuous. Another Penan usage shows this clearly, although Needham (*2*), who also records it, rejects an explanation which in fact seems very plausible. The reciprocal terms 'grandparent' and 'grandchild' replace the usual, closer terms for members of the same nuclear family when one of the two persons involved is in mourning. Is not the point that the person in mourning is looked upon as having moved over somewhat towards death and so further away than he was from his closest relatives? Death loosens the ties of kinship network. Needham is unwilling to allow this because he regards what is in fact one problem as several: the mourner does not call a son, daughter, nephew or niece or their spouse 'grandchild' because the same mourning directly or indirectly affects them but quite simply by way of reciprocity. All the examples Needham mentions confirm this except that of a young child who suffers a slight mishap (has fallen down, received a blow or whose food has been stolen by a dog) and is called on that occasion by the necronym normally reserved for those who have lost a grandparent. But my account covers this case also since the child is placed metaphorically in mourning by the damage done to him and, due to his tender years, a slight injury to his well-being (actual in the case of a fall or potential in that of a loss of food) is enough to drive him back towards death.

other ceases to do so are merged in one of the classes of relations of which the system is composed.

Some societies jealously watch over their names and make them last practically for ever, others squander them and destroy them at the end of every individual existence. They then get rid of them by forbidding them and coin other names in their place. But these apparently contradictory attitudes in fact merely express two aspects of a constant property of systems of classification: they are finite and inflexible in form. By its rules and customs, each society, to impose a structure on the continuous flux of generation, does no more than apply to a rigid and discontinuous grid, and a slight shift in its logic is enough to secure this in one position or the other: either the system of proper names forms the finest mesh of the filter of which it is, consequently, an essential part; or alternatively, it is left outside while retaining all the same the function of individuating the continuous and thus setting up in a formal manner discontinuity, which can then be seen as a preliminary condition of classification. In both cases, too, the dead as their distance from the grid increases, lose their names which are either taken by the living as symbols of positions which must always be filled* or are done away with under the impact of the same movement which, at the other end of the grid, extinguishes the names of the living.

The Tiwi system of naming, to which I have referred several times, is intermediate between these two forms. In the first place, proper names are meticulously confined to a single bearer:

> It is impossible for any two people to have the same name . . . Although the Tiwi number nearly eleven hundred people at the present time, and each one of these has on an average three names, a careful study of these three thousand three hundred names failed to reveal any two as being identical (Hart, p. 281).

This proliferation of names is further increased by the number and variety of prohibitions relating to them. These prohibitions extend

* In the Fox myth of the origin of death, the person in mourning is told: Now this is what you are to do. You, i.e. you and the deceased, must always release each other (i.e. hold an adoption feast). Then the soul of the dead will safely and speedily go yonder. You must adopt someone. And you must think exactly the same of that toward them. And you will be related to him exactly (as you were to the dead). That is the only way the soul of your relative may depart safely and speedily (Michelson, I, p. 411). The text is eloquent about the fact that, in this case too, the quick drive out the dead.

in two directions. As I mentioned in an example,* they attach in the first instance to all the words in current use which sound like the names of the deceased; and they apply not only to the latter, but also to all the names which the deceased gave to others, whether they were his own or someone else's children. A young child with only one name, given by his father, would become nameless if his father died and would remain so until another name came to him from elsewhere (l.c., p. 282). Every time a woman remarries, her husband gives new names not just to his predecessor's children but to all the children his wife has borne throughout her life whoever was their father. As the Tiwi practise a form of polygyny chiefly favouring old men, a man has little hope of marriage before the age of thirty-five and women pass from husband to husband. This is due to the difference in age between husband and wife which makes it very likely that a husband will die before his wife. No one can therefore boast a definitive name until his mother's death (id., p. 283).

A system as strange as this would remain incomprehensible were it not for an hypothesis which suggests an explanation of it, namely, that relations and positions are here put on the same footing. In addition, the abolition of a relation involves in each case that of the proper names which were a function of it either socially (names bestowed by the deceased) or linguistically (words which resemble the deceased's names). And every creation of a new relation starts a process of renaming within the domain of the relation.

Some ethnographers have approached the problem of proper names from the angle of kinship terms:

> Logically, terms of relationship may be regarded as ranking between proper names and pronouns. They occupy a position between both and might be called individualized pronouns or generalized proper names (Thurnwald, p. 357).

But if this transition is likewise possible it is because from the ethnological point of view, proper names always appear as terms which are generalized or have a generalizing function. In this respect they do not differ fundamentally from the names of species, as is shown by the popular tendency to attribute names of human beings to birds in accordance with their respective species. In French, the sparrow is 'Pierrot', the parrot 'Jacquot', the magpie 'Margot', the

* pp. 176–7.

finch 'Guillaume', the wren 'Bertrand' or 'Robert', the water-rail 'Gerardine', the sparrow-owl 'Claude', the eagle-owl 'Hubert', the crow 'Colas', the swan 'Godard' . . . This last name also refers to a significant social condition for it was applied to husbands whose wives were in labour (Witkowski, pp. 501–2).* Names of species for their part seem to have some of the features of proper names. Following Brondal,† Gardiner admits this in the case of the scientific terminology of zoology and botany:

> The name *Brassica rapa* easily evokes the thought of a botanist classifying a number of specimens which to the lay mind are much alike, and to one of which he gives the name *Brassica rapa*, just as a parent names his baby. We have no such thought about the word *turnip*, and *Brassica rapa* is simply the scientific name for the ordinary turnip. We may find confirmatory support for regarding *Brassica rapa* as a proper name, or at least as much more of a proper name than turnip, in the fact that we do not say *This is a Brassica rapa*, or *These are fine specimens of Brassica rapa*. In so saying we appeal to the name of any single example of the type, whereas in speaking of a certain vegetable as a turnip, we appeal to the similarity of that vegetable to others of its kind. The difference of linguistic attitude is a mere nuance, but it is a real one. In the one instance the sound of the name, what we usually describe as 'the name itself', is more in the foreground than in the other instance (Gardiner, p. 52).

This account illustrates the author's central thesis that: 'proper names are identificatory marks recognizable, not by the intellect, but by the senses' (l.c., p. 41). Now, we justified the assimilation of botanical and zoological terms to proper names by showing that in a very large number of societies proper names are constructed in the same way as species named in the natural sciences. A conclusion diametrically opposed to Gardiner's follows from this. Proper names seemed to us to have close affinities with species names, in particular when their role was clearly that of class indicators, that is, when

* It is very significant that even so limited and simple a series includes terms from different logical sphere. 'Pierrot' can be a class indicator since one can say 'There are three *pierrots* on the balcony'. But 'Godard' is a term of address. As the author of the article on this word in the Dictionary de Trevoux (1732 ed.) so excellently puts it: 'Godard is the name given to swans. When one calls them, when one wants them to come, one says to them: "*Godard*, *Godard*, come *Godard*, come. Here *Godard*". Jacquot and perhaps Margot seem to have an intermediate role.' (Cf. Rolland, *Faune*, Vol. II on the human proper names given to birds.)

† From the point of view of eternity, particular species of plants and animals and simple substances are unique things of the same kind as, for example, Sirius or Napoleon (Brondal, p. 230).

they belonged to a meaningful system. Gardiner, on the other hand, attempts to explain this same analogy by the meaningless nature of scientific terms, which he reduces, like proper names, to mere distinctive sounds. If he were right, we should arrive at an odd paradox. *Brassica rapa* is certainly reducible to a distinctive sound so far as the layman, unversed in Latin and botany, is concerned, but he does

Fig 10 Brassica rapa (from Ed. Lambert, *Traite pratique de Botanique*, Paris, 1883).

not know what it expresses. Without extraneous information, he could not therefore recognize this term as a proper name but only as a word of unknown sense, if not indeed a *flatus vocis*. This is in fact the situation in some Australian tribes in which totemic species are given names from sacred language which have no animal or plant associations for the uninitiated. If, therefore, *Brassica rapa* does look like a proper name, it can do so only to the botanist, who alone can say 'What good specimens of *Brassica rapa*'. For the botanist, however, what is in question is something quite different from a distinctive sound, for he knows both the meaning of the Latin words and the rules of the taxonomy.

So it appears the Gardiner's account must be confined to the case of the semi-initiated who recognize *Brassica rapa* as the name of a botanical species without knowing which plant is in question. In spite of the author's protestations (p. 51), this is a return to Vendryes' bizarre idea (p. 222) that a bird's name becomes a proper name when the observer is unable to distinguish the species to which it belongs. However, everything said so far suggests that the connection between proper names and species names is not a contingent one. It rests on the fact that a phrase like *Brassica rapa* is 'outside discourse' in two ways: because it derives from scientific language and because it is composed of Latin words. It is therefore only with difficulty that it is included in the syntagmatic chain. Its paradigmatic nature thus comes to the fore. Similarly, it is because of the paradigmatic role of proper names in a system of signs external to thc system of the language that their insertion in the syntagmatic chain makes a perceptible break in the latter's continuity: in French, by the absence of an article before them and by writing them with a capital letter.

The Navaho seem to have gained a fairly clear conception of the problems just discussed. One of their myths sets aside Gardiner's account in advance:

> One day Mouse met Bear and asked him if his name was Cac. This made Bear angry and he tried to hit Mouse, who ran behind Bear and set fire to his fur. Bear couldn't put it out, so he gave four songs as offerings to Mouse, begging him to put out the fire; nowadays if you carry mouse hair with you, no bear will touch you (adapted from Haile-Wheelwright, p. 46).*

The myth humorously underlines the difference between species names and distinctive sounds. One of the reasons for this difference so far as the Navaho are concerned, lies in the fact that names of species are, at least in part, proper names. In the story quoted above Mouse offends Bear because he addresses him incorrectly and using a ridiculous word. Now, the botanical terms of the Navaho (whose zoological vocabulary has not been so well studied) generally consist of a trinome, the first element of which is the name proper, the second describes the plant's use and the third its appearance. Most people apparently know only the descriptive term. The 'real name' is a term of address which priests use when they speak to the plant: a proper name therefore and one which it is essential to be well

* [Ed. note.] The usage of capitals and articles in the text is quite haphazard and corresponds neither to any feature in the Navaho language nor to any principle of English usage. In this regard English is similar to French usage and the text has therefore been adapted for the sake of the clarity of the illustration.

acquainted with and to pronounce correctly (Wyman and Harris; Leighton).

We do not ourselves use scientific nomenclature for conversing with plants and animals. We do however readily give animals, and borrow from plants, some of the names serving as terms of address between people: girls are sometimes called Rose or Violet and conversely several animal species are allowed to share christian names commonly borne by men or women. But why should it, as we have already seen, particularly be birds who profit from this liberal attitude? They are further removed than dogs from men in their anatomical structure, their physical structure and their mode of life, and human christian names cannot be given to dogs without causing uneasiness or even mild offence. The explanation is already contained in what has just been said.

Birds are given human christian names in accordance with the species to which they belong more easily than are other zoological classes, because they can be permitted to resemble men for the very reason that they are so different. They are feathered, winged, oviparous and they are also physically separated from human society by the element in which it is their privilege to move. As a result of this fact, they form a community which is independent of our own but, precisely because of this independence, appears to us like another society, homologous to that in which we live: birds love freedom; they build themselves homes in which they live a family life and nurture their young; they often engage in social relations with other members of their species; and they communicate with them by acoustic means recalling articulated language.

Consequently everything objective conspires to make us think of the bird world as a metaphorical human society: is it not after all literally parallel to it on another level? There are countless examples in mythology and folklore to indicate the frequency of this mode of representation. Consider for instance the comparison mentioned above which the Chickasaw Indians make between the society of birds and a human community.*

* Cf. above, p. 118.

My account is inversely confirmed by the cases of those animals which are likewise given human christian names, although they are not birds: 'Jean Lapin', 'Robin Mouton', 'Bernard (or Martin) l'Ane', 'Pierre (or Alain) le Renard', 'Martin l'Ours', etc. (Sebillot, II, p. 97, III, pp. 19–20). These animals do not form a natural series: some are domestic, some wild; some are herbivorous, others carnivorous; some are loved (or scorned) and others feared. What we have

Now, this metaphorical relation which is imagined between the society of birds and the society of men, is accompanied by a procedure of naming, itself of a metonymical order (we need not in this work regard ourselves as bound by grammarians' refinements, and I shall not treat synecdoche – a species of metonymy according to Littré – as a distinct figure of speech): when species of birds are christened 'Pierrot', 'Margot' or 'Jacquot', these names are drawn from a portion which is the preserve of human beings and the relation of bird names to human names is thus that of part to whole.

The position is exactly the reverse in the case of dogs. Not only do they not form an independent society; as 'domestic' animals they are part of human society, although with so low a place in it that we should not dream of following the example of some of the Australians and Amerindians in designating them in the same way as human beings – whether what is in question are proper names or kinship term.* On the contrary, we allot them a special series: 'Azor', 'Medor', 'Sultan', 'Fido', 'Diane' (the last of these is of course a human christian name but in the first instance conceived as mythological). Nearly all these are like stage names, forming a series parallel to the names people bear in ordinary life or, in other words, metaphorical names. Consequently when the relation between (human and animal) species is socially conceived as metaphorical, the relation between the respective systems of naming takes on a metonymical character; and when the relation between species is conceived as metonymical, the system of naming assumes a metaphorical character.

Let us now consider another case, that of cattle, the social position of which is metonymical (they form part of our technical and economic system) but different from that of dogs in that cattle are more overtly treated as 'objects' and dogs as 'subjects' (this is suggested, first, by the collective name we use to designate the former and, secondly, by the taboo on the eating of dogs in our culture; the situation is different among the African pastoral peoples who treat cattle as we treat dogs). Now, the names given to cattle belong to a different series from birds' or dogs'. They are generally descriptive

here is therefore an artificial system, based on characteristic oppositions between temperaments and ways of life and tending to reconstruct a small-scale model of human society in the animal kingdom. The *Roman de Renart* offers a typical illustration of this.

* Cf. above, pp. 167–8; and even less named human beings in terms of them – as the Dayak do: father (or mother) of this or that dog . . . (Geddes).

terms, referring to the colour of their coats, their bearing or temperament: 'Rustaud', 'Rousset', 'Blanchette', 'Douce', etc. (cf. Lévi-Strauss 2, p. 280). These names often have a metaphorical character but they differ from the names given to dogs in that they are epithets coming from the syntagmatic chain, while the latter come from a paradigmatic series; the former thus tend to derive from speech, the latter from language.

Finally, let us consider the names given to horses – not ordinary horses whose place approximates more or less closely to that of cattle or that of dogs according to the class and occupation of their owner, and is made even more uncertain by the rapid technological changes of recent times, but racehorses, whose sociological position is clearly distinguishable from the cases already examined. The first question is how to define their position. They cannot be said to constitute an independent society after the manner of birds, for, they are products of human industry and they are born and live as isolated individuals juxtaposed in stud farms devised for their sake. On the other hand, they do not form part of human society either as subjects or as objects. Rather, they constitute the desocialized condition of existence of a private society: that which lives off race-courses or frequents them. Another difference, in the system of naming, corresponds to these, although two reservations must be made in drawing this comparison: the names given to racehorses are chosen in accordance with particular rules which differ for thoroughbreds and half-breds and they display an eclecticism which draws on learned literature rather than oral tradition. This said, there is no doubt that there is a significant contrast between the names of racehorses and those of birds, dogs or cattle. They are rigorously individualized since, as among the Tiwi, two individuals cannot have the same name; and, although they share with the names given to cattle the feature of being formed by drawing upon the syntagmatic chain: 'Ocean', 'Azimuth', 'Opera', 'Belle-de-Nuit', 'Telegraphe', 'Luciole', 'Orvietan', 'Weekend', 'Lapis-Lazuli', etc., they are distinguished from them by the absence of descriptive connotation. Their creation is entirely unrestricted so long as they satisfy the requirement of unambiguous individuation and adhere to the particular rules referred to above. Thus, while cattle are given descriptive names formed out of words of discourse, the names assigned to racehorses are words from discourse which rarely, if ever, describe them. The former type of name perhaps resembles a nickname and these latter perhaps merit the title of sub-names* as it is in this second domain that the most extreme arbitrariness reigns.

To sum up: birds and dogs are relevant in connection with human society either because they suggest it by their own social life (which men look on as an imitation of theirs), or alternatively because, having no social life of their own, they form part of ours.

Cattle, like dogs, form part of human society, but as it were, asocially, since they verge on objects. Finally racehorses, like birds, form a series disjoined from human society, but like cattle, lacking in intrinsic sociability.

If, therefore, birds are *metaphorical human beings* and dogs, *metonymical human beings*, cattle may be thought of as *metonymical inhuman beings* and racehorses as *metaphorical inhuman beings*. Cattle are contiguous only for want of similarity, racehorses similar only for want of contiguity. Each of these two categories offers the converse image of one of the two other categories, which themselves stand in the relation of inverted symmetry.

The linguistic equivalent of this system of psycho-sociological differences is to be found on the plane of appellations. Bird and dog names are derived from language. But, although they have the same paradigmatic character, they differ in that the former are real, while the latter are conventional christian names. The names of birds are taken from the preserve of ordinary human christian names, of which they constitute a part; while the names of dogs in effect reproduce in its entirety a portion of names formally similar to human christian names although rarely borne by ordinary human beings.

The names of cattle and horses derive rather from speech, since they are in both cases taken from the syntagmatic chain. But the names of cattle remain closest to it for, as descriptive terms, they are scarcely proper names. A cow habitually said to be gentle ('douce') is called 'Douce'. The names given to cattle thus survive as testimony of a bygone discourse, and they can at any moment resume their function of epithets in discourse: even when one talks to cattle, their character as objects never allows them to be anything but *what is spoken about*. The names of racehorses are 'within discourse' in a different fashion: not 'still in discourse' but 'made of discourse'. To find horses' names it is necessary to take the syntagmyatic chain to pieces and to transform its discrete units into proper

* The opposition here comes out more clearly in the French where nickname 'surnom' is apposed to sub-name 'sous-nom' [trans. note].

names which will not be able to figure in discourse in any other capacity unless the ambiguity is dispelled by the context. The difference here is due to the fact that cattle are ranked in the inhuman part of human society, while racehorses (who, objectively speaking, belong to the same category) primarily present the image of an anti-society to a restricted society which owes its existence entirely to them. The system of naming applied to them is the most frankly inhuman of all and the technique of linguistic demolition employed to construct it likewise the most barbarous.

When all is said and done, we arrive at a three-dimensional system:

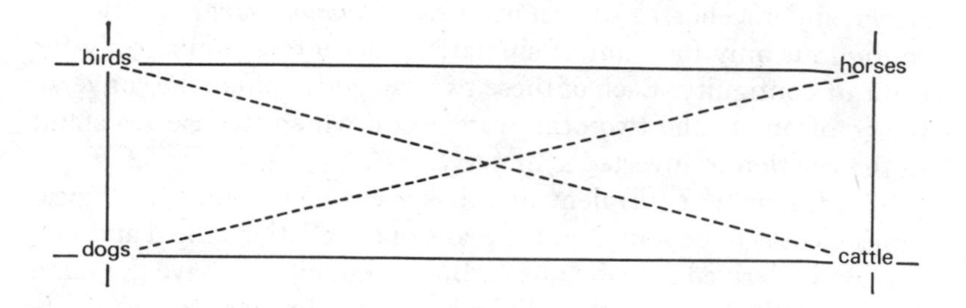

The upper line on the horizontal plane corresponds to the positive or negative metaphorical relation between human and animal society (birds) or between the society of men and the anti-society of horses, and the lower to the metonymical relation between the society of men on the one hand and dogs and cattle on the other which are members of the former in the capacity either of subjects or of objects.

The left-hand column on the vertical plane associates birds and dogs which have a metaphorical or a metonymical relation with social life. The right-hand column associates horses and cattle, which have no relation with social life, although cattle form part of it (metonymy) and racehorses bear a negative resemblance to it (metaphor).

Finally, two oblique axes have to be added, for the names given to birds and cattle are formed by metonymical appropriation (either from a paradigmatic set or from a syntagmatic chain), while the names given to dogs and horses are formed by metaphorical reproduction (either of a paradigmatic set or of a syntagmatic chain). What we have here is therefore a coherent system.

The systematic relations between these usages are not their only interesting feature from our point of view.* Although borrowed from our civilization where their place is a minor one, they offer ready access to other usages which are given extreme importance by the societies which employ them. The attention we have paid to certain aspects of our customs which some may consider futile is justified for two reasons. In the first place, we hope thereby to gain a clearer and more general idea of the nature of proper names. Secondly and above all, we are led to inquire into the hidden motives underlying ethnographic curiosity: the fascination exercised over us by customs apparently far removed from ours, the contradictory feeling of proximity and strangeness with which they affect us, stem perhaps from the fact these customs are very much closer to our own than they appear and present us with an enigmatic image which needs deciphering. In any case this is what seems to be shown by a comparison of the facts just analysed with some features of the Tiwi naming systems which were provisionally left on one side.

It will be remembered that the Tiwi have an inordinate consumption of names: first, because each person has several names; secondly, because all the names have to be distinct; thirdly, because every re-marriage (and we have seen that they are frequent) involves giving new names to all the children a woman already has; and finally, because a person's death results in a prohibition not only of the names he has borne but also of all those which he may have been led to bestow in the course of this life.† How, one may ask, do the Tiwi constantly manage to fabricate new names in these circumstances?

Several cases have to be distinguished. A proper name can be put back into circulation by the son of the deceased if he decides to take it after the period during which its use is forbidden. Many names are thus put in reserve and constitute a sort of onomastic fund which can be drawn on at will. Nevertheless, if one assumes a constant rate of births and deaths, the pool is likely to diminish on account of the prolonged duration of the taboo, unless a sudden demographic

* This book was already completed when M. M. Houis kindly drew my attention to the work of V. Larock. Although I have not made use of it because its context is so different from my own, I feel it right to pay tribute to it as the first tentative account of names of people from an ethnographic point of view.

† Cf. above, p. 199.

disequilibrium should act as a compensating factor. The system must therefore have other procedures at its disposal.

The chief of these, and there are in fact several, stems from extending to common nouns the prohibition on proper names, when it is noticed that the two are phonetically similar. These common nouns, which are withdrawn from circulation in daily life, are not however entirely destroyed: they pass into the sacred language, reserved for ritual, where they progressively lose their meaning, the sacred language being by definition incomprehensible to the uninitiated and partly freed of any meaningful function so far as the initiated themselves are concerned. Now, sacred words, which have lost their sense, can be used to construct proper names by the addition of a suffix. Thus the word *matirandijingli* from sacred language, the meaning of which is obscure, turns into the proper name *Materandjingimirli*. This procedure is systematically employed and it has been possible to say that the sacred language is mainly composed of words which have become taboo, *Pukimani*, on account of the contamination of ordinary language by the prohibition attaching to the names of the dead. Sacred language is itself exempt from this contamination (Hart).

These facts are important from two points of view. In the first place, it is clear that this complicated system is perfectly coherent: proper names contaminate common nouns; common nouns, banished from ordinary language, pass into sacred language, which in turn allows the formation of proper names. This cyclical movement is, as it were, sustained by a double pulsation: proper names originally lacking in meaning acquire one by being attached to common nouns and the latter relinquish their meaning on passing into the sacred language, which allows them to become proper names again. The system thus functions by pumping semantic charge alternately from common nouns to proper names and from the profane language to the sacred language. In the last analysis, the energy consumed derives from ordinary language, which coins new words for the needs of communication in proportion as the old words are taken from it. This example is an admirable demonstration of the subsidiary nature of the interpretations proposed, whether by ethnologists or by the native, to explain the prohibition on the names of the dead. For a system as well adjusted as this could not have been born of a fear of ghosts. Rather, the latter has come to be grafted on to it.

That this is so seems even more certain when one notices that the Tiwi system has striking analogies, on the human plane, with the system in our own society, to which I drew attention in analysing the various ways of naming animals, where, it is hardly necessary to say, fear of the dead plays no part. Among the Tiwi also, the system rests on a sort of arbitrage, exercised by means of proper names, between a syntagmatic chain (that of ordinary language) and a paradigmatic set (the sacred language, which is essentially of this nature since the words there become progressively unfitted to form a syntagmatic chain as they lose their meaning). In addition, proper names are metaphorically connected with common nouns through a positive phonetic resemblance, while sacred words are metonymically connected with proper names (as means or ends) through a negative resemblance, based on the absence or poverty of semantic content.

Even if one defines it, on the most general level, as consisting in an exchange of words between the profane and the sacred language, through the medium of proper names, the Tiwi system clarifies phenomena which minor aspects of our culture allowed us only to do so much as broach. We are better able to understand how terms like *Brassica rapa* which belong to a language 'sacred' in two respects (being Latin and scientific) can have the character of proper names, not, as Gardiner suggests and Hart seems prepared to admit, because they are devoid of meaning but because, in spite of appearances, they are part of a whole system in which meaning is never entirely lost. Were this not so, the sacred language of the Tiwi would not be a language but a conglomeration of oral gestures. There can, however, be no doubt that even an obscure sacred language retains potential meaning. I shall come back to this aspect of the question later.

For the moment we must distinguish another type of 'sacred' language which we employ, in the manner of the Tiwi, to introduce proper names into ordinary language, even transforming the common nouns from the domain in question into proper names. Thus, as we have already seen, we use flower names as proper names for girls, but we do not stop at this, since the inventiveness of horticulturalists provides newly introduced flowers with proper names taken over from human beings. This chassé-croisé has some notable peculiarities. The names we take from flowers and give (mainly to persons of the female sex) are common nouns belonging to ordinary language (a girl may perhaps be called Rosa but definitely not *Rosa centifolia*); those we give them in return, however, come from a 'sacred' language: a title is added to the patronym or christian name and lends it a mysterious dignity. A new flower is not usually called 'Elizabeth', 'Doumer', or 'Brigitte' but 'Queen-Elizabeth', 'President-Paul-Doumer', 'Madame-Brigitte-Bardot'.* Moreover, no account is taken of the bearer's sex (in this case the grammatical gender of the name of the flower) in naming it: a rose or a gladiolus (feminine and masculine respectively in French) can be given either a man's or a woman's name indifferently. This recalls one of the rules for the attribution of 'umbilical' names among the Wik Munkan.†

Now, these usages, whether also taken from our own culture or from that of Australian islanders, clearly derive from the same group as all those we have been considering; we observe the same equivalence between metonymical and metaphorical relations which has seemed to play the part of common denominator between them from the start. The names we take over from flowers to make into proper names have the force of metaphors: fair as a rose, modest as a violet, etc. But the names drawn from 'sacred' language which flowers receive in exchange have the force of metonymy, in two ways: *Brassica rapa* removes the self-sufficiency of cabbage-turnip to make it a species of a genus, part of a whole. The name 'Impératrice-Eugénie', given to a new variety of flower, performs a converse transformation, since it takes place at the level of the signifying instead of at that of the signified: this time the flower is designated *by means of* part of a whole; not any Eugénie but a particular Eugénie; Eugénie de Montijo not before her marriage but after it; not a biological individual but a person in a determined social role, etc.‡ One type of 'sacred' name is thus 'metonymizing' and the other

* This tendency is already apparent in popular tradition which, when it attributes human christian names to certain flowers, generally inserts them in a phrase: 'Beau Nicolas' for the rose campion, 'Marie Cancale' for the cornflower, 'Joseph Foireux' for the cowslip, etc. (Rolland, Flore, vol. II). Similarly in English, the flower names: 'Jack in the Pulpit', 'Jack behind the Garden Gate', etc.

† Cf. above, p. 184.

‡ Note the inversion of the cycle as compared to the Tiwi system. Among ourselves, the cycle goes from ordinary language to proper name, from proper name to the 'sacred' language, to return finally to ordinary language. Ordinary

'metonymized', and this opposition holds in the case examined above. It will be remembered that, as well as taking names from flowers, human beings give certain of their names to birds. These names are also 'metonymizing' for they most commonly consist of diminutives drawn from the popular language and treat the community of birds (inversely to that of flowers) as equivalent, as a whole, to a humble and well-behaved sub-group of human society. Similarly, it will readily be agreed that the metaphorical names given to dogs and cattle place the role of the figure of speech at the level of the signifying and the signified respectively.

Systematic as the set of naming procedures we have reviewed may seem, they nevertheless raise a problem. These equivalent procedures, connected with each other by relations of transformation, operate at different levels of generality. The human christian names given to birds apply to any member of a determinate species: any magpie is called 'Margot'. But the names given to flowers: Queen-Elizabeth, Impératrice-Eugénie, etc., cover no more than the variety or sub-variety. The field of application of the names given to dogs and cattle is even more restricted. The animal's owner intends them to refer to a single individual, even though in fact each can be borne by several: there is not just one dog called 'Médor'. Only the names of racehorses and other pedigree animals are absolutely individualized. No other trotting horse than the one already so christened can be called Orvietan III in the twenty-six years of the alphabetical cycle.*

This is, however, in my view, the clearest proof one could wish for that proper names and species names form part of the same group so that there is no fundamental difference between the two types of name. Or rather the reason for the difference lies not in their linguistic nature but in the way in which each culture divides up reality and in the variable limits it assigns to the enterprise of classification, depending on the problems it raises (which can differ for each particular group within the total society). It is thus by virtue of an

language furnishes the common name rose which first becomes Rose, a woman's christian name and then returns to ordinary language through the intermediary of the sacred language in the form: Princess Margaret-Rose, naming a variety of rose of which (if the flower is a success) it will rapidly become the common name.

* The alphabetical cycle refers to the system whereby the initial letter of a pedigree animal should correspond to the year of its birth, and that the letters succeed one another in alphabetical order [trans. note].

extrinsic determination that a certain level of classification requires appellations, which can be common nouns or proper names according to the circumstances. But this does not, however, bring us back to the Durkheimian thesis of the social origin of logical thought. Although there is undoubtedly a dialectical relation between the social structure and systems of categories, the latter are not an effect or result of the former: each, at the cost of laborious mutual adjustments, translates certain historical and local modalities of the relations between man and the world, which form their common substratum.

These clarifications were necessary to enable us to emphasize, without risk of misunderstanding, the sociological and at the same time relative nature of the notion of a species as well as of an individual. From the biological point of view, men who belong to the same race (assuming that a precise sense can be given to this term) are comparable to the individual flowers which blossom, open and wither on the same tree: they are so many specimens of a variety or sub-variety. Similarly, all the members of the species *Homo sapiens* are logically comparable to the members of any other animal or plant species. However, social life effects a strange transformation in this system, for it encourages each biological individual to develop a personality; and this is a notion no longer recalling specimens within a variety but rather types of varieties or of species, probably not found in nature (although there is a suggestion of it now and again in the tropical environment) and which could be termed 'mono-individual'. What disappears with the death of a personality is a synthesis of ideas and modes of behaviour as exclusive and irreplaceable as the one a floral species develops out of the simple chemical substances common to all species. When the loss of someone dear to us or of some public personage such as a politician or writer or artist moves us, we suffer much the same sense of irreparable privation that we should experience were *Rosa centifolia* to become extinct and its scent to disappear for ever. From this point of view it seems not untrue to say that some modes of classing, arbitrarily isolated under the title of totemism, are universally employed: among ourselves this 'totemism' has merely been humanized. Everything takes place as if in our civilization every individual's own personality were his totem: it is the signifier of his signified being.

In so far as they derive from a paradigmatic set,* proper names thus form the fringe of a general system of classification: they are both its extension and its limit. When they come on to the stage the curtain rises for the last act of the logical performance. But the length of the play and the number of acts are a matter of the civilization, not of the language. The more or less 'proper' nature of names is not intrinsically determinable nor can it be discovered just by comparing them with the other words in the language. It depends on the point at which a society declares its work of classifying to be complete. To say that a name is perceived as a proper name is to say that it is assigned to a level beyond which no classification is requisite, not absolutely but within a determinate cultural system. Proper names always remain on the margin of classification.

In every system, therefore, proper names represent the *quanta of signification* below which one no longer does anything but point. This brings us to the root of the parallel mistakes committed by Peirce and by Russell, the former in defining proper names as 'indices' and the latter in believing that he had discovered the logical model of proper names in demonstrative pronouns. This amounts in effect to allowing that the act of naming belongs to a continuum in which there is an imperceptible passage from the act of signifying to that of pointing. I hope that I have succeeded in showing that this passage is in fact discontinuous although each culture fixes its thresholds differently. The natural sciences put theirs on the level of species, varieties or subvarieties as the case may be. So terms of different degrees of generality will be regarded each time as proper names. The same mental operation is involved when the native sage – and sometimes scientist – also practising these modes of classification, extends them to individual members of the social group or, more precisely, to the single positions which individuals – each constituting a sub-class – can occupy at the same time or successively. From a formal point of view there is thus no fundamental difference

* Even Vercingetorix which Gardiner regards as a perfect example of an 'embodied' name. Without speculating on the place of Vercingetorix in the system of Gallic names, it is clear that for us it refers to the warrior of ancient times who enjoyed an exclusive name of curious consonance and is not Attila nor Genseric nor Jugurtha nor Ghengiz Khan. As for Popocatepetl, another example dear to Gardiner, every schoolboy, even if ignorant of geography, knows that it must belong to the same class as Titicaca. One classes as best one can.

between the zoologist or the botanist who allots a recently discovered plant the position *Elephantopus spicatus* Aubl., arranged for it by the system (if it has not indeed already been written into it), and the Omaha priest who defines the social paradigms of a new member of the group by conferring the available name *Old-bison's-worn-hoof* on him. They know what they are doing in both cases.

CHAPTER EIGHT

TIME REGAINED

Taking an overall view of the devices and procedures which I have so far been primarily concerned to list, one is first of all struck by the systematic nature of the relations between them. Two aspects of this system are also immediately apparent: its internal coherence and its practically unlimited capacity for extension.

As the examples given show, the structure is in all cases supported by an axis (which it is convenient to picture as vertical). This connects the general with the particular, the abstract with the concrete; but the classificatory intention can always reach its limits whichever direction is in question. These are defined in terms of an implicit axiomatic according to which all classification proceeds by pairs of contrasts: classification only ceases when it is no longer possible to establish oppositions. Strictly speaking, therefore, the system knows no checks. Its internal dynamism is progressively weakened as it proceeds along its axis in either direction. And when the system comes to a halt, this is not because of any unforeseen obstacles presented by empirical properties of beings or things nor through any jamming of its mechanism but because it has completed its course and wholly fulfilled its function.

When the classificatory intention ascends, as it were, towards the greatest generality and most extreme abstraction, no diversity prevents it from applying a scheme through the operation of which reality undergoes a series of progressive purifications, whose final term will be provided, as intended, in the form of a simple binary opposition (high and low, right and left, peace and war, etc.), and beyond which it is, for intrinsic reasons, useless as well as impossible to go. The same operation can be repeated on other planes: on that of the internal organization of the social group, which the so-called totemic classifications allow to grow to the dimensions of an international society by application of a similar scheme of organization to an ever-greater number of groups; or again on the spatio-temporal plane, thanks to a mythical geography which, as an Aranda myth mentioned above* shows, permits the organization of an inexhaustible variety of landscapes by successive reductions which once again terminate in a binary opposition (in this case between directions and elements, since the contrast here is between land and water).

At the lower end there is no external limit to the system either, since it succeeds in treating the qualitative diversity of natural species as the symbolic material of an order, and its progress towards the concrete, particular and individual is not even arrested by the obstacle of personal appellations: even proper names can serve as terms for a classification.

What is in question is thus a total system, which ethnologists in vain tried to pull to pieces in order to fashion them into distinct institutions, of which totemism continues to be the most famous example. But in this way one is led only into paradoxes bordering on the absurd. Thus, Elkin (4, pp. 153–4), in an otherwise admirable work of synthesis, taking totemism as the point of departure for his analysis of the religious thought and organization of Australian natives, when confronted by its theoretical wealth, evades the difficulty by introducing a special heading, 'classificatory totemism'. He thus treats classification as a special form of totemism when in fact, as I hope I have established, it is totemism or so-called totemism, which constitutes not even a mode of classification, but an aspect or moment of it. Comte knew nothing of totemism (and it was no doubt this which saved him from being deceived by a phantom), and though he lacked the evidence which would have confirmed his thesis, yet he had roughly gauged the importance in the history of thought of a classificatory system, whose organization and tenor he understood better than ethnologists of the present day:

> Never since that epoch have human conceptions been able to recover to a degree at all comparable, that great unity of method and homogeneity of doctrine which constitutes the fully normal state of our intelligence, and which it had then acquired spontaneously . . . (Comte, 53e leçon, p. 58).

* Cf. above, pp. 168–9.

No doubt Comte assigns this 'savage mind' to a period of history – to the ages of fetishism and polytheism – while in this book it is neither the mind of savages nor that of primitive or archaic humanity, but rather mind in its untamed state as distinct from mind cultivated or domesticated for the purpose of yielding a return. This latter has appeared at certain points of the globe and at certain moments in history, and it is natural that Comte, lacking ethnographic data (and that ethnographic sense which can be acquired only by the collection and handling of data of this type) should have apprehended the former in its retrospective form, as a mode of mental activity anterior in time to the latter. We are better able to understand today that it is possible for the two to co-exist and interpenetrate in the same way that (in theory at least) it is possible for natural species, of which some are in their savage state and others transformed by agriculture and domestication, to co-exist and cross, although – from the very fact of their development and the general conditions it requires – the existence of the latter threatens the former with extinction. But, whether one deplores or rejoices in the fact, there are still zones in which savage thought, like savage species, is relatively protected. This is the case of art, to which our civilization accords the status of a national park, with all the advantages and inconveniences attending so artificial a formula; and it is particularly the case of so many as yet 'uncleared' sectors of social life, where, through indifference or inability, and most often without our knowing why, primitive thought continues to flourish.

The exceptional features of this mind which we call savage and which Comte described as spontaneous, relate principally to the extensive nature of the ends it assigns itself. It claims at once to analyse and to synthesize, to go to its furthest limits in both directions, while at the same time remaining capable of mediating between the two poles. Comte noted the analytical orientation very well:

> The very superstitions which seem most absurd to us today ... originally had a truly progressive philosophical character, in that they provided, as a rule, a forcible stimulation to persistent observation of phenomena, the exploration of which could not, at that time, directly have inspired any sustained interest (id., p. 70).

The error of judgment of which Comte was guilty in the last proposition explains why he was so entirely mistaken about the synthetical aspect. Contemporary savages were slaves of 'the infinite variety of phenomena' and were, as he thought 'discerning exploration' of them confirmed, unacquainted with any 'nebulous symbolization' (p. 63). Now, 'the discerning exploration of contemporary savages', which is precisely what ethnography practises, invalidates the positivist preconception on both these points. If savage thought is definable both by a consuming symbolic ambition such as humanity has never again seen rivalled, and by scrupulous attention directed entirely towards the concrete, and finally by the implicit conviction that these two attitudes are but one, it is surely precisely because it rests, from a theoretical as well as a practical point of view, on this 'sustained interest' of which Comte denies it to be capable. When man observes, experiments, classifies, and theorizes, he is not impelled by arbitrary superstitions any more than by the vagaries of chance, to which it would, as we saw at the beginning of this book, be naïve to attribute a part in the discovery of the arts of civilization.*

Given only these two explanations to choose from, one would prefer Comte's, provided it were first rid of the paralogism on which it rests. For Comte, all intellectual evolution really proceeds from 'the inevitable primitive dominance of theological philosophy', that is to say, from the fact that originally man found it impossible to interpret natural phenomena without assimilating them 'to his own actions, the only ones whose essential mode of production he could ever believe himself to understand' (id., 51e leçon, IV, p. 347). But how could he have done this without simultaneously making the opposite move of attributing a power and efficacy comparable to that of natural phenomena to his own actions? This man, externalized by man, can serve to shape a god only if the forces of nature have already been internalized in him. The mistake made by Comte and the majority of his successors was to believe that man could at all plausibly have peopled nature with wills comparable to his own without ascribing some of the attributes of this nature, in which he detected himself, to his desires; for the mere sense of his own impotence, had he started with this alone, would never have furnished him with a principle of explanation.

Indeed, the difference between practical action, which produces returns, and magical or ritual action, which lacks efficiency, is not

* Cf. pp. 13–14.

that which one thinks one perceives in defining them in terms of their objective or subjective orientation respectively. This might seem true when one considers things from the outside, but the relation is the opposite from the point of view of the agent: he conceives practical actions as subjective in their principle and centrifugal in their orientation, since they result from his interference in the physical world. Magical operations, on the other hand, appear to him as additions to the objective order of the universe: they present the same necessity to those performing them as the sequence of natural causes, in which the agent believes himself simply to be inserting supplementary links through his rites. He therefore supposes that he observes them from outside and as if they did not emanate from himself.

This rectification of traditional perspectives enables us to dispose of the spurious problem which some see in the 'normal' recourse to fraud and trickery during magical operations. For, if the system of magic rests entirely on the belief that man can intervene in natural determinism to complete or modify its course, then it hardly matters whether he does so a little more or a little less: fraud is consubstantial with magic and, strictly speaking, the sorcerer never 'cheats'. The difference between his theory and his practice is one of degree, not of kind.

Secondly, light is thrown on the question of the relations between magic and religion which is so controversial. For, although it can, in a sense, be said that religion consists in a *humanization of natural laws* and magic in a *naturalization of human actions* – the treatment of certain human actions *as if* they were an integral part of physical determinism – these are not alternatives or stages in an evolution. The anthropomorphism of nature (of which religion consists) and the physiomorphism of man (by which we have defined magic) constitute two components which are always given, and vary only in proportion. As we noticed earlier, each implies the other. There is no religion without magic any more than there is magic without at least a trace of religion. The notion of a supernature exists only for a humanity which attributes supernatural powers to itself and in return ascribes the powers of its superhumanity to nature.

There is therefore no need to invoke the exercise of vanished faculties or the employment of some supernumerary sensibility to understand the penetration which so-called primitives show in their observation and interpretation of natural phenomena. The procedure of the American Indian who follows a trail by means of imperceptible clues or the Australian who unhesitatingly identifies the footprints left by any member of his group (Meggitt) is no different from our procedure when we drive a car and assess the moment to pass or avoid a vehicle at a glance, by a slight turn of the wheels, a fluctuation in the normal speed of the engine or even the supposed intention of a look. This comparison is highly instructive, however incongruous it may seem, for, what sharpens our faculties, stimulates our perception, gives assurance to our judgments is, on the one hand, that the means we command and the risks we run are immeasurably increased by the mechanical power of the engine and, on the other, that the tension resulting from the feeling of this incorporated force exercises itself in a series of dialogues with other drivers whose intentions, similar to our own, are translated into signs which we set about deciphering precisely because they are signs, and call for intellection.

This reciprocity of perspectives, in which man and the world mirror each other and which seems to us the only possible explanation of the properties and capacities of the savage mind, we thus find transposed to the plane of mechanized civilization. An exotic observer would certainly declare the traffic in the centre of a large town or on a motorway to be beyond the scope of human faculties; and so in effect it is, in as much as it is neither men nor natural laws which are brought exactly face to face but systems of natural forces humanized by drivers' intentions and men transformed into natural forces by the physical energy of which they make themselves the mediators. It is no longer a case of the operation of an agent on an inert object, nor of the return action of an object, promoted to the role of an agent, on a subject dispossessing itself in its favour without demanding anything of it in return; in other words, it is no longer situations involving a certain amount of passiveness on one side or the other which are in question. The beings confront each other face to face as subjects and objects at the same time; and, in the code they employ, a simple variation in the distance separating them has the force of a silent adjuration.

This enables us to understand how it is that attentive, meticulous observation turned entirely on the concrete finds both its principle and its result in symbolism. Savage thought does not distinguish the moment of observation and that of interpretation any more than, on observing them, one first registers an interlocutor's signs and then tries to understand them: when he speaks, the signs expressed carry with them their meaning. Articulated language decomposes into elements, each of which is not a sign but rather the medium of a sign: a distinctive unit which could not be replaced by another without a change of meaning, which it expresses by being joined or opposed to other units.

This conception of classificatory systems as systems of meaning will be thrown into relief even more clearly if two traditional problems are briefly discussed; the problem of the relation between so-called totemism and sacrifice, and the problem raised by the similarities exhibited throughout the world by the myths used to explain the origin of clan appellations.

That it should have been possible to regard totemism as the origin of sacrifice in the history of religion remains, after so long, a matter of astonishment. Even if, for convenience, one were to agree to grant totemism a semblance of reality, the two institutions would only look the more contrasting and incompatible, as Mauss, not without hesitation and afterthought, was often led to affirm.

I am not claiming that segmentary societies in which clans are called by animal or plant names could not have practised some forms of sacrifice. The example of the sacrifice of dogs among the Iroquois is sufficient to prove the contrary. But the dog does not serve as any clan's eponym among the Iroquois, and the system of sacrifice is thus independent of that of clan affinities. Above all, there is another reason for which the two systems are mutually exclusive. Granting that in both cases there is an implicit or explicit recognition of an affinity between a man or group of men, and an animal or plant (in the capacity of an eponym of the group of men or in that of a sacrified object replacing a man, or, again, in that of a medium to the human sacrificer), it is clear that in the case of totemism no other species or natural phenomenon is substitutable for the eponym: one beast can never be taken for another. If I am a member of the bear clan, then I cannot belong to the eagle clan, since, as we have seen, the system's sole reality consists in a network of differentiation between terms posited as discontinuous. The opposite is true in the case of sacrifice. Although distinct things are often destined in a preferential manner, for certain deities or certain types of sacrifice, the fundamental principle is that of substitution: in default of the prescribed object, any other can replace it, so long as the intention, the only thing of consequence, persists and although the zeal itself can vary. Sacrifice therefore belongs to the realms of continuity:

> When a cucumber is used as a sacrificial victim Nuer speak of it as an ox. In doing so they are asserting something rather more than that it takes the place of an ox. They do not, of course, say that cucumbers are oxen, and in speaking of a particular cucumber as an ox in a sacrificial situation they are only indicating that it may be thought of as an ox in that particular situation. And they act accordingly by performing the sacrificial rites as closely as possible to what happens when the victim is an ox. The resemblance is conceptual, not perceptual. The 'is' rests on qualitative analogy. And the expression is asymmetrical, a cucumber is an ox, but an ox is not a cucumber (Evans-Pritchard 2, p. 128).

There are therefore two fundamental differences between the system of totemism and that of sacrifice. The former is a quantified system while the latter permits a continuous passage between its terms: a cucumber is worth an egg as a sacrificial victim, an egg a fish, a fish a hen, a hen a goat, a goat an ox. And this gradation is oriented: a cucumber is sacrificed if there is no ox but the sacrifice of an ox for want of a cucumber would be an absurdity. In totemism, or so-called totemism, on the other hand, relations are always reversible. In a system of clan appellations in which both figured, the oxen would be genuinely equivalent to the cucumbers, in the sense that it would be impossible to confound them and that they would be equally suitable for manifesting the differentiation between the groups they respectively connote. But they can only play this part in so far as totemism (as distinct from sacrifice) proclaims them to be distinct and not substitutable for each other.

The underlying reason for these differences is to be found in the respective roles assigned to natural species in each system. Totemism is based on a postulation of homology between two parallel series – that of natural species and that of social groups – whose respective terms, it must be remembered, do not resemble each other in pairs. It is only the relation between the series as a whole which is homomorphic: a formal correlation between two systems of differences, each constituting a pole of opposition. In sacrifice, the series of natural species (continuous and no longer discontinuous, oriented and no longer reversible) plays the part of an intermediary between two polar terms, the sacrificer and the deity, between which there is initially no homology nor even any sort of relation. For, the object of the sacrifice precisely is to establish a relation, not of resemblance but of contiguity, by means of a series of successive identifications. These can be made in either direction, depending on whether the sacrifice is expiatory or represents a rite of communion: thus, either of the person offering the sacrifice with the sacrificer, of the sacrificer with the victim, of the sacralized victim with the deity; or in the reverse order.

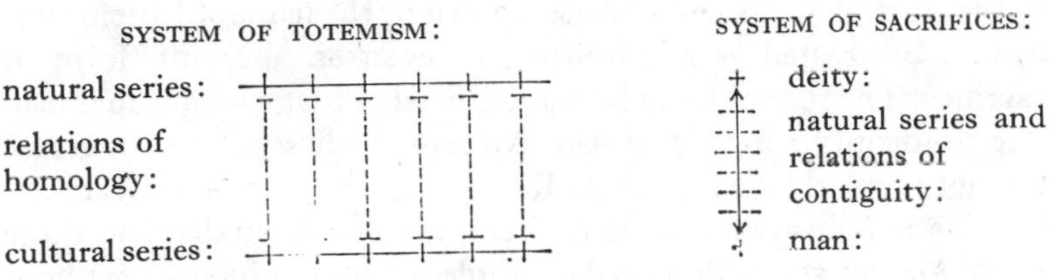

This is not all. Once the relation between man and the deity is secured by sacralization of the victim, the sacrifice breaks it by destroying this same victim. Human action thus brings about an interruption of continuity, and, as it had previously established communication between the human reservoir and the divine reservoir, the latter will automatically fill the gap by discharging the anticipated benefit. The scheme of sacrifice consists in an irreversible operation (the destruction of the victim) with a view to setting off an equally irreversible operation on another plane (the granting of divine grace), which is required by the fact that two 'recipients', situated at different levels, have previously been brought into communication.

So sacrifice is an *absolute* or *extreme* operation which relates to an *intermediary* object. From this point of view, it resembles, though it is at the same time opposed to them, the rites termed 'sacrilegious', such as incest, bestiality, etc., which are *intermediary* operations relating to *extreme* objects. This was shown in an earlier chapter in the case of a minor sacrilege: the appearance of a menstruating woman while the rites of eagle hunting are in progress, among the Hidatsa Indians.* Sacrifice seeks to establish a desired connection between two initially separate domains. As

* Cf. above, p. 51 seq.

language so well expresses it, its object is to bring to pass the *fulfilment* of human prayers by a distant deity. It claims to achieve this by first bringing together the two domains through a sacralized victim (an ambiguous object, in effect attaching to both), and then eliminating this connecting term. The sacrifice thus creates a lack of contiguity, and by the purposive nature of the prayer, it induces (or is supposed to induce) a compensating continuity to arise on the plane where the initial deficiency experienced by the sacrificer traced the path which leads to the deity, in advance and, as it were, by a dotted line.

It follows that the eating of totemic species, sometimes occurring in the Australian rites of increase known by the name of Intichiuma, cannot be treated as a primitive, or even an aberrant, form of sacrifice. The resemblance is as superficial as that which would lead one to identify whales and fish. Moreover, these rites of increase are not regularly connected with so-called totemic classifications; they do not always accompany them, even in Australia, and there are numerous and widespread examples of rites of increase without 'totemism' and of 'totemism' without rites of increase.

Above all, the structure of rites of the Intichiuma type and the implicit ideas on which they rest are very far removed from those we have discerned in sacrifice. In such societies (magical) production and (real) consumption of natural species are normally separate as a result of an identity postulated between each group of men and a totemic species, and a proclaimed or ascertained distinction between different social groups on the one hand and different natural species on the other. The role of the Intichiuma is therefore periodically and momentarily to re-establish the contiguity between production and consumption, as though human groups and natural species had from time to time to count themselves two by two and in pairs of allies, before each taking their own place in the game: species nourishing the men who do not 'produce' them, and men 'producing' the species which they are forbidden to eat. In the Intichiuma, consequently, men momentarily confirm their substantial identity with their respective totemic species, by the two-fold rule that each group is to produce what it consumes and consume what it produces, and these things are the same for each and different for all. Thanks to this, there will no longer be a risk of the normal play of reciprocity creating confusions between fundamental definitions which must be repeated periodically. If the natural series is presented by capitals and the social series by small letters,

A B C D E..........N

a *b* *c* *d* *e*..........*n*

then the Intichiuma recalls the affinity between A and *a*, B and *b*, C and *c*, N and *n*, attesting that when, in the normal course of events, group *b* incorporates, by eating, species A, C, D, E . . . N, group *a* species B, C, D, E . . . N, and so on, what is in question is an exchange between social groups and an arbitrage between resemblance and contiguity, not the replacement of one resemblance by another resemblance nor one contiguity by another contiguity.* Sacrifice turns to comparison as a means of effacing differences and in order to establish contiguity; the so-called totemic meals institute contiguity, but only with a view to making possible a comparison, the anticipated result of which is to confirm differences.

The two systems are therefore opposed by their orientation, metonymical in one case and metaphorical in the other. But this anti-symmetry leaves them still on the same plane, when in fact they are on different levels from the epistemological point of view.

Totemic classifications have a doubly objective basis. There really are natural species, and they do indeed form a discontinuous series; and social segments for their part also exist. Totemism, or so-called totemism, confines itself to conceiving a homology of structure between the two series, a perfectly legitimate hypothesis, for social segments are instituted, and it is in the power of each society to render the hypothesis plausible by shaping its rules and representations accordingly. The system of sacrifice, on the other

* The Indians of eastern Canada do not eat deer-meat while they are hunting the deer, nor trout during the trout-fishing season (Jenness, I, p. 60). So they eat only when they are not killing and kill only when they are not eating. The reciprocity between man and animal species is of the same type as that between two groups of men in some Australian tribes, *the occasion for which* is provided by a natural species. On the other hand, what is in question in Canada is diachronic, and not as in Australia synchronic, reciprocity. The same difference can also be seen among the Keresan group of the Pueblo: 'Each year the . . . toraikatsi chief of the wilderness would select a few wild plant foods and game animals upon which they would concentrate their efforts to bring forth an abundance. They would alter the list of plants and animals somewhat from year to year' (L. A. White, p. 306). This is thus an Intichiuma, but situated on the axis of successiveness instead of the axis of simultaneity.

hand, makes a non-existent term, divinity, intervene; and it adopts a conception of the natural series which is false from the objective point of view, for, as we have seen, it represents it as continuous. To express this difference in level between totemism and sacrifice it is not, then, enough to say that the former is a system of reference and the latter a system of operations, that one works out a schema of interpretation while the other sets up (or claims to set up) a technique for obtaining certain results: that one is true, and the other is false. Rather, to put it precisely, classificatory systems belong to the levels of language: they are codes which, however well or badly made, aim always to make sense. The system of sacrifice, on the other hand, represents a private discourse wanting in good sense for all that it may frequently be pronounced.

In another work I briefly mentioned the myths of origin of so-called totemic institutions, and showed that even in regions distant from each other and despite the difference in their stories, these myths all teach the same lesson, namely: (1) that so-called totemic institutions are based on a global correspondence between two series, not on particular correspondences between their terms; (2) that the correspondence in question is metaphorical, and not metonymical; and (3) that it becomes evident only after each series has first been impoverished by a suppression of elements so that their internal discontinuity emerges clearly (Lévi-Strauss 6, pp. 19–20 and 26–7).

There is a singular contrast between the precision and wealth of this lesson (the more striking as the myths analysed are known to us only in abridged or mutilated versions)* and the insignificance of myths accounting for the appellations of each clan. The latter are all very much alike throughout the world, but notably in their poverty. Certainly Australia possesses complex myths which lend themselves to a semantic analysis inspired by that which we have applied to myths of other regions (Stanner 2). Nevertheless, specialists on this continent are used to collecting myths in which the attribution of a half-human, half-animal ancestor to a totemic group rests on a mere statement: the myth establishes that the ancestor appeared at such and such a place, followed such and such a course, performed certain actions in this or that place,

* Firth (2) has just published more complete versions of Tikopia myth.

which mark him out as the originator of geographical features which can still be seen, finally that he stopped or disappeared in a particular spot. Properly speaking, therefore, the myth amounts to the description of an itinerary and adds little or nothing to the remarkable facts which it claims to establish: that a particular course, and the water-points, thickets, or rocks which mark it, are of sacred value for a human group and that this group proclaims its affinity with this or that natural species: caterpillar, ostrich, or kangaroo.

No doubt, as T. G. H. Strehlow has pointed out, the exclusive use of *pidgin* for a long time forced enquirers to content themselves with sketchy and ridiculous versions. But, in the first place, we now have plenty of texts with interlinear translations and of adaptations which are the work of competent specialists; and, secondly, myths of exactly the same type are found in other regions of the world where the linguistic difficulties were more quickly overcome. I shall restrict myself to three examples, all from America. The first two come from the Northern and Southern United States respectively, and the third from Central Brazil.

The Menomini explain their clan names by saying that when the bear was endowed with human form, he settled down with his wife not far from the mouth of the Menomini river. Here they fished the sturgeons which constituted their only food (the bear and sturgeon clans belong to the same phratry). One day, three thunder birds perched on the great ledge of rock which projects into Lake Winnebago, near the place called Fond du Lac. After changing into men, they visited the bears and came to an agreement with them to convoke several animals whose place of birth or residence is specified by the myth. They all set off. When they arrived at Green Bay on Lake Michigan an obliging wave carried the wolf, who could not swim, to the other bank. In token of his gratitude, he adopted the wave as one of his clan totems. An analogous incident, placed near Mackinaw, also on Lake Michigan, resulted in the association of the black bear and the bald eagle. The relations between the other clans (elk, crane, dog, deer, beaver, etc.) were likewise established through fortuitous meetings and services rendered (Hoffman, pp. 39–42 ; Skinner I, p. 8, ff.).

The reason why the Hopi wild mustard clan bears this name as well as those of oak, chaparral-cock, and warrior is that, during a legendary migration, they tried to stop a child crying by offering it mustard leaves and a branch of oak, gathered and cut on the way. After this, they met the cock and then the warrior. The badger and butterfly clan is so-called because its ancestors took with them a man-badger whose acquaintance they had made a short time before they caught a butterfly to amuse a child; but the child was ill and it was Badger who cured him with simples. The ancestors of the rabbit and tobacco clan found the plant and met the animal. Those of the Patki clan took the names of lake, cloud, rain, snow, and fog as a result of various incidents on their journey. Somewhere between the actual site of Phoenix (Arizona) and the Little Colorado, the ancestors of the bear clan came upon a dead bear, whence their name; but another band found the skin, from which small rodents had taken the hair to line their holes. They made hide straps out of the skin, and since then the hide strap and bear clans have been associated. A third band took the name of the rodents and was allied to the former clans (Voth 4, Parsons, pp. 26–30).

Let us now turn to South America. The Bororo say that the sun and moon belong to the Badedgeba clan of the Cera moiety on account of a dispute between a father and son, who both wanted to appropriate the names of these heavenly bodies. A compromise gave the father the names of Sun and Bath-of-the-Sun. Tobacco belongs to the Paiwe clan because an Indian belonging to it happened by chance to discover its leaves in the innards of a fish he was gutting in order to cook. The chief of the 'black' Badedgeba clan at one time possessed some black and some red birds (*Phimosus infuscatus* and *Ibis rubra* respectively), but his colleague 'red' Babedgeba stole them from him and he had to agree to a division according to colour (Colbacchini).

All these myths of origin of clan appellations are so similar that it is unnecessary to cite examples from other parts of the world, such as Africa where they also abound. What, then, are their common characteristics? In the first place, they all have in common a brevity leaving room for none of those apparent digressions which often have a wealth of concealed meaning. A story reduced to its essential outlines has no surprises in store for the analyst. Secondly, these myths are falsely aetiological (supposing that a myth could be genuinely so) in as much as the kind of explanation they give is reducible to a scarcely modified statement of the initial position; from this point of view they appear redundant. Their role seems to be demarcative, rather than aetiological; they do not really explain an origin or indicate a cause; what they do is to invoke an origin or cause (*insignificant* in itself), to make the most of some detail or to 'stress' a species. This detail or that species acquires a differential value not because of the particular origin attributed to it but just because it is endowed with an origin when other details or species are not. History is surreptitiously introduced into the structure in a modest, almost negative way: it does not account for the present, but it makes a selection between its elements, according only some of them the privilege of having a past. The poverty of totemic myths is therefore due to the fact that the function of each is only to establish a difference as a difference: they are the constitutive units of a system. The question of significance does not arise at the level of each myth taken in isolation but at that of the system of which they form the elements.

Now, here we again encounter a paradox discussed earlier:* the systems with which we are concerned are not easily 'mythologizable' as systems because their virtually synchronic nature is engaged in a never-ending struggle with diachrony. *Ex hypothesi* the elements of the system are on this side of myth, but, in terms of its destination, the set lies always beyond; myth, as it were, runs after it to catch up with it. It only exceptionally succeeds because the system is constantly being drawn in by history; and when one thinks it has succeeded a new doubt makes itself felt: do mythical representations correspond to an actual structure which models social and religious practices or do they translate only the congealed image by means of which native philosophers give themselves the illusion of fixing a reality which escapes them? Important as Marcel Griaule's discoveries in Africa are, one often wonders to which of these interpretations they relate.

The earliest theories on totemism are, as it were, contaminated by this paradox, which they were unable to formulate clearly. The reason why McLennan, and later Robertson Smith and Frazer (IV, pp. 73–6, 264–5) were so convinced that totemism was anterior to exogamy (a proposition which I find meaningless) was that the former appeared to them simply denotative, whereas they divined the systematic nature of the latter. Now, systems can be established only between elements which are already denoted. But to perceive totemism too as a system it would have been necessary to place it in the linguistic, taxonomic, mythical, and ritual context from

* Cf. above, pp. 66–71.

which, in their concern to trace the contours of an arbitrary institution, they began by isolating it.

In fact, as I have tried to show, matters are not so simple. The ambiguity of totemism is real, even if the institution we have imagined in the hope of getting rid of it is not. Indeed, so-called totemism may either present or preclude the characteristics of a system, depending on the point of view adopted: it is a grammar fated to degenerate into a lexicon. Unlike other systems of classification, which are primarily *conceived* (like myths) or *acted* (like rites), totemism is always *lived*, that is to say, it attaches to concrete groups and concrete individuals because it is an *hereditary system of classification.**

This enables us to understand the appearance of a permanent conflict between the structural nature of the classification and the statistical nature of its demographic basis. The classification tends to be dismantled like a palace swept away upon the flood, whose parts, through the effect of currents and stagnant waters, obstacles and straits, come to be combined in a manner other than that intended by the architect. In totemism, therefore, function inevitably triumphs over structure. The problem it has never ceased presenting to theorists is that of the relation between structure and event. And the great lesson of totemism is that the form of the structure can sometimes survive when the structure itself succumbs to events.

There is thus a sort of fundamental antipathy between history and systems of classification. This perhaps explains what one is tempted to call the 'totemic void', for in the bounds of the great civilizations of Europe and Asia there is a remarkable absence of anything which might have reference to totemism, even in the form of remains. The reason is surely that the latter have elected to explain themselves by history and that this undertaking is incompatible with that of classifying things and beings (natural and social) by means of finite groups. Totemic classifications no doubt divide their groups into an original and a derivative series: the former contains zoological and botanical species in their supernatural aspect, the latter human groups in their cultural aspect, and the former is asserted to have existed before the latter, having in some sort engendered it. The original series, however, lives on in diachrony through animal and plant species, alongside the human series.

* No doubt some forms of totemism are not, properly speaking, hereditary; but even in this case, the system is sustained by concrete men.

The two series exist in time but under an atemporal regime, since, being both real, they sail through time together, remaining such as they were at the moment of separation. The original series is always there, ready to serve as a system of reference for the interpretation and rectification of the changes taking place in the derivative series. In theory, if not in practice, history is subordinated to system.

When, however, a society sides with history, classification into finite groups becomes impossible because the derivative series, instead of reproducing the original series, merges with it to form a single series in which each term is derivative in relation to the one preceding it and original in relation to the one coming after it. Instead of a once-for-all homology between two series each finite and discontinuous in its own right, a continuous evolution is postulated within a single series that accepts an unlimited number of terms.

Some Polynesian mythologies are at the critical point where diachrony irrevocably prevails over synchrony, making it impossible to interpret the human order as a fixed projection of the natural order by which it is engendered; it is prolongation, rather than a reflection, of the natural order:

> Fire and water married, and from them sprung the earth, rocks, trees, and everything. The cuttle-fish fought with the fire and was beaten. The fire fought with the rocks, and the rocks conquered. The large stones fought with the small ones; the small ones conquered. The small stones fought with the grass, and the grass conquered. The trees fought with the creepers, the trees were beaten and the creepers conquered. The creepers rotted, swarmed with maggots, and from maggots they grew to be men (G. Turner, pp. 6–7).

This evolutionism precludes any synthesis of a totemic type, for things and natural beings do not afford the static model of a likewise static diversity between human groups: they are ordered as the genesis of a humanity whose advent they prepare. But this incompatibility in turn raises a problem, namely: how, if it exists, do classificatory systems succeed in eliminating history or, when that is impossible, integrating it?

I have suggested elsewhere that the clumsy distinction between 'peoples without history' and others could with advantage be replaced by a distinction between what for convenience I called 'cold' and 'hot' societies: the former seeking, by the institutions they give themselves, to annul the possible effects of historical factors on their equilibrium and continuity in a quasi-automatic fashion; the latter resolutely internalizing the historical process and making it the moving power of their development (Charbonnier, pp. 35–47; Lévi-Strauss 4, pp. 41–3). Several types of historical sequences will still need to be distinguished. Some, while existing in duration, are of a recurrent nature; the annual cycle of the seasons, for instance, or that of individual life or that of exchanges of goods and services within the social group. These sequences raise no problem because they are periodically repeated in duration without their structure necessarily undergoing any change; the object of 'cold' societies is to make it the case that the order of temporal succession should have as little influence as possible on their content. No doubt they do not succeed perfectly; but this is the norm they set themselves. Apart from the fact that the procedures they employ are more efficacious than some contemporary ethnologists (Vogt) are willing to admit, the real question is not what genuine results they obtain but rather by what lasting purpose they are guided, for their image of themselves is an essential part of their reality.

It is tedious as well as useless, in this connection, to amass arguments to prove that all societies are in history and change: that this is so is patent. But in getting embroiled in a superfluous demonstration, there is a risk of overlooking the fact that human societies react to this common condition in very different fashions. Some accept it, with good or ill grace, and its consequences (to themselves and other societies) assume immense proportions through their attention to it. Others (which we call primitive for this reason) want to deny it and try, with a dexterity we underestimate, to make the states of their development which they consider 'prior' as permanent as possible. It is not sufficient, in order that they should succeed, that their institutions should exercise a regulating action on the recurrent sequences by limiting the incidence of demographic factors, smoothing down antagonisms which manifest themselves within the group or between groups and perpetuating the framework in which individual and collective activities take place.* It is also necessary that these

* At the beginning of a recent study, G. Balandier announced with much ceremony that it is high time that the social sciences 'grasped society in its actual

non-recurrent chains of events whose effects accumulate to produce economic and social upheavals, should be broken as soon as they form, or that the society should have an effective procedure to prevent their formation. We are acquainted with this procedure, which consists not in denying the historical process but in admitting it as a form without content. There is indeed a before and an after, but their sole significance lies in reflecting each other. It is thus that all the activities of the Northern Aranda reproduce those that their totemic ancestors are still believed to perform:

The *gurra* ancestor hunts, kills, and eats bandicoots; and his sons are always engaged upon the same quest. The witchetty grub men of Lukara spend every day of their lives in digging up grubs from the roots of acacia trees. . . . The *ragia* (wild plum tree) ancestor lives on the *ragia* berries which he is continually collecting into a large wooden vessel. The crayfish ancestor is always building fresh weirs across the course of the moving flood of water which he is pursuing; and he is for ever engaged in spearing fish . . . if the myths gathered in the Northern Aranda area are treated collectively, a full and very detailed account will be found of all the occupations which are still practised in Central Australia. In his myths we see the native at his daily task of hunting, fishing, gathering vegetable food, cooking, and fashioning his implements. All occupations originated with the totemic ancestors; and here, too, the native follows tradition blindly: he clings to the primitive weapons used by his forefathers, and no thought of improving them ever enters his mind (T.G.H. Strehlow, pp. 34–5).

I select this in preference to all the other evidence to the same purpose available from other parts of the world because it emanates from an ethnologist born and brought up among the natives, speaking their language fluently and remaining deeply attached to

life and development'. After which he describes, in very pertinent fashion moreover, institutions whose object is, to use his own terms, to 'regroup' lineages threatened with dispersion; to 'allay' their crumbling; to 'recall' their solidarity, 'establish' communication with the ancestors, 'prevent separated members of the clan from becoming strangers to each other', furnish 'an instrument of protection against conflicts', 'control' and 'master' antagonisms and subversions by means of a 'minutely regulated' ritual which is 'a factor reinforcing social and political structures'. One is easily in agreement with him (while, however, questioning whether he is so with his own premises), that the institutions he began by denying to have been founded on 'logical relations' and 'fixed structures' (p. 23) demonstrate in fact the 'prevalence of traditional social logic' (p. 33), and that 'the classical system thus reveals, over a long period, a surprising capacity for "assimilating" . . .' (p. 34). The only surprising thing in all this is the author's own surprise.

them. He can be suspected of neither incomprehension nor ill-will. It is no doubt difficult for us (as it is for him, judging by what follows in the text) not to pass an unfavourable judgment on an attitude so flagrantly in contradiction with the avid need for change characteristic of our own civilization. However, the obstinate fidelity to a past conceived as a timeless model, rather than as a stage in the historical process, betrays no moral or intellectual deficiency whatsoever. It expresses a consciously or unconsciously adopted attitude, the systematic nature of which is attested all over the world by that endlessly repeated justification of every technique, rule, and custom in the single argument: the ancestors taught it to us. As for us in other domains until recently, antiquity and continuance are the foundations of legitimacy. But the antiquity is conceived as absolute, for it goes back to the origin of the world, and the continuance admits neither of orientation or of degree.

Mythical history thus presents the paradox of being both disjoined from and conjoined with the present. It is disjoined from it because the original ancestors were of a nature different from contemporary men: they were creators and these are imitators. It is conjoined with it because nothing has been going on since the appearance of the ancestors except events whose recurrence periodically effaces their particularity. It remains to be shown how the savage mind succeeds not only in overcoming this twofold contradiction, but also in deriving from it the materials of a coherent system in which diachrony, in some sort mastered, collaborates with synchrony without the risk of further conflicts arising between them.

Thanks to ritual, the 'disjoined' past of myth is expressed, on the one hand, through biological and seasonal periodicity and, on the other, through the 'conjoined' past, which unites from generation to generation the living and the dead. This synchro-diachronic system has been well analysed by Sharp (p. 71), who divides the rites of the Australian tribes of the Cape York Peninsula into three categories. The *rites of control* are positive or negative. They aim to increase or restrict species or totemic phenomena, sometimes for the benefit of, sometimes to the detriment of the group, by fixing the quantity of spirits or spirit-substance allowed to emanate from the totemic centres established by the ancestors at various points in the tribal territory. The commemorative or *historical rites* recreate the sacred and beneficial atmosphere of mythical times –

the 'dream age', as the Australians call it – mirroring its protagonists and their great deeds. The *mourning rites* correspond to an inverse procedure: instead of charging living men with the personification of remote ancestors, these rites assure the conversion of men who are no longer living men into ancestors. It can thus be seen that the function of the system of ritual is to overcome and integrate three oppositions: that of diachrony and synchrony; that of the periodic or non-periodic features which either may exhibit; and, finally, within diachrony, that of reversible and irreversible time, for, although present and past are theoretically distinct, the historical rites bring the past into the present and the rites of mourning the present into the past, and the two processes are not equivalent: mythical heroes can truly be said to return, for their only reality lies in their personification; but human beings die for good. Hence the schema:

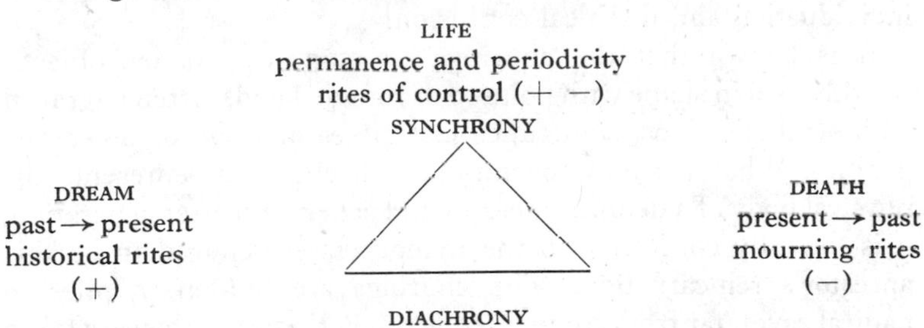

In central Australia, this system is completed or reinforced by the usage of the churinga or tjurunga which has given rise to a great deal of past and present speculation. The above considerations help to explain it. The commemorative and funeral rites postulate that the passage between past and present is possible in both directions. They do not furnish the proof of it. They pronounce on diachrony but they still do so in terms of synchrony since the very fact of celebrating them is tantamount to changing past into present. It is therefore understandable that some groups should have sought to give tangible confirmation of the diachronic essence of diachrony at the very heart of synchrony. From this point of view it is significant that the importance of the churinga is especially great among the Western and Northern Aranda and diminishes until it disappears altogether as one progresses northwards. The problem of the relation between diachrony and synchrony is indeed made even thornier among the Aranda groups by the fact that they represent the totemic ancestors not, in the manner of the Arabanna and Warramunga (Spencer and Gillen, pp. 161–2), as individualized heroes from whom the members of the totemic group are supposed to be directly descended, but as an indistinct multitude and this ought to exclude, in principle, the very notion of genealogical continuity. In fact, as we saw earlier,* among the Aranda, from one point of view it is as if every individual had before his birth drawn an anonymous ancestor by lot, of whom he then became the reincarnation. No doubt because of the refinements of their social organization which lavishes on synchrony the benefits of clear-cut distinctions and precise definitions, even the relation between past and present appeared to them in terms of synchrony. The role of the churinga would therefore be to offset the correlative impoverishment of the diachronic dimension. They are the past materially present and they provide the means of reconciling empirical individuation and mythical confusion.

It is known that the churinga are stone or wooden objects, roughly oval in shape with pointed or rounded ends, often engraved with symbolic signs, sometimes just pieces of wood or unworked pebbles. Whatever its appearance, each churinga represents the physical body of a definite ancestor and generation after generation, it is formally conferred on the living person believed to be this ancestor's reincarnation. The churinga are hidden in piles in natural caves, far from frequented ways. Periodically they are taken out to be inspected and handled, and on these occasions they are always polished, greased and coloured, and prayers and incantations are addressed to them. Their role and the treatment accorded to them thus have striking analogies with the documentary archives which we secrete in strongboxes or entrust to the safe-keeping of solicitors and which we inspect from time to time with the care due to sacred things, to repair them if necessary or to commit them to smarter dossiers. On these occasions we too are prone to recite great myths recalled to us by the contemplation of the torn and yellowed pages: the deeds and achievements of our ancestors, the history of our homes from the time they were built or first acquired.

It is not therefore profitable to look as far afield as Durkheim did to discover the reason for the sacred character of the churinga. When an exotic custom fascinates us in spite of (or on account of) its apparent singularity, it is generally because it presents us with a

* **Cf. above, p. 81.**

distorted reflection of a familiar image, which we confusedly recognize as such without yet managing to identify it. Durkheim (pp. 120–3) would have it that the churinga were sacred because they bore the totemic mark, drawn or engraved on them. But, in the first place, it is now known that this is not always so. T.G.H Strehlow draws attention, among the Northern Aranda, to stone churinga, valued above the rest which he describes as 'insignificant and rude objects, roughly polished by being rubbed together during increase ceremonies' (p. 54); and among the Southern Aranda he saw churinga which are 'plain pieces . . . of wood, devoid of markings and heavily coated with a thick lumpy mixture of red ochre and grease' (p. 73). The churinga can even be a smooth pebble, a natural rock or a tree (p. 95). Secondly, according to Durkheim's own argument, his account of the churinga had to confirm one of his fundamental theses, that of the emblematic nature of totemism. The sacredness of the churinga, the most sacred objects known to the Aranda, had to be explained by an emblematic figuration of the totem to show that the represented totem is more sacred than the real one. But, as I have already said, there is no such thing as the real totem;* the individual animal plays the part of the signifying, and the sacredness attaches neither to it nor to its icon but to the signified, which either can stand for. After all, a document does not become sacred by virtue of bearing a stamp which has prestige, such as that of the *Archives Nationales*: it bears the stamp because it has first been acknowledged to be sacred, and it would remain so without it.

Nor can it be said, following another explanation which Durkheim moreover relates to the preceding one, that the churinga *is* the ancestor's body. This Aranda formula, quoted by C. Strehlow, must be taken in its metaphorical sense. The ancestor does not lose his body because at the moment of conception he surrenders his

* Cf. above, p. 148.
There is no single chief ruling an entire Indian tribe, but a chief in every band; similarly there is no single boss for every species of animal or plant, but a boss in each locality. The bosses are always larger than other plants and animals of their kind, and in the case of birds, fish, and animals, always white. Now and then the Indians see and kill them, but generally they keep out of sight of human beings. They are like the government in Ottawa, an old Indian remarked. An ordinary Indian can never see the 'government'. He is sent from one office to another, is introduced to this man and to that, each of whom sometimes claims to be the 'boss', but he never sees the real government, who keeps himself hidden (Jenness, I, p. 61).

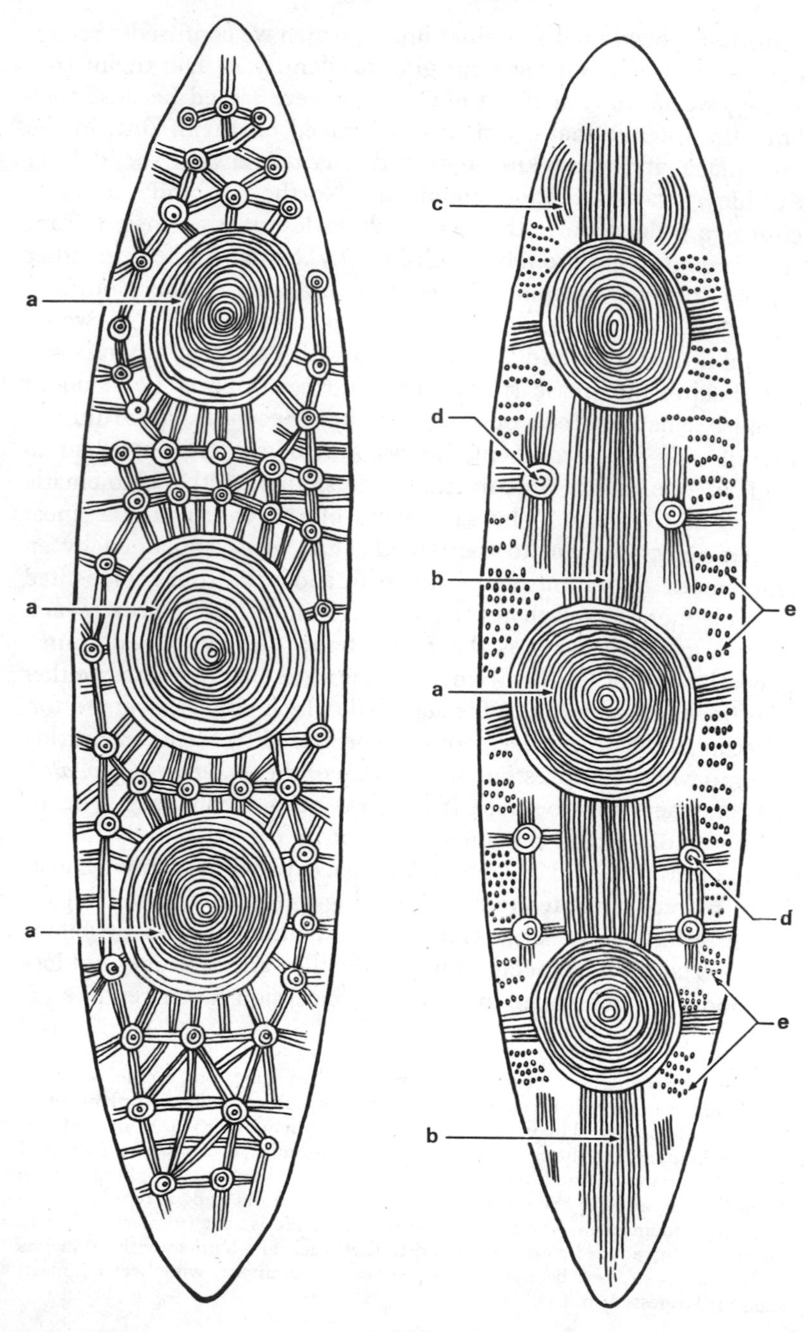
a
a
a
c
d
b
e
a
d
e
b

churinga (or one of them) to the next incarnation. Rather, the churinga furnishes the tangible proof that the ancestor and his living descendant are of one flesh. Were this not so, how could it be that if the original churinga is not discovered on the site where the woman was mystically fertilized, another is fabricated to take its place? This probative feature of the churinga is another respect in which they resemble documentary archives, particularly title-deeds, which pass through the hands of all the successive purchasers (and can be restored in case of loss or destruction), but that, in their case, it is a question of a moral and physical personality held by a usufructurary, and not of the real property of an owner. And although in our case also archives are the most valuable and sacred of all goods, we, like the the Aranda, sometimes come to entrust them to foreign groups. And if we send Louis XIV's will to the United States or the United States lends France the Declaration of Independence or the Liberty Bell, this is proof that, in the Aranda informant's own words:

> . . . we are living at peace with our neighbours: we cannot engage in strife or fight with men who are guarding our tjuringa and who have entrusted their tjuringa to our safe-keeping (T. G. H. Strehlow, p. 161).

But why do we set such store by our archives? The events to which they relate are independently attested, in innumerable ways: they survive in the present and in our books; in themselves they are devoid of meaning; they acquire it entirely through their historical repercussions and the commentaries which explain them by relating them to other events. Paraphrasing an argument of Durkheim's, we might say of archives that they are after all only pieces of paper.* They need only all have been published, for our know-

* . . . in themselves, the churinga are objects of woods and stone like . . . [so many] others . . . (Durkheim, p. 122).

Fig 11 *Churinga of an Aranda man of the Frog totem.* The large concentric circles (*a*) represent three celebrated trees which mark the totemic site near the Hugh River. The straight lines between them (*b*) depict their large roots, and the curved lines (*c*) their smaller roots. The small concentric circles (*d*) represent less important trees with their roots, and the dotted lines (*e*) are the tracks of the frogs as they hop about in the sand of the river bed. The frogs themselves are represented on one side of the churinga (see the left) by the complicated network of lines (their limbs) linking small concentric circles (their bodies) (from B. Spencer and F. J. Gillen, *The Native Tribes of Central Australia*, new ed., London, 1938, pp. 145–7).

ledge and condition to be totally unaffected were a cataclysm to destroy the originals. We should, however, feel this loss as an irreparable injury that strikes to the core of our being. And not without reason: if my account of churinga is correct, their sacredness attaches to the function of diachronic significance which they alone attest in a system which, being classificatory, is displayed in its entirety in a synchrony that succeeds even in assimilating duration. The churinga are the palpable proofs of mythical times, the *Alcheringa*, which could still be conceived without them but of which there would no longer be any physical evidence. Similarly, our past would not disappear if we lost our archives: it would be deprived of what one is inclined to call its diachronic flavour. It would still exist as a past but preserved in nothing but contemporary or recent books, institutions, or even a situation. So it too would be exhibited in synchrony.

The virtue of archives is to put us in contact with pure historicity. As I have already said about myths concerning the origin of totemic appellations, their value does not lie in the intrinsic significance of the events evoked: these can be insignificant or even entirely absent, if what is in question is a few lines of autograph or a signature out of context. But think of the value of Johann Sebastian Bach's signature to one who cannot hear a bar of his music without a quickening of his pulse. As for events themselves, I have pointed out that they are attested otherwise than by the authentic documents, and generally better. Archives thus provide something else: on the one hand they constitute events in their radical contingence (since only interpretation, which forms no part of them, can ground them in reason), and, on the other, they give a physical existence to history, for in them alone is the contradiction of a completed past and a present in which it survives, surmounted. Archives are the embodied essence of the event.

By this approach we recover, at the very centre of the savage mind, that pure history to which we were already led by totemic myths. It is not inconceivable that some of the events they relate are genuine, even if the picture they paint of them is symbolic and distorted (Elkin 4, p. 210). However, this is not at issue, for all historical events are to a large extent the products of the historian's choice of categories. Even if mythical history is false, it at least manifests in a pure and accentuated form (the more so, one might say, because it *is* false) the characteristic traits of an historical event.

These depend on the one hand on its contingent status (the ancestor appeared in such and such a spot; he went here, then there; he performed this and that deed . . .) and on the other on its power of arousing intense and varied feelings:

> The Northern Aranda clings to his native soil with every fibre of his being. He will always speak of his own 'birthplace' with love and reverence. Today, tears will come into his eyes when he mentions an ancestral home site which has been, sometimes unwittingly desecrated by the white usurpers of his group territory. . . . Love of home, longing for home, these are dominating motives which constantly re-appear also in the myths of the totemic ancestors (T. G. H. Strehlow, pp. 30–1).

Now, this passionate love of the soil is primarily accounted for historically:

> Mountains and creeks and springs and water-holes are, to him [the native] not merely interesting or beautiful scenic features . . .; they are the handiwork of ancestors from whom he himself has descended. He sees recorded in the surrounding landscape the ancient story of the lives and the deeds of the immortal beings whom he reveres; beings, who for a brief space may take on human shape once more; beings, many of whom he has known in his own experience as his fathers and grandfathers and brothers, and as his mothers and sisters. The whole countryside is his living, age-old family tree. The story of his own doings at the beginning of time, at the dim dawn of life, when the world as he knows it now was being shaped and moulded by all-powerful hands (ibid., pp. pp. 30–31).

When it is noted that these events and sites are the same as those which furnished the materials of the symbolic systems to which the previous chapters were devoted, it must be acknowledged that so-called primitive peoples have managed to evolve not unreasonable methods for inserting irrationality, in its dual aspect of logical contingence and emotional turbulence, into rationality. Classificatory systems thus allow the incorporation of history, even and particularly that which might be thought to defy the system. For make no mistake: the totemic myths which solemnly relate futile incidents and sentimentalize over particular places are comparable only to minor, lesser history: that of the dimmest chroniclers. Those same societies, whose social organization and marriage rules require the efforts of mathematicians for their interpretation, and whose cosmology astonishes philosophers, recognize no break in the continuity between the lofty theorizing to which they devote themselves in these domains and a history which is that not of a Burckhardt or Spengler but of a Lenôtre and a La Force. Considered in this light, the style of the Aranda water colourists will perhaps appear less unexpected. And nothing in our civilization more closely resembles the periodic pilgrimages made by the initiated Australians, escorted by their sages, than our conducted tours to Goethe's or Victor Hugo's house, the furniture of which inspires emotions as strong as they are arbitrary. As in the case of the churinga, the main thing is not that the bed is the selfsame one on which it is proved Van Gogh slept: all the visitor asks is to be shown it.

CHAPTER NINE

HISTORY AND DIALECTIC

In the course of this work I have allowed myself, not without ulterior motive, to borrow a certain amount of Sartre's vocabulary. I wanted to lead the reader to face a problem, the discussion of which will serve to introduce my conclusion. The problem is to what extent thought that can and will be both anecdotal and geometrical may yet be called dialectical. The savage mind totalizes. It claims indeed to go very much further in this direction than Sartre allows dialectical reason, for, on the one hand, the latter lets pure seriality escape (and we have just seen how classificatory systems succeed in incorporating it) and, on the other, it excludes schematization, in which these same systems reach their consummation. In my view, it is in this intransigent refusal on the part of the savage mind to allow anything human (or even living) to remain alien to it, that the real principle of dialectical reason is to be found. But my idea of the latter is very different from Sartre's.

In reading the *Critique* it is difficult to avoid feeling that Sartre vacillates between two conceptions of dialectical reason. Sometimes he opposes dialectical and analytical reason as truth and error, if not as God and the devil, while at other times these two kinds of reason are apparently complementary, different routes to the same truths. The first conception not only discredits scientific knowledge and finally even leads to suggesting the impossibility of a science of biology, it also involves a curious paradox; for the work entitled *Critique de la raison dialectique* is the result of the author's exercise of his own analytical reason: he defines, distinguishes, classifies and opposes. This philosophical treatise is no different in kind from the works it examines and with which it engages in discussion, if only to condemn them. It is difficult to see how analytical reason could be applied to dialectical reason and claim to establish it, if the two are defined by mutually exclusive characteristics. The second conception is open to a different objection: if dialectical and analytical reason ultimately arrive at the same results, and if their respective truths merge into a single truth, then, one may ask in what way they are opposed and, in particular, on what grounds the former should be pronounced superior to the latter. Sartre's endeavour seems contradictory in the one case and superfluous in the other.

How is the paradox to be explained, and avoided? Sartre attributes a reality *sui generis* to dialectical reason in both the hypotheses between which he hesitates. It exists independently of analytical reason, as its antagonist or alternatively its complement. Although in both our cases Marx is the point of departure of our thought, it seems to me that the Marxist orientation leads to a different view, namely, that the opposition between the two sorts of reason is relative, not absolute. It corresponds to a tension within human thought which may persist indefinitely *de facto*, but which has no basis *de jure*. In my view dialectical reason is always constitutive: it is the bridge, forever extended and improved, which analytical reason throws out over an abyss; it is unable to see the further shore but it knows that it is there, even should it be constantly receding. The term dialectical reason thus covers the perpetual efforts analytical reason must make to reform itself if it aspires to account for language, society and thought; and the distinction between the two forms of reason in my view rests only on the temporary gap separating analytical reason from the understanding of life. Sartre calls analytical reason reason in repose; I call the same reason dialectical when it is roused to action, tensed by its efforts to transcend itself.

In Sartre's terminology I am therefore to be defined as a transcendental materialist and aesthete. I am a transcendental materialist (p. 124) because I do not regard dialectical reason as *something other than* analytical reason, upon which the absolute originality of a human order would be based, but as *something additional in* analytical reason: the necessary condition for it to venture to undertake the resolution of the human into the non-human. And I count as an aesthete since Sartre applies this term to anyone purporting to study men as if they were ants (p. 183). But apart from the fact that this seems to me just the attitude of any scientist who is an agnostic, there is nothing very compromising about it, for ants with their artificial tunnels, their social life and their chemical messages, already present a sufficiently tough resistance to the enterprises of analytical reason . . . So I accept the characterization of aesthete in so far as I believe the ultimate goal of the human sciences to be not to constitute, but to dissolve man. The pre-eminent value of anthropology is that it represents the first step in a procedure which involves others. Ethnographic analysis tries to arrive at invariants beyond the empirical diversity of human societies; and, as the present work shows, these are sometimes to be found at the most unforeseen points. Rousseau (2, ch. VIII) foresaw this with his usual acumen: 'One needs to look near at hand if one wants to study men; but to study man one must learn to look from afar; one must first observe differences in order to discover attributes'. However, it would not be enough to reabsorb particular humanities into a general one. This first enterprise opens the way for others which Rousseau would not have been so ready to accept and which are incumbent on the exact natural sciences: the reintegration of culture in nature and finally of life within the whole of its physico-chemical conditions.*

However, in spite of the intentionally brutal turn given to my thesis, I am not blind to the fact that the verb 'dissolve' does not in any way imply (but even excludes) the destruction of the constituents of the body subjected to the action of another body. The solution of a solid into a liquid alters the disposition of its molecules. It also often provides an efficacious method of putting them by so that they can be recovered in case of need and their properties be better studied. The reductions I am envisaging are thus legitimate, or indeed possible, only if two conditions are satisfied. First, the phenomena subjected to reduction must not be impoverished; one must be certain that everything contributing to their distinctive richness and originality has been collected around them. For it is pointless to pick up a hammer unless to hit the nail on the head.

Secondly, one must be ready to accept, as a consequence of each reduction, the total overturning of any preconceived idea concerning the level, whichever it may be, one is striving to attain. The idea of some general humanity to which ethnographic reduction leads, will bear no relation to any one may have formed in advance. And when we do finally succeed in understanding life as a function of

* The opposition between nature and culture to which I attached much importance at one time (1, ch. 1 and 2) now seems to be of primarily methodological importance.

inert matter, it will be to discover that the latter has properties very different from those previously attributed to it. Levels of reduction cannot therefore be classed as superior and inferior, for the level taken as superior must, through the reduction, be expected to communicate retroactively some of its richness to the inferior level to which it will have been assimilated. Scientific explanation consists not in moving from the complex to the simple but in the replacement of a less intelligible complexity by one which is more so.

Seen in this light, therefore, my self is no more opposed to others than man is opposed to the world: the truths learnt through man are 'of the world', and they are important for this reason.* This explains why I regard anthropology as the principle of all research, while for Sartre it raises a problem in the shape of a constraint to overcome or a resistance to reduce. And indeed what can one make of peoples 'without history' when one has defined man in terms of dialectic and dialectic in terms of history? Sometimes Sartre seems tempted to distinguish two dialectics: the 'true' one which is supposed to be that of historical societies, and a repetitive, short-term dialectic, which he grants so-called primitive societies whilst at the same time placing it very near biology. This imperils his whole system, for the bridge between man and nature which he has taken such pains to destroy would turn out to be surreptitiously re-established through ethnography, which is indisputably a human science and devotes itself to the study of these societies. Alternatively Sartre resigns himself to putting a 'stunted and deformed' humanity on man's side (p. 203), but not without implying that its place in humanity does not belong to it in its own right and is a function only of its adoption by historical humanity: either because it has begun to internalize the latter's history in the colonial context, or because, thanks to anthropology itself, historical humanity has given the blessing of meaning to an original humanity which was

*This even holds for mathematical truths of which a contemporary logician, however, says that 'The characteristic of mathematical thought is that it does not convey truth about the external world' (Heyting, pp. 8–9). But mathematical thought at any rate reflects the free functioning of the mind, that is, the activity of the cells of the cerebral cortex, relatively emancipated from any external constraint and obeying only its own laws. As the mind too is a thing, the functioning of this thing teaches us something about the nature of things: even pure reflection is in the last analysis an internalization of the cosmos. It illustrates the structure of what lies outside in a symbolic form: 'Logic and logistics are empirical sciences belonging to ethnography rather than psychology' (Beth, p. 151).

without it. Either way the prodigious wealth and diversity of habits, beliefs and customs is allowed to escape; and it is forgotten that each of the tens or hundreds of thousands of societies which have existed side by side in the world or succeeded one another since man's first appearance, has claimed that it contains the essence of all the meaning and dignity of which human society is capable and, reduced though it may have been to a small nomad band or a hamlet lost in the depths of the forest, its claim has in its own eyes rested on a moral certainty comparable to that which we can invoke in our own case. But whether in their case or our own, a good deal of egocentricity and naïvety is necessary to believe that man has taken refuge in a single one of the historical or geographical modes of his existence, when the truth about man resides in the system of their differences and common properties.

He who begins by steeping himself in the allegedly self-evident truths of introspection never emerges from them. Knowledge of men sometimes seems easier to those who allow themselves to be caught up in the snare of personal identity. But they thus shut the door on knowledge of man: written or unavowed 'confessions' form the basis of all ethnographic research. Sartre in fact becomes the prisoner of his Cogito: Descartes made it possible to attain universality, but conditionally on remaining psychological and individual; by sociologizing the Cogito, Sartre merely exchanges one prison for another. Each subject's group and period now take the place of timeless consciousness. Moreover, Sartre's view of the world and man has the narrowness which has been traditionally credited to closed societies. His insistence on tracing a distinction between the primitive and the civilized with the aid of gratuitous contrasts reflects, in a scarcely more subtle form, the fundamental opposition he postulates between myself and others. Yet there is little difference between the way in which this opposition is formulated in Sartre's work and the way it would have been formulated by a Melanesian savage, while the analysis of the practico-inert quite simply revives the language of animism.*

Descartes, who wanted to found a physics, separated Man from

*It is precisely because all these aspects of the savage mind can be discovered in Sartre's philosophy, that the latter is in my view unqualified to pass judgment on it: he is prevented from doing so by the very fact of furnishing its equivalent. To the anthropologist, on the contrary, this philosophy (like all the others) affords a first-class ethnographic document, the study of which is essential to an understanding of the mythology of our own time.

Society. Sartre, who claims to found an anthropology, separates his own society from others. A Cogito – which strives to be ingenuous and raw – retreats into individualism and empiricism and is lost in the blind alleys of social psychology. For it is striking that the situations which Sartre uses as a starting point for extracting the formal conditions of social reality – strikes, boxing matches, football matches, bus-stop queues – are all secondary incidentals of life in society; and they cannot therefore serve to disclose its foundations.

This axiomatic, so far removed from the anthropologist's, is all the more disappointing when he feels himself very close to Sartre whenever the latter applies himself, with incomparable artistry, to grasping, in its dialectical movement, a present or past social experience within our own culture. Sartre then does what every anthropologist tries to do in the case of different cultures: to put himself in the place of the men living there, to understand the principle and pattern of their intentions, and to perceive a period or a culture as a significant set. In this respect we can often learn from him, but these are lessons of a practical, not a theoretical, nature. It is possible that the requirement of 'totalization' is a great novelty to some historians, sociologists and psychologists. It has been taken for granted by anthropologists ever since they learned it from Malinowski. But Malinowski's deficiencies have also taught us that this is not where explanation ends. It only begins when we have succeeded in constituting our object. The role of dialectical reason is to put the human sciences in possession of a reality with which it alone can furnish them, but the properly scientific work consists in decomposing and then recomposing on a different plane. With all due respect to Sartrian phenomenology, we can hope to find in it only a point of departure, not one of arrival.

Furthermore, dialectical reason must not let itself be carried away by its own elan, nor must the procedure leading to the comprehension of an *other* reality attribute to it, in addition to its own dialectical features, those appertaining to the procedure rather than to the object: it does not follow from the fact that all knowledge of others is dialectical, that others are wholly dialectical in every respect. By making analytical reason an anti-comprehension, Sartre often comes to refuse it any reality as an integral part of the object of comprehension. This paralogism is already apparent in his manner of invoking history, for one is hard put to it to see whether it is meant to be the history men make unconsciously, history of men consciously made by historians, the philosopher's interpretation of the history of men or his interpretation of the history of historians. The difficulty becomes even greater, however, when Sartre endeavours to explain the life and thought of the present or past members not of his own society but of exotic societies.

He thinks, rightly, that this attempted comprehension stands no chance of succeeding unless it is dialectical; and he concludes, wrongly, that the relationship between native thought and his knowledge of it, is that of a constitutive to a constituted dialectic, and thus, by an unforeseen detour, he repeats all the illusions of theorists of primitive mentality on his own account. It seems even less tolerable to him than to Levy-Bruhl that the savage should possess 'complex understanding' and should be capable of analysis and demonstration. Of the Ambrym native, made famous by Deacon's work, who was able to show the field-worker the functioning of his marriage rules and kinship system by a diagram in the sand (an aptitude in no way exceptional as plenty of similar cases are recorded in ethnographic literature) Sartre says: 'It goes without saying that this construction is not a thought: it is a piece of manual work governed by unexpressed synthetical knowledge' (p. 505). Granted: but then the same must be said of a professor at the Ecole Polytechnique demonstrating a proof on the blackboard, for every ethnographer capable of dialectical comprehension is intimately persuaded that the situation is exactly the same in both cases. So it would follow that all reason is dialectical, which for my part I am prepared to concede, since dialectical reason seems to me like analytical reason in action; but then the distinction between the two forms of reason which is the basis of Sartre's enterprise would become pointless.

I must now confess to having myself unintentionally and unwittingly lent support to these erroneous ideas, by having seemed all too often in *Les structures élémentaires de la parenté* as if I were seeking out an unconscious genesis of matrimonial exchange. I should have made more distinction between exchange as it is expressed spontaneously and forcefully in the *praxis* of groups and the conscious and deliberate rules by which these same groups – or their philosophers – spend their time in codifying and controlling it. If there is anything to be learnt from the ethnographic enquiries of the last twenty years, it is that this latter aspect is much more important than has generally been realized by observers, who labour under the same delusion as Sartre. Thus we must, as Sartre advocates, apply dialectical reason to the knowledge of our own and other societies. But we must not lose sight of the fact that analytical reason occupies a considerable place in all of them and that, as it is present, the approach we adopt must also allow us to rediscover it there.

But even were it not present, Sartre's position would not be improved. For in this case exotic societies would merely confront us, in a more general manner than others, with an unconscious teleology, which, although historical, completely eludes human history: that of which certain aspects are revealed by linguistics and psycho-analysis and which rests on the interplay of biological mechanisms (structure of the brain, lesions, internal secretions) and psychological ones. There, it seems to me, is 'the bone' (to borrow a phrase from Sartre) which his critique does not manage to break, and moreover cares nothing about, which is the most serious charge one could level at it. For language does not consist in the analytical reason of the old-style grammarians nor in the dialectic constituted by structural linguistics nor in the constitutive dialectic of individual *praxis* facing the practico-inert, since all three presuppose it. Linguistics thus presents us with a dialectical and totalizing entity but one outside (or beneath) consciousness and will. Language, an unreflecting totalization, is human reason which has its reasons and of which man knows nothing. And if it is objected that it is so only for a subject who internalizes it on the basis of linguistic theory, my reply is that this way out must be refused, for this subject is one who *speaks*: for the same light which reveals the nature of language to him also reveals to him that it was so when he did not know it, for he already made himself understood, and that it will remain so tomorrow without his being aware of it, since his discourse never was and never will be the result of a conscious totalization of linguistic laws. But if, as speaking subject, man can find his apodictic experience in an *other* totalization, there seems no longer any reason why, as living subject, he should not have access to the same experience in other, not necessarily human, but living beings.

This method could also lay claim to the name 'progressive-regressive'; in fact, what Sartre describes as such is the very method anthropologists have been practising for many years. But Sartre restricts it to its preliminary step. For our method is progressive-regressive not once but twice over. In the first stage, we observe the datum of experience, analyse it in the present, try to grasp its historical antecedents as far as we can delve into the past, and bring all these facts back to the light of day to incorporate them into a meaningful totality. The second stage, which repeats the first on a different plane and at a different level, then begins. This internalized human thing which we have sought to provide with all its wealth and originality, only fixes the distance analytical reason must cover, the leap it must make, to close the gap between the ever unforeseen complexity of this new object and the intellectual means at its disposal. It must therefore transform itself as dialetical reason, in the hope that once flexible, widened and strengthened, by its agency this unforeseen object will be assimilated to others, this novel totality will be merged into other totalities and that thus little by little clambering on to the mass of its conquests, dialectical reason will descry other horizons and other objects. No doubt the procedure would go astray if it were not, at every stage and, above all, when it seemed to have run its course, ready to retrace its steps and to double back on itself to preserve the contact with that experienced totality which serves both as its end and means. This return on itself is in my view a verification, rather than, as Sartre regards it, a demonstration, for, as I see it, a conscious being aware of itself as such poses a problem to which it provides no solution. The discovery of the dialectic subjects analytical reason to an imperative requirement: to account also for dialectical reason. This standing requirement relentlessly forces analytical reason to extend its programme and transform its axiomatic. But dialectical reason can account neither for itself nor for analytical reason.

It will be objected that this expansion is illusory since it is always accompanied by a contraction in meaning, and we should abandon the substance for the shadow, clarity for obscurity, the manifest for the conjectural, truth for science fiction (Sartre, p. 129). Again, Sartre would have to show that he himself avoids this dilemma, inherent in every attempt at explanation. The real question is not whether our endeavour to understand involves a gain or a loss of meaning, but whether the meaning we preserve is of more value than that we have been judicious enough to relinquish. In this respect Sartre seems to have remembered only half of Marx's and Freud's combined lesson. They have taught us that man has meaning only on the condition that he view himself as meaningful. So far I agree with Sartre. But it must be added that *this meaning is never the right one*: superstructures are *faulty acts* which have 'made it' socially. Hence it is vain to go to historical consciousness for the truest meaning. What Sartre calls dialectical reason is only a reconstruction, by what he calls analytical reason, of hypothetical moves about which it is impossible to know – unless one should perform them without thinking them – whether they bear any relation at all to what he tells us about them and which, if so, would be definable in terms of analytical reason alone. And so we end up in the paradox of a system which invokes the criterion of historical consciousness to distinguish the 'primitive' from the 'civilized' but – contrary to its claim – is itself ahistorical. It offers not a concrete image of history but an abstract schema of men making history of such a kind that it can manifest itself in the trend of their lives as a synchronic totality. Its position in relation to history is therefore the same as that of primitives to the eternal past: in Sartre's system, history plays exactly the part of a myth.

Indeed, the problem raised by the *Critique de la raison dialectique* is reducible to the question: under what conditions is the myth of the French Revolution possible? And I am prepared to grant that the contemporary Frenchman must believe in this myth in order fully to play the part of an historical agent and also that Sartre's analysis admirably extracts the set of formal conditions necessary if this result is to be secured. But it does not follow that his meaning, just because it is the richest (and so most suited to inspire practical action), should be the truest. Here the dialectic turns against itself. This truth is a matter of context, and if we place ourselves outside it – as the man of science is bound to do – what appeared as an experienced truth first becomes confused and finally disappears altogether. The so-called men of the Left still cling to a period of contemporary history which bestowed the blessing of a congruence between practical imperatives and schemes of interpretation. Perhaps this golden age of historical consciousness has already passed; and that this eventuality can at any rate be envisaged proves that what we have here is only a contingent context like the fortuitous 'focusing' of an optical instrument when its object-glass and eye-piece move in relation to each other. We are still 'in focus' so far as the French Revolution is concerned, but so we should have been in relation to the Fronde had we lived earlier. The former will rapidly cease to afford a coherent image on which our action can be modelled, just as the latter has already done. What we learn from reading Retz is that thought is powerless to extract a scheme of interpretation from events long past.

At first sight, there seems no doubt: on one side the privileged, on the other the humble and exploited; how could we hesitate? We are Frondeurs. However, the people of Paris were being manoeuvred by noble houses, whose sole aim was to arrange their own affairs with the existing powers, and by one half of the royal family which wanted to oust the other. And now we are already only half Frondeurs. As for the Court, which took refuge at Saint-Germain, it appears at first to have been a faction of good for nothings vegetating on their privileges and growing fat on exactions and usury at the expense of the collectivity. But no, it had a function all the same since it retained military power; it conducted the struggle against foreigners, the Spaniards, whom the Frondeurs invited without hesitation to invade the country and impose their wills on this same Court which was defending the fatherland. The scales, however, tilt the other way again: the Frondeurs and Spaniards together formed the party of peace. The Prince de Condé and the Court only sought warlike adventures. We are pacifists and once again become Frondeurs. But nevertheless did not the military exploits of Mazarin and the Court extend France to its present frontiers, thus founding the state and the nation? Without them we should not be what we are today. So here we are on the other side again.

It suffices therefore for history to move away from us in time or for us to move away from it in thought, for it to cease to be internalizable and to lose its intelligibility, a spurious intelligibility attaching to a temporary internality. I am not however suggesting that man can or should sever himself from this internality. It is not in his power to do so and wisdom consists for him in seeing himself live it, while at the same time knowing (but in a different register) that what he lives so completely and intensely is a myth – which will appear as such to men of a future century, and perhaps to himself a few years hence, and will no longer appear at all to men of a future millenium. All meaning is answerable to a lesser meaning, which gives it its highest meaning, and if this regression finally ends in recognizing 'a contingent law of which one can say only: *it is thus*, and not otherwise' (Sartre, p. 128), this prospect is not alarming to those whose thought is not tormented by transcendence even in a latent form. For man will have gained all he can reasonably hope for if, on the sole condition of bowing to this contingent law, he succeeds in determining his form of conduct and in placing all else in the realm of the intelligible.

Sartre is certainly not the only contemporary philosopher to have valued history above the other human sciences and formed an almost mystical conception of it. The anthropologist respects history, but he does not accord it a special value. He conceives it as a study complementary to his own: one of them unfurls the range of human societies in time, the other in space. And the difference is even less great than it might seem, since the historian strives to reconstruct the picture of vanished societies as they were at the points which for them corresponded to the present, while the ethnographer does his best to reconstruct the historical stages which temporally preceded their existing form.

This symmetry between history and anthropology seems to be rejected by philosophers who implicitly or explicitly deny that distribution in space and succession in time afford equivalent perspectives. In their eyes some special prestige seems to attach to the temporal dimension, as if diachrony were to establish a kind of intelligibility not merely superior to that provided by synchrony, but above all more specifically human.

It is easy to explain, if not to justify, this preference. The diversity of social forms, which the anthropologist grasps as deployed in space, present the appearance of a discontinuous system. Now, thanks to the temporal dimension, history seems to restore to us, not separate states, but the passage from one state to another in a continuous form. And as we believe that we apprehend the trend of our personal history as a continuous change, historical knowledge appears to confirm the evidence of inner sense. History seems to do more than describe beings to us from the outside, or at best give us intermittent flashes of insight into internalities, each of which are so on their own account while remaining external to each other: it appears to re-establish our connection, outside ourselves, with the very essence of change.

There would be plenty to say about this supposed totalizing continuity of the self which seems to me to be an illusion sustained by the demands of social life – and consequently a reflection of the external on the internal – rather than the object of an apodictic experience. But there is no need to resolve this philosophical problem in order to perceive that the proposed conception of history corresponds to no kind of reality. As historical knowledge is claimed to be privileged, I feel entitled (as I would not otherwise feel) to make the point that there is a twofold antinomy in the very notion of an historical fact. For, *ex hypothesi*, a historical fact is what really took place, but where did anything take place? Each episode in a revolution or a war resolves itself into a multitude of individual psychic movements. Each of these movements is the translation of unconscious development, and these resolve themselves into cerebral, hormonal or nervous phenomena, which themselves have reference to the physical or chemical order. Consequently, historical facts are no more *given* than any other. It is the historian, or the agent of history, who constitutes them by abstraction and as though under the threat of an infinite regress.

What is true of the constitution of historical facts is no less so of their selection. From this point of view, the historian and the agent of history choose, sever and carve them up, for a truly total history would confront them with chaos. Every corner of space conceals a multitude of individuals each of whom totalizes the trend of history in a manner which cannot be compared to the others; for any one of these individuals, each moment of time is inexhaustibly rich in physical and psychical incidents which all play their part in his totalization. Even history which claims to be universal is still only a juxtaposition of a few local histories within which (and between which) very much more is left out than is put in. And it would be vain to hope that by increasing the number of collaborators and making research more intensive one would obtain a better result. In so far as history aspires to meaning, it is doomed to select regions, periods, groups of men and individuals in these groups and to make them stand out, as discontinuous figures, against a continuity barely good enough to be used as a backdrop. A truly total history would cancel itself out – its product would be nought. What makes history possible is that a sub-set of events is found, for a given period, to have approximately the same significance for a contingent of individuals who have not necessarily experienced the events and may even consider them at an interval of several centuries. History is therefore never history, but history-for.* It is partial in the sense of being

* Quite so, will be the comment of the supporters of Sartre. But the latter's whole endeavour shows that, though the subjectivity of history-for-me can make way for the objectivity of history-for-us, the 'I' can still only be converted into 'we' by condemning this 'we' to being no more than an 'I' raised to the power of two, itself hermetically sealed off from the other 'we's. The price so paid for the

biased even when it claims not to be, for it inevitably remains partial – that is, incomplete – and this is itself a form of partiality. When one proposes to write a history of the French Revolution one knows (or ought to know) that it cannot, simultaneously and under the same heading, be that of the Jacobin and that of the aristocrat. *Ex hypothesi*, their respective totalizations (each of which is anti-symmetric to the other) are equally true. One must therefore choose between two alternatives. One must select as the principal either one or a third (for there are an infinite number of them) and give up the attempt to find in history a totalization of the set of partial totalizations; or alternatively one must recognize them all as equally real: but only to discover that the French Revolution as commonly conceived never took place.

History does not therefore escape the common obligation of all knowledge, to employ a code to analyse its object, even (and especially) if a continuous reality is attributed to that object.* The distinctive features of historical knowledge are due not to the absence of a code, which is illusory, but to its particular nature: the code consists in a chronology. There is no history without dates. To be convinced of this it is sufficient to consider how a pupil succeeds in learning history: he reduces it to an emaciated body, the skeleton of which is formed by dates. Not without reason, there has been a reaction against this dry method, but one which often runs to the opposite extreme. Dates may not be the whole of history, nor what is most interesting about it, but they are its *sine qua non*, for history's entire originality and distinctive nature lie in apprehending the relation between *before* and *after*, which would perforce dissolve if its terms could not, at least in principle, be dated.

Now, this chronological coding conceals a very much more complex nature than one supposes when one thinks of historical dates

illusion of having overcome the insoluble antinomy (in such a system) between my self and others, consists of the assignation, by historical consciousness, of the metaphysical function of Other to the Papuans. By reducing the latter to the state of means, barely sufficient for its philosophical appetite, historical reason abandons itself to a sort of intellectual cannibalism much more revolting to the anthropologist than real cannibalism.

* In this sense too, one can speak of an antinomy of historical knowledge: if it claims to reach the continuous it is impossible, being condemned to an infinite regress; but to render it possible, events must be quantified and thereafter temporality ceases to be the privileged dimension of historical knowledge because as soon as it is quantified each event can, for all useful purposes, be treated as if it were the result of a choice between possible pre-existents.

as a simple linear series. In the first place, a date denotes a moment in a succession: *d* 2 is after *d* 1 and before *d* 3. From this point of view dates only perform the function of ordinal numbers. But each date is also a cardinal number and, as such, expresses a *distance* in relation to the dates nearest to it. We use a large number of dates to code some periods of history; and fewer for others. This variable quantity of dates applied to periods of equal duration are a gauge of what might be called the pressure of history: there are 'hot' chronologies which are those of periods where in the eyes of the historian numerous events appear as differential elements; others, on the contrary, where for him (although not of course for the men who lived through them) very little or nothing took place. Thirdly and most important, a date is a *member* of a class. These classes of dates are definable by the meaningful character each date has within the class in relation to other dates which also belong to it, and by the absence of this meaningful character with respect to dates appertaining to a different class. Thus the date 1685 belongs to a class of which 1610, 1648 and 1715 are likewise members; but it means nothing in relation to the class composed of the dates: 1st, 2nd, 3rd, 4th millenium, nor does it mean anything in relation to the class of dates: 23 January, 17 August, 30 September, etc.

On this basis, in what would the historian's code consist? Certainly not in dates, since these are not recurrent. Changes of temperature can be coded with the help of figures, because the reading of a figure on the thermometer evokes the return of an earlier situation: whenever I read 0° C, I know that it is freezing and put on my warmest coat. But a historical date, taken in itself, would have no meaning, for it has no reference outside itself: if I know nothing about modern history, the date 1643 makes me none the wiser. The code can therefore consist only of classes of dates, where each date has meaning in as much as it stands in complex relations of correlation and opposition with other dates. Each class is defined by a frequency, and derives from what might be called a corpus or a domain of history. Historical knowledge thus proceeds in the same way as a wireless with frequency modulation: like a nerve, it codes a continuous quantity – and as such an asymbolic one – by frequencies of impulses proportional to its variations. As for history itself, it cannot be represented as an aperiodic series with only a fragment of which we are acquainted. History is a discontinuous set composed of domains of history, each of which is defined by a characteristic frequency and by a differential coding of *before* and *after*. It is no more possible to pass between the dates which composε the different domains than it is to do so between natural and irrational numbers. Or more precisely: the dates appropriate to each class are irrational in relation to all those of other classes.

It is thus not only fallacious but contradictory to conceive of the historical process as a continuous development, beginning with prehistory coded in tens or hundreds of millenia, then adopting the scale of millenia when it gets to the 4th or 3rd millenium, and continuing as history in centuries interlarded, at the pleasure of each author, with slices of annual history within the century, day to day history within the year or even hourly history within a day. All these dates do not form a series: they are of different species. To give just one example, the coding we use in prehistory is not preliminary to that we employ for modern and contemporary history. Each code refers to a system of meaning which is, at least in theory, applicable to the virtual totality of human history. The events which are significant for one code are no longer so for another. Coded in the system of prehistory, the most famous episodes in modern and contemporary history cease to be pertinent; except perhaps (and again we know nothing about it) certain massive aspects of demographic evolution viewed on a world-wide scale, the invention of the steam-engine, the discovery of electricity and of nuclear energy.

Given that the general code consists not in dates which can be ordered as a linear series but in classes of dates each furnishing an autonomous system of reference, the discontinuous and classificatory nature of historical knowledge emerges clearly. It operates by means of a rectangular matrix:

. . . .

. . . .

. . . .

. . . .

. . . .

. . . .

where each line represents classes of dates, which may be called hourly, daily, annual, secular, millenial for the purposes of schematization and which together make up a discontinuous set. In a system of this type, alleged historical continuity is secured only by dint of fraudulent outlines.

Furthermore, although the internal gaps in each class cannot be filled in by recourse to other classes, each class taken as a whole nevertheless always refers back to another class, which contains the principle of an intelligibility to which it could not itself aspire. The history of the 17th century is 'annual' but the 17th century, as a domain of history belongs to another class, which codes it in relation to earlier and later centuries; and this domain of modern times in its turn becomes an element of a class where it appears correlated with and opposed to other 'times': the middle ages, antiquity, the present day, etc. Now, these various domains correspond to histories of different power.

Biographical and anecdotal history, right at the bottom of the scale, is low-powered history, which is not intelligible in itself and only becomes so when it is transferred *en bloc* to a form of history of a higher power than itself; and the latter stands in the same relation to a class above it. It would, however, be a mistake to think that we progressively reconstitute a total history by dint of these dovetailings. For any gain on one side is offset by a loss on the other. Biographical and anecdotal history is the least explanatory; but it is the richest in point of information, for it considers individuals in their particularity and details for each of them the shades of character, the twists and turns of their motives, the phases of their deliberations. This information is schematized, put in the background and finally done away with as one passes to histories of progressively greater 'power'.* Consequently, depending on the level on which he places himself, the historian loses in information what he gains in comprehension or vice versa, as if the logic of the concrete wished

* Each domain of history is circumscribed in relation to that immediately below it, inscribed in relation to that above it. So each low-powered history of an inscribed domain is complementary to the powerful history of the circumscribed domain and contradictory to the low-powered history of this same domain (in so far as it is itself an inscribed domain). Each history is thus accompanied by an indeterminate number of anti-histories, each complementary to the others: to a history of grade 1, there corresponds an anti-history of grade 2, etc. The progress of knowledge and the creation of new sciences take place through the generation of anti-histories which show that a certain order which is possible only on one plane ceases to be so on another. The anti-history of the French Revolution envisaged by Gobineau is contradictory on the plane on which the Revolution had been thought of before him. It becomes logically conceivable

to remind us of its logical nature by modelling a confused outline of Gödel's theorem in the clay of 'becoming'. The historian's relative choice, with respect to each domain of history he gives up, is always confined to the choice between history which teaches us more and explains less, and history which explains more and teaches less. The only way he can avoid the dilemma is by getting outside history: either by the bottom, if the pursuit of information leads him from the consideration of groups to that of individuals and then to their motivations which depend on their personal history and temperament, that is to say to an infra-historical domain in the realms of psychology and physiology; or by the top, if the need to understand incites him to put history back into prehistory and the latter into the general evolution of organized beings, which is itself explicable only in terms of biology, geology and finally cosmology.

There is, however, another way of avoiding the dilemma without thereby doing away with history. We need only recognize that history is a method with no distinct object corresponding to it to reject the equivalence between the notion of history and the notion of humanity which some have tried to foist on us with the unavowed aim of making historicity the last refuge of a transcendental humanism: as if men could regain the illusion of liberty on the plane of the 'we' merely by giving up the 'I's that are too obviously wanting in consistency.

In fact history is tied neither to man nor to any particular object. It consists wholly in its method, which experience proves to be indispensable for cataloguing the elements of any structure whatever, human or non-human, in their entirety. It is therefore far from being the case that the search for intelligibility comes to an end in history as though this were its terminus. Rather, it is history that serves as the point of departure in any quest for intelligibility. As we say of certain careers, history may lead to anything, provided you get out of it.

This further thing to which history leads for want of a sphere of reference of its own shows that whatever its value (which is

(which does not mean that it is true) if one puts oneself on a new plane, which incidentally Gobineau chose clumsily; that is to say: if one passes from a history of 'annual' or 'secular' grade (which is also political, social and ideological) to a history of 'millenial' or 'multi-millenial' grade (which is also cultural and anthropological), a procedure not invented by Gobineau which might be called: Boulainvilliers' 'transformation'.

indisputable) historical knowledge has no claim to be opposed to other forms of knowledge as a supremely privileged one. We noted above* that it is already found rooted in the savage mind, and we can now see why it does not come to fruition there. The characteristic feature of the savage mind is its timelessness; its object is to grasp the world as both a synchronic and a diachronic totality and the knowledge which it draws therefrom is like that afforded of a room by mirrors fixed on opposite walls, which reflect each other (as well as objects in the intervening space) although without being strictly parallel. A multitude of images forms simultaneously, none exactly like any other, so that no single one furnishes more than a partial knowledge of the decoration and furniture but the group is characterized by invariant properties expressing a truth. The savage mind deepens its knowledge with the help of *imagines mundi*. It builds mental structures which facilitate an understanding of the world in as much as they resemble it. In this sense savage thought can be defined as analogical thought.

But in this sense too it differs from domesticated thought, of which historical knowledge constitutes one aspect. The concern for continuity which inspires the latter is indeed a manifestation, in the temporal order, of knowledge which is interstitial and unifying rather than discontinuous and analogical: instead of multiplying objects by schemes promoted to the role of additional objects, it seems to transcend an original discontinuity by relating objects to one another. But it is this reason, wholly concerned with closing gaps and dissolving differences, which can properly be called 'analytical'. By a paradox on which much stress has recently been laid, for modern thought 'continuity, variability, relativity, determinism go together' (Auger, p. 475).

This analytic, abstract continuity will doubtless be opposed to that of the *praxis* as concrete individuals live it. But this latter continuity seems no less derivative than the former, for it is only the conscious mode of apprehending psychological and physiological processes which are themselves discontinuous. I am not disputing that reason develops and transforms itself in the practical field: man's mode of thought reflects his relations to the world and to men. But in order for *praxis* to be living thought, it is necessary first (in a logical and not a historical sense) for thought to exist: that is to say, its initial conditions must be given in the form of an objective

* Pp. 242–3.

structure of the psyche and brain without which there would be neither *praxis* nor thought.

When therefore I describe savage thought as a system of concepts embedded in images, I do not come anywhere near the *robinsonnades** (Sartre, pp. 642–3) of a constitutive constituent dialectic: all constitutive reason presupposes a constituted reason. But even if one allowed Sartre the circularity which he invokes to dispel the 'suspect character' attaching to the first stages of his synthesis, what he proposes really are 'robinsonnades', this time in the guise of descriptions of phenomena, when he claims to restore the sense of marriage exchange, the potlatch or the demonstration of his tribe's marriage rules by a Melanesian savage. Sartre then refers to a comprehension which has its being in the *praxis* of their organizers, a bizarre expression to which no reality corresponds, except perhaps the capacity which any foreign society presents to anyone looking at it from the outside, and which leads him to project the lacunae in his own observation on to it in the form of positive attributes. Two examples will show what I mean.

No anthropologist can fail to be struck by the common manner of conceptualizing initiation rites employed by the most diverse societies throughout the world. Whether in Africa, America, Australia or Melanesia, the rites follow the same pattern: first, the novices, taken from their parents, are symbolically 'killed' and kept hidden in the forest or bush where they are put to the test by the Beyond; after this they are 'reborn' as members of the society. When they are returned to their natural parents, the latter therefore simulate all the phases of a new delivery, and begin a re-education even in the elementary actions of feeding or dressing. It would be tempting to interpret this set of phenomena as a proof that at this stage thought is wholly embedded in *praxis*. But this would be seeing things back to front, for it is on the contrary scientific *praxis* which, among ourselves, has emptied the notions of death and birth of everything not corresponding to mere physiological processes and rendered them unsuitable to convey other meanings. In societies with initiation rites, birth and death provide the material for a rich and varied conceptualization, provided that these notions (like so many others) have not been stripped by any form of scientific

* This term alludes to Robinson Crusoe and the Swiss family Robinson whose 'creation' of civilization was not a genuine invention but merely an application of their pre-existing knowledge. [Trans. note.]

knowledge oriented towards practical returns–which they lack–of the major part of a meaning which transcends the distinction between the real and the imaginary: a complete meaning of which we can now hardly do more than evoke the ghost in the reduced setting of figurative language. What looks to us like being embedded in *praxis* is the mark of thought which quite genuinely takes the words it uses seriously, whereas in comparable circumstances we only 'play' on words.

The taboos on parents-in-law furnish the matter for a cautionary tale leading to the same conclusion by a different route. Anthropologists have found the frequent prohibition of any physical or verbal contact between close affines so strange that they have exercised their ingenuity in multiplying explanatory hypotheses, without always making sure that the hypotheses are not rendered redundant by one another. Elkin for instance explains the rarity of marriage with the patrilateral cousin in Australia by the rule that as a man has to avoid any contact with his mother-in-law, he will be wise to choose the latter among women entirely outside his own local group (to which his father's sisters belong). The aim of the rule itself is supposed to be to prevent a mother and daughter from being rivals for the affections of the same man; finally, the taboo is supposed to be extended by contamination to the wife's maternal grandmother and her husband. There are thus four concurrent interpretations of a single phenomenon: as a function of a type of marriage, as the result of a psychological calculation, as protection against instinctive tendencies and as the product of association by contiguity. This, however, still does not satisfy Elkin, for in his view the taboo on the father-in-law rests on a fifth explanation: the father-in-law is the creditor of the man to whom he has given his daughter, and the son-in-law feels himself to be in a position of inferiority in relation to him (Elkin 4, pp. 66–7, 117–20).

I shall content myself with the last explanation which perfectly covers all the cases considered and renders the others worthless by bringing out their naïvety. But why is it so difficult to put these usages into their proper place? The reason is, I think, that the usages of our own society which could be compared with them and might furnish a landmark to identify them by, are in a dissociated form among ourselves, while in these exotic societies they appear in an associated one which makes them unrecognizable to us.

We are acquainted with the taboo on parents-in-law or at least with its approximate equivalent. By the same token we are forbidden to address the great of this world and obliged to keep out of their way. All protocol asserts it: one does not speak first to the Queen of England or the President of the French Republic; and we adopt the same reserve when unforeseen circumstances create conditions of closer proximity between a superior and ourselves than the social distance between us warrants. Now, in most societies the position of wife-giver is accompanied by social (and sometimes also economic) superiority, that of wife-taker by inferiority and dependence. This inequality between affines may be expressed objectively in institutions as a fluid or stable hierarchy, or it may be expressed subjectively in the system of interpersonal relations by means of privileges and prohibitions.

There is therefore nothing mysterious about these usages which our own experience enables us to see from the inside. We are disconcerted only by their constitutive conditions, different in each case. Among ourselves, they are sharply separated from other usages and tied to an unambiguous context. In exotic societies, the same usages and the same context are as it were embedded in other usages and a different context: that of family ties, with which they seem to us incompatible. We find it hard to imagine that, in private, the son-in-law of the President of the French Republic should regard him as the head of the state rather than as his father-in-law. And although the Queen of England's husband may behave as the first of her subjects in public, there are good reasons for supposing that he is just a husband when they are alone together. It is either one or the other. The superficial strangeness of the taboo on parents-in-law arises from its being both at the same time.

Consequently, and as we have already found in the case of operations of understanding, the system of ideas and attitudes is here presented only as *embodied*. Considered in itself, this system has nothing about it to baffle the anthropologist. My relation to the President of the Republic is made up entirely of negative observances, since, in the absence of other ties, any relations we may have are wholly defined by the rule that I should not speak unless he invites me to do so and that I should remain a respectful distance from him. But this abstract relation need only be clothed in a concrete relation and the attitudes appropriate to each to accumulate, for me to find myself as embarrassed by my family as an

Australian aborigine. What appears to us as greater social ease and greater intellectual mobility is thus due to the fact that we prefer to operate with detached pieces, if not indeed with 'small change', while the native is a logical hoarder: he is forever tying the threads, unceasingly turning over all the aspects of reality, whether physical, social or mental. We traffic in our ideas; he hoards them up. The savage mind puts a philosophy of the finite into practice.

This is also the source of the renewed interest in it. This language with its limited vocabulary able to express any message by combinations of oppositions between its constitutive units, this logic of comprehension for which contents are indissociable from form, this systematic of finite classes, this universe made up of meanings, no longer appears to us as retrospective witnesses of a time when: '. . . le ciel sur la terre Marchait et respirait dans un peuple de dieux',* and which the poet only evokes for the purpose of asking whether or not it is to be regretted. This time is now restored to us, thanks to the discovery of a universe of information where the laws of savage thought reign once more: 'heaven' too, 'walking on earth' among a population of transmitters and receivers whose messages, while in transmission, constitute objects of the physical world and can be grasped both from without and from within.

The idea that the universe of primitives (or supposedly such) consists principally in messages is not new. But until recently a negative value was attributed to what was wrongly taken to be a distinctive characteristic, as though this difference between the universe of the primitives and our own contained the explanation of their mental and technological inferiority, when what it does is rather to put them on a par with modern theorists of documentation.† Physical science had to discover that a semantic universe possesses all the characteristics of an object in its own right for it to be recognized that the manner in which primitive peoples conceptualize their

* i.e. 'when heaven walked and breathed on earth among a population of Gods'. From A. de Musset 'Rolla' 1833 reprinted in *Poesies Nouvelles*. [Trans. note.]

† The documentalist neither disallows nor disputes the substance of the works he analyses in order to derive the constitutive units of his code or to adapt them, either by combining them among themselves or, if necessary, decomposing them into finer units. He thus treats the authors as gods whose revelations are written down, instead of being inscribed into beings and things, but which have the same sacred value, which attaches to the supremely meaningful character that, for methodological or ontological reasons, it is *ex hypothesi* necessary to recognize in them in both cases.

world is not merely coherent but the very one demanded in the case of an object whose elementary structure presents the picture of a discontinuous complexity.

The false antinomy between logical and prelogical mentality was surmounted at the same time. The savage mind is logical in the same sense and the same fashion as ours, though as our own is only when it is applied to knowledge of a universe in which it recognizes physical and semantic properties simultaneously. This misunderstanding once dispelled, it remains no less true that, contrary to Levy-Bruhl's opinion, its thought proceeds through understanding, not affectivity, with the aid of distinctions and oppositions, not by confusion and participation. Although the term had not yet come into use, numerous texts of Durkheim and Mauss show that they understood that so-called primitive thought is a quantified form of thought.

It will be objected that there remains a major difference between the thought of primitives and our own: Information Theory is concerned with genuine messages whereas primitives mistake mere manifestations of physical determinism for messages. Two considerations, however, deprive this argument of any weight. In the first place, Information Theory has been generalized, and it extends to phenomena not intrinsically possessing the character of messages, notably to those of biology; the illusions of totemism have had at least the merit of illuminating the fundamental place belonging to phenomena of this order, in the internal economy of systems of classification. In treating the sensible properties of the animal and plant kingdoms as if they were the elements of a message, and in discovering 'signatures' – and so signs – in them, men have made mistakes of identification: the meaningful element was not always the one they supposed. But, without perfected instruments which would have permitted them to place it where it most often is – namely, at the microscopic level – they already discerned 'as through a glass darkly' principles of interpretation whose heuristic value and accordance with reality have been revealed to us only through very recent inventions: telecommunications, computers and electron microscopes.

Above all, during the period of their transmission, when they have an objective existence outside the consciousness of transmitters and receivers, messages display properties which they have in common with the physical world. Hence, despite their mistakes with regard to physical phenomena (which were not absolute but relative to the level where they grasped them) and even though they interpreted them as if they were messages, men were nevertheless able to arrive at some of their properties. For a theory of information to be able to be evolved it was undoubtedly essential to have discovered that the universe of information is part of an aspect of the natural world. But the validity of the passage from the laws of nature to those of information once demonstrated, implies the validity of the reverse passage – that which for millenia has allowed men to approach the laws of nature by way of information.

Certainly the properties to which the savage mind has access are not the same as those which have commanded the attention of scientists. The physical world is approached from opposite ends in the two cases: one is supremely concrete, the other supremely abstract; one proceeds from the angle of sensible qualities and the other from that of formal properties. But the idea that, theoretically at least and on condition no abrupt changes in perspective occurred, these two courses were destined to meet, explains why both, independently of each other in time and space, should have led to two distinct though equally positive sciences: one which flowered in the neolithic period, whose theory of the sensible order provided the basis of the arts of civilization (agriculture, animal husbandry, pottery, weaving, conservation and preparation of food, etc.) and which continues to provide for our basic needs by these means; and another which places itself from the start at the level of intelligibility, and of which contemporary science is the fruit.

We have had to wait until the middle of this century for the crossing of long separated paths: that which arrives at the physical world by the detour of communication, and that which as we have recently come to know, arrives at the world of communication by the detour of the physical. The entire process of human knowledge thus assumes the character of a closed system. And we therefore remain faithful to the inspiration of the savage mind when we recognize that, by an encounter it alone could have foreseen, the scientific spirit in its most modern form will have contributed to legitimize the principles of savage thought and to re-establish it in its rightful place.

12 June–16 October 1961

BIBLIOGRAPHY

ALVIANO, F. DE: 'Notas etnograficas sobre os Ticunas do Alto Solimões', *Revista do Instituto Historico e Geografico Brasileiro*, vol. 180, 1943.

ANDERSON, A. J. O. and DIBBLE, Ch. E.: *Florentine Codex, Book 2*, Santa Fé, N. M., 1951.

ANDERSON, E.: *Plants, Man and Life*, London, 1954.

ANTHONY, H. G.: *Field Book of North American Mammals*, New York, 1928.

AUGER, P.: 'Structures et complexités dans l'univers de l'antiquité à nos jours', *Cahiers d'histoire mondiale*, vol. 6, no. 3, Neuchâtel, 1960.

BALANDIER, G.: 'Phénomènes sociaux totaux et dynamique sociale', *Cahiers internationaux de sociologie*, vol. 30, Paris, 1961.

BALZAC, H. DE: *La Comédie humaine*, 10 vol, Bibl. de la Pléiade, Paris, 1940–50.

BARRETT, S. A.: 'Totemism among the Miwok', *Journal of American Folklore*, vol. 21, Boston-New York, 1908.

BARROWS, D. P.: *The Ethno-Botany of the Coahuila Indians of Southern California*, Chicago, 1900.

BATESON, G.: *Naven*, Cambridge, 1936.

BEATTIE, J. H. M.: 'Nyoro Personal Names', *The Uganda Journal*, vol. 21, no. 1, Kampala, 1957.

BECKWITH, M. W.: 'Mandan-Hidatsa Myths and Ceremonies', *Memoirs of the American Folklore Society*, vol. 32, New York, 1938.

BENEDICT, P. K.: 'Chinese and Thai Kin numeratives', *Journal of the American Oriental Society*, vol. 65, 1945.

BEIDELMAN, T. O.: 'Right and Left Hand among the Kaguru: A note on Symbolic Classification', *Africa*, vol. 31, no. 3, London, 1961.

BERGSON, H.: *The two sources of morality and religion* (translated from the French by R. Ashley Audra and Cloudesley Brereton), New York, 1956.

BETH, E.W.: *The Foundations of Mathematics*, Amsterdam, 1959.

BOAS, F.: (1) Introduction to: James Teit, 'Traditions of the Thompson River Indians of British Columbia', *Memoirs of the American Folklore Society*, vol. 6, 1898.

(2) 'Handbook of American Indian Languages', Part 1, *Bulletin 40, Bureau of American Ethnology*, Washington, D.C., 1911.

(3) 'The Origin of Totemism', *American Anthropologist*, vol. 18, 1916.

(4) 'Ethnology of the Kwakiutl', *35th Annual Report, Bureau of American Ethnology*, 2 vol. (1913–14), Washington, D.C., 1921.

(5) 'Mythology and Folk-Tales of the North American Indians', reprinted in: *Race, Language and Culture*, New York, 1940.

BOCHET, G.: 'Le Poro des Dieli', *Bulletin de l'Institut Français d'Afrique noire*, vol. 21, nos. 1–2, Dakar, 1959.

BOWERS, A.W.: *Mandan Social and Ceremonial Organization*, Chicago, 1950.

BRÖNDAL, V.: *Les Parties du discours*, Copenhagen, 1928.

BROUILLETTE, B.: *La Chasse des animaux à fourrure au Canada*, Paris, 1934.

CAPELL, A.: 'Language and World View in the Northern Kimberley, W. Australia', *Southwestern Journal of Anthropology*, vol. 16, no. 1, Albuquerque, 1960.

CARPENTER, E.: (Personal communication, 26.10.61.)

CHARBONNIER, G.: 'Entretiens avec Claude Lévi-Strauss', *Les Lettres Nouvelles* 10, Paris, 1961.

COGHLAN, H.H.: 'Prehistoric Copper and some Experiments in Smelting', *Transactions of the Newcomen Society*, vol. 20, London, 1939–40.

COLBACCHINI, P.A. et ALBISETTI, P.C.: *Os Bororos Orientais*, São Paulo-Rio de Janeiro, 1942.

COMTE, A.: *Cours de philosophie positive*, 6 vol., Paris, n. ed., 1908.

CONKLIN, H.C.: (1) *The Relation of Hanunóo Culture to the Plant World*, Doctoral Dissert., Yale, 1954 (microfilm).

(2) 'Hanunóo Color Categories', *Southwestern Journal of Anthropology*, vol. 11, no. 4, Albuquerque, 1955.

(3) 'Betel Chewing among the Hanunóo', *Proceedings of the 4th Far-eastern Prehistoric Congress*, Paper no. 56, Quezon City (Nat. Res. Council of the Philippines), 1958.

(4) 'Lexicographical Treatment of Folk Taxonomies', *International Journal of American Linguistics*, vol. 28, New York, 1962.

COOKE, Ch.A.: 'Iroquois Personal Names – Their Classification', *Proceedings of the American Philosophical Society*, vol. 96, fasc. 4, Philadelphia, 1952.

CRUZ, M.: 'Dos nomes entre os Bororos', *Revista do Instituto Historico e Geografico Brasileiro*, vol. 175 (1940), 1941.

CUNNISON, I. G.: *The Luapala Peoples of Northern Rhodesia*, Manchester, 1959.

DELATTE, A.: 'Herbarius: Recherches sur le cérémonial usité chez les anciens pour la cueillette des simples et des plantes magiques', *Bibl. de la Fac. de Phil. et Let. Univ. de Liège*, fasc. LXXXI, Liège-Paris, 1938.

DENNETT, R. E.: *Nigerian Studies*, London, 1910.

DENNLER, J. G.: 'Los nombres indígenas en guaraní', *Physis*, no. 16, Buenos Aires, 1939.

DENSMORE, F.: (1) 'Papago Music', *Bulletin 90, Bureau of American Ethnology*, Washington, D.C., 1929.
(2) 'Mandan and Hidatsa Music', *Bulletin 80, Bureau of American Ethnology*, Washington, D.C., 1923.

DIAMOND, S.: 'Anaguta Cosmography: The Linguistic and Behavioral Implications', *Anthropological Linguistics*, vol. 2, no. 2, 1960.

DICKENS, Ch.: *Great Expectations*, Complete Works, 30 vol., New York and London, n.d.

DIETERLEN, G.: (1) 'Les Correspondances cosmo-biologiques chez les Soudanais', *Journal de Psychologie normale et pathologique*, 43rd year, no. 3, Paris, 1950.
(2) 'Classification des végétaux chez les Dogon', *Journal de la Société des Africanistes*, tome XXII, Paris, 1952.
(3) 'Parenté et Mariage chez les Dogon (Soudan français)', *Africa*, vol. 26, no. 2, London, April 1956.
(4) 'Mythe et organisation sociale au Soudan français', *Journal de la Société des Africanistes*, tome XXV, fasc. I et II, 1955.
(5) 'Mythe et organisation sociale en Afrique occidentale', *Journal de la Société des Africanistes*, tome XXIX, fasc. I, Paris, 1959.
(6) 'Note sur le totémisme Dogon', *L'Homme*, II, 1, Paris, 1962.

DORSEY, G. A. and KROEBER, A. L.: 'Traditions of the Arapaho', *Field Columbian Museum, Publ. 81, Anthropological Series*, vol. 5, Chicago, 1903.

DORSEY, J. O.: (1) 'Osage Traditions', *6th Annual Report, Bureau of American Ethnology* (1884–5), Washington, D.C., 1888.
(2) 'Siouan Sociology', *15th Annual Report, Bureau of American Ethnology* (1893–4), Washington, D.C., 1897.

DUPIRE, M.: 'Situation de la femme dans une société pastorale (Peul nomades du Niger)', *in*: D. Paulme ed., *Femmes d'Afrique Noire*, Paris-La Haye, 1960.

DURKHEIM, E.: *The Elementary Forms of the Religious Life* (translated from the French by J. W. Swain), London, 1915.

DURKHEIM, E. and MAUSS, M.: *Primitive Classification* (translated from the French by R. Needham), London, 1963.

ELKIN, A. P.: (1) 'Studies in Australian Totemism. Sub-Section, Section and Moiety Totemism', *Oceania*, vol. 4, no. 1, 1933–4.
(2) 'Studies in Australian Totemism. The Nature of Australian Totemism', *Oceania*, vol. 4, no. 2, 1933–4.
(2*a*) 'Cult Totemism and Mythology in Northern South Australia', *Oceania*, vol. 5, no. 2, 1934.
(3) 'Kinship in South Australia', *Oceania*, vol. 8, 9, 10, 1937–40.
(4) *The Australian Aborigines*, Sydney-London, 3rd ed., 1961.

ELMENDORF, W. W. and KROEBER, A. L.: 'The Structure of Twana Culture', *Research Studies, Monographic Supplement no. 2*, Pullman, Washington, 1960.

ELMORE, F. H.: 'Ethnobotany of the Navajo', *The University of New Mexico Bulletin, Monograph Series*, vol. 1, no. 7, Albuquerque, 1943.

EVANS-PRITCHARD, E. E.: (1) 'Witchcraft', *Africa*, vol. 8, no. 4, London, 1955.
(2) *Nuer Religion*, Oxford, 1956.
(3) 'Zande Clans and Totems', *Man*, vol. 61, art. no. 147, London, 1961.

FIRTH, R.: (1) 'Totemism in Polynesia', *Oceania*, vol. 1, nos. 3 and 4, 1930, 1931.
(2) *History and Traditions of Tikopia*, Wellington, 1961.

FISCHER, J. L., FISCHER, A., and MAHONY, F.: 'Totemism and Allergy', *The International Journal of Social Psychiatry*, vol. 5, no. 1, 1959.

FLETCHER, A. C.: (1) 'A Pawnee Ritual used when changing a Man's name', *American Anthropologist*, vol. 1, 1899.
(2) 'The Hako: A Pawnee Ceremony', *22nd Annual Report, Bureau of American Ethnology* (1900–1), Washington, D.C., 1904.

FLETCHER, A. C. and LA FLESCHE, F.: 'The Omaha Tribe', *27th Annual Report, Bureau of American Ethnology* (1905–6), Washington, D.C., 1911.

FORTUNE, R. F.: (1) 'Omaha Secret Societies', *Columbia University Contributions to Anthropology*, vol. 14, New York, 1932.
(2) *Sorcerers of Dobu*, New York, 1932.

FOURIE, L.: 'Preliminary Notes on Certain Customs of the Hei-/om Bushmen', *Journal of the Southwest Africa Scientific Society*, vol. 1, Windhoek, S.W.A., 1927.

FOX, C. E.: *The Threshold of the Pacific*, London, 1924.

FOX, R. B.: 'The Pinatubo Negritos: their useful plants and material culture', *The Philippine Journal of Science*, vol. 81 (1952), nos. 3–4, Manila, 1953.

FRAKE, Ch. O.: 'The Diagnosis of Disease among the Subanun of Mindanao', *American Anthropologist*, vol. 63, no. 1, 1961.

FRAZER, J. G.: *Totemism and Exogamy*, 4 vol., London, 1910.

FREEMAN, J. D.: 'Iban Augury', *Bijdragen tot de Taal-, Land- en Volkenkunde*, Deel 117, 1st Afl., 'S-Gravenhage, 1961.

FREUD, S.: *Totem and Taboo* (translated from the German by J. Strachey), London, 1950.

GARDINER, A. H.: *The Theory of Proper Names. A Controversial Essay*, London, 2nd ed., 1954.

GEDDES, W. R.: *The Land Dayaks of Sarawak*, Colonial Office, London, 1954.

GILGES, W.: 'Some African Poison Plants and Medicines of Northern Rhodesia', *Occasional Papers, Rhodes-Livingstone Museum*, no. 11, 1955.

GOLDENWEISER, A. A.: 'On Iroquois Work', *Summary Report of the Geological Survey of Canada*, Ottawa, Department of Mines, 1913.

GRZIMEK, B.: 'The Last Great Herds of Africa', *Natural History*, vol. 70, no. 1, New York, 1961.

HAILE, Father B.: *Origin Legend of the Navaho Flintway*, Chicago, 1943.

HAILE, Father B. and WHEELWEIGHT, M. C.: *Emergence Myth according to the Hanelthnayhe Upward-Reaching Rite*, Navajo Religion Series, vol. 3, Santa Fe, 1949.

HALLOWELL, A. I.: 'Ojibwa Ontology, Behavior and World View', *in*: S. Diamond, ed., *Culture in History. Essays in Honor of Paul Radin*, New York, 1960.

HAMPATÉ BA, A. and DIETERLEN, G.: 'Koumen. Texte initiatique des Pasteurs Peul', *Cahiers de l'Homme*, nouvelle série I, Paris-La Haye, 1961.

HANDY, E. S. Craighill and PUKUI, M. Kawena: 'The Polynesian Family System in Ka-'u, Hawai'i', parts VI and VII; and VIII, *Journal of the Polynesian Society*, vol. 62; and vol. 64, Wellington, N.Z., 1953 and 1955.

HARNEY, W. E.: 'Ritual and Behaviour at Ayers Rock', *Oceania*, vol. 31, no. 1, Sydney, 1960.

HARRINGTON, J. P.: 'Mollusca among the American Indians', *Acta Americana*, vol. 3, no. 4, 1945.

HART, C. W. M.: 'Personal Names among the Tiwi', *Oceania*, vol. 1, no. 3, 1930.

HEDIGER, H.: *Studies of the Psychology and Behaviour of Captive Animals in Zoos and Circus* (translated from German), London, 1955.

HENDERSON, J. and HARRINGTON, J. P.: 'Ethnozoology of the Tewa Indians', *Bulletin no. 56, Bureau of American Ethnology*, Washington, D.C., 1914.

HENRY, J.: *Jungle People. A Kaingáng Tribe of the Highlands of Brazil*, New York, 1941.

HERNANDEZ, Th.: 'Social Organization of the Drysdale River Tribes, North-West Australia,' *Oceania*, vol. II, no. 3, 1940–1.

HEYTING, A.: *Les Fondements des Mathématiques*, Paris, 1955.

HOFFMAN, W. J.: 'The Menomini Indians', *14th Annual Report. Bureau of American Ethnology*, part 1 (1892–3), Washington, D.C., 1896.

HOLLIS, A. C.: *The Nandi, their Language and Folklore*, Oxford, 1909.

HUBERT, R. and Mauss, M.: (1) *Mélanges d'histoire des religions*, 2nd ed., 1929.

(2) 'Esquisse d'une théorie générale de la magie', *L'Année Sociologique*, tome VII, 1902–3, *in*: Mauss, M. *Sociologie et Anthropologie*, Paris, 1950.

IVENS, W. G.: *Melanesians of the South-East Solomon Islands*, London, 1927.

JAKOBSON, R.: 'Concluding Statement: Linguistics and Poetics', *in*: Thomas A. Sebeok, ed. *Style in Language*, New York-London, 1960.

JAKOBSON, R. and HALLE, M.: *Fundamentals of Language*, 'S-Gravenhage, 1956.

JENNESS, D.: (1) 'The Indian's Interpretation of Man and Nature', *Proceedings and Transactions, Royal Society of Canada*, 3rd series, vol. XXIV, Section II, 1930.

(2) 'The Ojibwa Indians of Parry Island. Their Social and Religious Life', *Bulletins of the Canada Department of Mines, National Museum of Canada*, no. 78, Ottawa, 1935.

(3) 'The Carrier Indians of the Bulkley River', *Bulletin no. 133, Bureau of American Ethnology*, Washington, D.C., 1943.

JENSEN, B.: 'Folkways of Greenland Dog-Keeping', *Folk*, vol. 3, Copenhagen, 1961.

K., W.: 'How Foods Derive their Flavor', (report of a communication by E. C. Crocker to the *Eastern New York Section of the American Chemical Society*). *The New York Times*, May 2, 1948.

KELLY, C. Tennant: 'Tribes on Cherburg Settlement, Queensland', *Oceania*, vol. 5, no. 4, 1935.

KINIETZ, W. V.: 'Chippewa Village. The Story of Katikitegon', *Bulletin no. 25, Cranbrook Institute of Science*, Detroit, 1947.

KOPPERS, W.: *Die Bhil in Zentralindien*, Wien, 1948.

KRAUSE, A.: *The Tlingit Indians*, translated by E. Gunther, Seattle, 1956.

KRIGE, E. J. and J. D.: *The Realm of a Rain Queen*, Oxford, 1943.

KROEBER, A. L.: (1) 'Zuñi Kin and Clan', *Anthropological Papers of the American Museum of Natural History*, vol. 18, part 11, New York, 1917.

(2) 'Handbook of the Indians of California', *Bulletin 78, Bureau of American Ethnology*, Washington, D.C., 1925.

KROTT, P.: 'Ways of the Wolverine', *Natural History*, vol. 69, no. 2, New York, 1960.

LA BARRE, W.: 'Potato Taxonomy among the Aymara Indians of Bolivia', *Acta Americana*, vol. 5, Nos. 1–2, 1947.

LA FLESCHE, F.: (1) 'Right and Left in Osage Ceremonies', *Holmes Anniversary Volume*, Washington, D.C., 1916.

(2) 'The Osage Tribe. Rites of the Chiefs: Sayings of the Ancient Men', *36th Annual Report, Bureau of American Ethnology* (1914–15), Washington, D.C., 1921.

(3) 'The Osage Tribe. The Rite of Vigil', *39th Annual Report, Bureau of American Ethnology* (1917–18), Washington, D.C., 1925.

(4) 'The Osage Tribe. Child Naming Rite', *43rd Annual Report, Bureau of American Ethnology* (1925–6), Washington, D.C., 1928.

(5) 'The Osage Tribe. Rite of the Wa-Xo'-Be', *45th Annual Report, Bureau of American Ethnology* (1927–8), Washington, D.C., 1930.

LAGUNA, F. DE: 'Tlingit Ideas about the Individual', *Southwestern Journal of Anthropology*, vol. 10, no. 2, Albuquerque, 1954.

LAROCK, V.: *Essai sur la valeur sacrée et la valeur sociale des noms de personnes dans les sociétés inférieures*, Paris, 1932.

LÉVI-STRAUSS, C.: (1) *Les Structures élémentaires de la parenté*, Paris, 1949.

(2) *A World on the Wane*, (translated from the French by John Russell), London, 1961.

(3) 'Documents Tupi-Kawahib', *in*: *Miscellanea Paul Rivet, Octogenario Dicata*, Mexico, 1958.

(4) *Collège de France*, chaire d'Anthropologie sociale. *Leçon inaugurale* faite le mardi 5 janvier 1960. Paris, 1960.

(5) 'La Structure et la forme, réflexions sur un ouvrage de Vladimir Propp', *Cahiers de l'Institut de Science économique appliquée* (Recherches et dialogues philosophiques et économiques, 7), no. 99, Paris, 1960.

(6) *Totemism* (translated from the French by R. Needham), Boston, 1963.

(7) 'The Bear and the Barber', *Journal of the Royal Anthropological Society*, vol. 93, London, 1963.

LIENHARDT, G.: *Divinity and Experience. The Religion of the Dinka*, London, 1961.

LOEB, E. M.: 'Kuanyama Ambo Magic', *Journal of American Folklore*, vol. 69, 1956.

LONG, J. K.: *Voyages and Travels of an Indian Interpreter and Trader* (1791), Chicago, 1922.

MANU (The Laws of): *The Sacred Books of the East*, ed. by F. Max Müller, vol. 25, Oxford, 1886.

MCCLELLAN, C.: 'The Interrelations of Social Structure with Northern Tlingit Ceremonialism', *Southwestern Journal of Anthropology*, vol. 10, no. 1, Albuquerque, 1954.

McCONNEL, U.: 'The Wik-Munkan Tribe of Cape York Peninsula', *Oceania*, vol. 1, nos. 1 and 2, 1930–1.

MARSH, G.H. and LAUGHLIN, W.S.: 'Human Anatomical Knowledge among the Aleutian Islanders', *Southwestern Journal of Anthropology*, vol. 12, no. 1, Albuquerque, 1956.

MAUSS, M.: (cf. also HUBERT and MAUSS, DURKHEIM and MAUSS). 'L'âme et le prénom', *Bulletin de la Société française de Philosophie*, Séance du 1er juin 1929 (29e année).

MEGGITT, M.J.: 'The Bindibu and Others', *Man*, vol. 61, art. no. 172, London, 1961.

MICHELSON, T.: (1) 'Notes on Fox Mortuary Customs and Beliefs', *40th Annual Report, Bureau of American Ethnology* (1918–19), Washington, D.C., 1925.
(2) 'Fox Miscellany', *Bulletin 114, Bureau of American Ethnology*, Washington, D.C., 1937.

MIDDLETON, J.: 'The Social Significance of Lugbara Personal Names', *The Uganda Journal*, vol. 25, no. 1, Kampala, 1961.

MOONEY, J.: 'The Sacred Formulas of the Cherokee', *7th Annual Report, Bureau of American Ethnology*, Washington, D.C., 1886.

NEEDHAM, R.: (1) 'The System of Teknonyms and Death-Names of the Penan', *Southwestern Journal of Anthropology*, vol. 10, no. 4, Albuquerque, 1954.
(2) 'A Penan Mourning-Usage', *Bijdragen tot de Taal-, Land- en Volkenkunde*, Deel 110, 3rd Afl., 'S-Gravenhage, 1954.
(3) 'The Left Hand of the Mugwe: An Analytical Note on the Structure of Meru Symbolism', *Africa*, vol. 30, no. 1, London, 1960.
(4) 'Mourning Terms', *Bijdragen tot de Taal-, Land- en Volkenkunde*, Deel 115, 1st Afl., 'S-Gravenhage, 1959.

NELSON, E.W.: *Wild Animals of North America*, Washington, D.C., 1918.

NSIMBI, N.B.: 'Baganda Traditional Personal Names', *The Uganda Journal*, vol. 14, no. 2, Kampala, 1950.

PARSONS, E.C.: 'Hopi and Zuñi Ceremonialism', *Memoirs of the American Anthropological Association*, no. 39, Menasha, 1933.

PASO Y TRONCOSO, F. del: 'La Botanica entre los Nahuas', *Anales Mus. Nac. Mexic.*, tome III, Mexico, 1886.

PEIRCE, Ch.S.: 'Logic as Semiotic: the Theory of Signs', *in*: J. Buchler, ed. *The Philosophy of Peirce: Selected Writings*, London, 3rd ed., 1956.

PINK, O.: 'Spirit Ancestors in a Northern Aranda Horde Country', *Oceania*, vol. 4, no. 2, Sydney, 1933–4.

RADCLIFFE-BROWN, A.R.: (1) 'The Social Organization of Australian Tribes', *Oceania*, vol. 1, no. 2, 1930–1.
(2) 'The Comparative Method in Social Anthropology', Huxley

Memorial Lecture for 1951. *Journal of the Royal Anthropological Institute*, vol. 81, parts I and II, 1951 (Published 1952). Republished in: *Method in Social Anthropology*, Chicago, 1958, ch. v.

(3) 'Introduction' *in*: A. R. Radcliffe-Brown and Daryll Forde, eds. *African Systems of Kinship and Marriage*, Oxford, 1950.

RADIN, P.: (1) 'The Winnebago Tribe', *37th Annual Report, Bureau of American Ethnology* (1915–16), Washington, D.C., 1923.

(2) 'Mexican Kinship Terms', *University of California Publications in American Archaelogy and Ethnology*, vol. 31, Berkeley, 1931.

RASMUSSEN, K.: 'Intellectual Culture of the Copper Eskimos', *Report of the Fifth Thule Expedition*, vol. 9, Copenhagen, 1932.

READ, K.E.: 'Leadership and Consensus in a New Guinea Society', *American Anthropologist*, vol. 61, no. 3, 1959.

REICHARD, G. A.: (1) 'Navajo Classification of Natural Objects', *Plateau*, vol. 21, Flagstaff, 1948.

(2) *Navaho Religion. A Study of Symbolism*, 2 vol. Bollingen Series XVIII, New York, 1950.

REKO, B. P.: *Mitobotanica Zapoteca*, Tacubaya, 1945.

RETZ, Cardinal DE: *Mémoires*, Bibliothèque de la Pléiade, Paris, 1949.

RISLEY, H. H.: *Tribes and Castes of Bengal*, 4 vol., Calcutta, 1891.

RITZENTHALER, R.: 'Totemic Insult among the Wisconsin Chippewa', *American Anthropologist*, vol. 47, 1945.

RIVERS, W. H. R.: 'Island-Names in Melanesia', *The Geographical Journal*, London, May, 1912.

ROBBINS, W. W., HARRINGTON, J. P., and FREIRE-MARRECO, B.: 'Ethnobotany of the Tewa Indians', *Bulletin no. 55, Bureau of American Ethnology*, Washington, D.C., 1916.

ROCAL, G.: *Le Vieux Périgord*, 3rd ed., Paris, 1928.

ROLLAND, E.: (1) *Faune populaire de la France*, Tome II, 'Les Oiseaux sauvages', Paris, 1879.

(2) *Flore populaire de la France*, Tome II, Paris, 1899.

ROSCOE, J.: *The Baganda: An Account of their Native Customs and Beliefs*, London, 1911.

ROUSSEAU, J. J.: (1) *Discours sur l'origine et les fondements de l'inégalité parmi les hommes*, Œuvres melées, Tome II, Nouvelle ed., London, 1776.

(2) *Essai sur l'origine des langues*, Œuvres posthumes, Tome II, London, 1783.

RUSSELL, B.: 'The Philosophy of Logical Atomism', *The Monist*, 1918.

RUSSELL, F.: 'The Pima Indians', *26th Annual Report, Bureau of American Ethnology* (1904–5), Washington, D.C., 1908.

SARTRE, J. P.: *Critique de la raison dialectique*, Paris, 1960.

SAUSSURE, F. DE: *Course in General Linguistics*, (translated from the French by W. Baskin), London, 1960.

SCHOOLCRAFT, H. R.: Cf. WILLIAMS.
SEDEIS (Société d'Études et de Documentation Économiques, Industrielles et Sociales): *Bulletin* no. 796, supplement 'Futuribles', no. 2, Paris, 1961.
SHARP, R. Lauriston: 'Notes on Northeast Australian Totemism', *in*: *Studies in the Anthropology of Oceania and Asia, Papers of the Peabody Museum, Harvard University*, vol. 20, Cambridge, Mass., 1943.
SEBILLOT, P.: *Le Folklore de France*, Tome III, 'La Faune et la flore', Paris, 1906.
SIMPSON, G. G.: *Principles of Animal Taxonomy*, New York, 1961.
SKINNER, A.: (1) 'Social Life and Ceremonial Bundles of the Menomini Indians', *Anthropological Papers of the American Museum of Natural History*, vol. 13, part 1, New York, 1913.
(2) 'Observations on the Ethnology of the Sauk Indians', *Bulletins of the Public Museum of the City of Milwaukee*, vol. 5, no. 1, 1923–5.
(3) 'Ethnology of the Ioway Indians', *Bulletins of the Public Museum of the City of Milwaukee*, vol. 5, no. 4, 1926.
SMITH, A. H.: 'The Culture of Kabira, Southern Ryūkyū Islands', *Proceedings of the American Philosophical Society*, vol. 104, no. 2, Philadelphia, 1960.
SMITH BOWEN, E.: *Return to Laughter*, London, 1954.
SPECK, F. G.: (1) 'Reptile Lore of the Northern Indians', *Journal of American Folklore*, vol. 36, no. 141, Boston-New York, 1923.
(2) 'Penobscot Tales and Religious Beliefs', *Journal of American Folklore*, vol. 48, no. 187, Boston-New York, 1935.
SPENCER, B. and GILLEN, F. J.: *The Northern Tribes of Central Australia*, London, 1904.
STANNER, W. E. H.: (1) 'Durmugam, A Nangiomeri (Australia)', *in*: J. B. Casagrande, ed. *In the Company of Man*, New York, 1960.
(2) 'On Aboriginal Religion, IV, The Design-Plan of a Riteless Myth', *Oceania*, vol. 31, no. 4, 1961.
STEPHEN, A. M.: 'Hopi Journal', ed. by E. C. Parsons, 2 vol., *Columbia University Contributions to Anthropology*, vol. 23, New York, 1936.
STREHLOW, C.: *Die Aranda und Loritja-Stämme in Zentral Australien*, 4 vol., Frankfurt am Main, 1907–13.
STREHLOW, T. G. H.: *Aranda Traditions*, Melbourne, 1947.
STURTEVANT, W. C.: 'A Seminole Medicine Maker', *in*: J. B. Casagrande, ed. *In the Company of Man*, New York, 1960.
SWANTON, J. R.: (1) 'Social Organization and Social Usages of the Indians of the Creek Confederacy', *42nd Annual Report, Bureau of American Ethnology* (1924–5), Washington, D.C., 1928.
(2) 'Social and Religious Beliefs and Usages of the Chickasaw Indians', *44th Annual Report, Bureau of American Ethnology* (1926–7), Washington, 1928.

TESSMANN, G.: *Die Pangwe, Völkerkundliche Monographie eines westafrikanischen Negerstammes*, 2 vol., Berlin, 1913.

THOMAS, N. W.: *Kinship Organisations and Group Marriage in Australia*, Cambridge, 1906.

THOMSON, D. F.: 'Names and Naming in the Wik Monkan Tribes', *Journal of the Royal Anthropological Institute*, vol. 76, part II, London, 1946.

THURNWALD, R.: 'Bánaro Society. Social Organization and Kinship System of a Tribe in the Interior of New Guinea', *Memoirs of the American Anthropological Association*, vol. 3, no. 4, 1916.

THURSTON, E.: *Castes and Tribes of Southern India*, 7 vol., Madras, 1909.

TOZZER, A. M.: 'A Comparative Study of the Mayas and the Lacandones', *Archaeological Institute of America, Report of the fellow in American Archaeology* (1902–5), New York, 1907.

TURNER, G.: *Samoa a Hundred Years ago and Long Before . . .*, London, 1884.

TURNER, V. W.: (1) 'Lunda Rites and Ceremonies', *Occasional Papers, Rhodes-Livingstone Museum*, no. 10, Manchester, 1953.

(2) 'Ndembu Divination. Its Symbolism and Techniques', *The Rhodes-Livingstone Papers*, no. 31, Manchester, 1961.

TYLOR, E. B.: *Primitive Culture*, 2 vol., London, 1871.

VAN GENNEP, A.: *L'Etat actuel du problème totémique*, Paris, 1920.

VAN GULIK, R. H.: (1) *Erotic Colour Prints of the Ming Period*, 3 vol., Tokyo, 1951.

(2) *Sexual Life in Ancient China*, Leiden, 1961.

VANZOLINI, P. E.: 'Notas sôbre a zoologia dos Indios Canela', *Revista do Museu Paulista*, N.S., vol. 10, São Paulo, 1956–8.

VENDRYES, J.: *Le Langage. Introduction linguistique à l'histoire*, Paris, 1921.

VESTAL, P. A.: 'Ethnobotany of the Ramah Navaho', *Papers of the Peabody Museum, Harvard University*, vol. 40, no. 4, Cambridge, Mass., 1952.

VOGT, E. Z.: 'On the Concepts of Structure and Process in Cultural Anthropology', *American Anthropologist*, vol. 62, no. 1, 1960.

VOTH, H. R.: (1) 'The Oraibi Soyal Ceremony', *Field Columbian Museum, Publication 55. Anthropological Series*, vol. 3, no. 1, Chicago, 1901.

(2) 'The Oraibi Powamu Ceremony', *Field Columbian Museum, Anthropological Series*, vol. 3, no. 2, Chicago, 1901.

(3) 'Hopi Proper Names', *Field Columbian Museum, Publication 100, Anthropological Series*, vol. 6, no. 3, Chicago, 1905.

(4) 'The Traditions of the Hopi', *Field Columbian Museum Publication 96, Anthropological Series*, vol. 8, Chicago, 1905.

(5) 'Brief Miscellaneous Hopi Papers', *Field Museum of Natural History, Publication 157, Anthropological Series*, vol. XI, no. 2, Chicago, 1912.

WALKER, A. Raponda, and SILLANS, R.: *Les Plantes utiles du Gabon*, Paris, 1961.

WALLIS, W. D.: 'The Canadian Dakota', *Anthropological Papers of the American Museum of Natural History*, vol. 41, part 1, New York, 1947.

WARNER, W. Lloyd: *A Black Civilization*, revised edition, New York, 1958.

WATERMAN, T. T.: 'Yurok Geography', *University of California Publications in American Archaeology and Ethnology*, vol. 16, no. 5, Berkeley, 1920.

WHITE, C. M. N.: (1) 'Elements in Luvale Beliefs and Rituals', *The Rhodes-Livingstone Papers*, no. 32, Manchester, 1961.

(2) (J. CHINJAVATA and L. E. MUKWATO.) 'Comparative Aspects of Luvale Puberty Ritual', *African Studies*, Johannesburg, 1958.

WHITE, L. A.: 'New Material from Acoma', *in*: *Bulletin 136, Bureau of American Ethnology*, Washington, D.C., 1943.

WHITING, A. F.: 'Ethnobotany of the Hopi', *Bulletin no. 14, Museum of Northern Arizona*, Flagstaff, 1950.

WILLIAMS, M. L. W.: *Schoolcraft's Indian Legends*, Michigan U.P., 1956.

WILSON, G. L.: 'Hidatsa Eagle Trapping', *Anthropological Papers of the American Museum of Natural History*, vol. 30, part IV, New York, 1928.

WIRZ, P.: *Die Marind-Anim von Holländisch-Süd-Neu-Guinea*, I Band, Teil II, 1922.

WITKOWSKI, G. J.: *Histoire des accouchements chez tous les peuples*, Paris, 1887.

WOENSDREGT, J.: 'Mythen en Sagen der Berg-Toradja's van Midden-Celebes', *Verhandelingen van het Bataviaasch Genootschap van Kunsten en Wetenschappen*, vol. 65, no. 3, Batavia, 1925.

WORSLEY, P.: 'Totemism in a Changing Society', *American Anthropologist*, vol. 57, no. 4, 1955.

WYMAN, L. C. and HARRIS, S. K.: 'Navaho Ethnobotany', *University of New Mexico, Bulletin no. 366, Anthropological Series*, vol. 3, no. 4, Albuquerque, 1941.

ZAHAN, D.: *Sociétés d'initiation Bambara*, Paris-La Haye, 1960.

ZEGWAARD, G. A.: 'Headhunting Practices of the Asmat of Netherlands New Guinea', *American Anthropologist*, vol. 61, no. 6, 1959.

ZELEǸINE, D.: *Le culte des idoles en Sibérie*, French translation, Paris, 1952.

INDEX

Abstraction, 1–5, 107, 135–60, 164, 166, 175, 182, 217–20, 257, 266, 269
Affectiveness, 37–9
Agriculture, 52, 73–4, 110–3
ALBERTUS MAGNUS, 42
ALBISETTI, P.C. See COLBACCHINI
Algonkin, 31–2, 50, 57, 70, 99, 117, 142, 166–7, 173, 187, 189, 196
Allergy, 98
Aluridja, 165, 167
ALVIANO, F. DE, 106
Ambo, 62
Analytical reason, 245–69
ANDERSON, A. J. O., 46 n.
ANDERSON, E., 73
Animals, names given to, 204–8, 213
Animism, 249
ANTHONY, H. G., 53 n.
Arabanna, Arabana, 81–2, 84–7, 238
Aranda, 81–8, 102–3, 109, 112–3, 118, 150, 165, 167–8, 170, 174, 218, 235, 237–41, 243–4
Arbitrary. See Motivation
Archetypes, 65
Archives, 239–44
ARON, R., 70
Art, 22–36, 156, 182
Artemisia, 46–8
Arunta. See Aranda
Ashanti, 133 n.
Asmat, 60
Astrology, 42
Athapaskan, 50
AUGER, P., 263
Aurora, 76–80
Aymara, 43
Azande, 11

BACH, J. S., 242
Baganda, 112–3, 178
Bahima, 150
BALANDIER, G., 234–5 n.
Balovale, 6
BALZAC, H. DE, 130
Bambara, 163
Banyoro, 150, 179–80
Bard, 65, 184
BARROWS, D. P., 5
Bateso, 151
BATESON, G., 174, 177
BEATTIE, J. H. M., 179–80
BECKWITH, M. W., 50
BEIDELMAN, T. O., 144
Bemba, 62
BENEDICT, P. K., 189
BERGSON, H., 137
BETH, E. W., 248 n.
Bhil, 120-1
Birds, 54–61, 96, 147, 149, 189
Birds, names given to, 203, 213

Birth, 46–8, 61, 76–81, 131, 168, 177, 184, 189–98, 264
Blackfoot, 10
BOAS, F., 1, 21, 135–6, 189
BOCHET, G., 154
Bororo (Africa), 145
Bororo (Brazil), 39 n., 99, 114, 173, 178, 230
BOULAINVILLIERS (Boulainviller), Comte H. DE, 261–2 n.
Bouriate, 8–9
BOWERS, A.W., 50
Brassica rapa, 201–3, 211–2
Bricolage, 16–36, 150 n.
BRÖNDAL, V., 185 n., 201 n.
BROUILLETTE, B., 50
BURCKHARDT, J., 244
Bushmen, 103–4

CALAME-GRIAULE, G., 163
Canela, 40 n.
Cannibalism, 78, 105, 257–8 n.
CAPELL, A., 57
Carcajou (*Gulo luscus*), 50–3
CARPENTER, E., 64
Caste, 113–33, 162
Chance, 14, 184–5, 187, 220
CHARBONNIER, G., 234
Cherburg, 180–1 n.
CHEVAL (the postman), 17
Chickasaw, 117, 119, 126, 164, 204
Chinese, 65 n., 106, 165 n.
Chinook, 1
Chippewa, 102, 116, 167
Churinga, 87–8, 237–44
Classification, 39–74, 135–221, 229–44, 259–62, 267–8
CLOUET, F., 22, 24, 26–7
Coahuila, 5
Code, 90–8, 106, 111, 119, 137–40, 149–50, 172, 222, 228, 258–62
CODRINGTON, R.H., 76, 78
COGHLAN, H.H., 14 n.
Cogito, 250
Coifs, 90
COLBACCHINI, P.A., 39 n., 114, 230
Colla, 43
Colours, 40, 55, 64–5
Comprehension, 20, 137, 153, 264–5
Computer, 89, 151
COMTE, A., 163–4, 218–20
Concept, conceptual, 1–5, 18–21, 90, 107, 117, 119, 129–31, 135–60, 223–4, 264–5 and *passim*
CONKLIN H.C., 3, 7–8, 39 n., 55, 62, 138–9, 141, 153
Continuous and discontinuous, 137–9, 172, 195–200, 215–6, 224–8, 232–4, 256–64, 268
COOKE, CH. A., 178 n.
Couvade, 195–6, 201
Creek, 59–60, 118
Crow, 112
CRUZ, M., 173
CUNNISON, I.G., 62
CUSHING, F.H., 42

Dakota, 189
Dates, 258–62
Dayak, 54, 56, 205 n.
DEACON, B., 251
Death, 31–2, 65, 76–81, 84, 144, 158, 177, 184–5, 189, 191–200, 210, 236–44, 264
DELATTE, A., 42
Delaware, 142
Demography, 66–74, 111–2, 155, 187, 209–10, 232, 234, 260
DENNETT, R.E., 133
DENNLER, J.G., 44 n.
DENSMORE, F., 50, 165 n.
DESCARTES, R., 249
DETAILLE, E., 28
Determinism, geographical, 94–6
Devanga, 120
Diachrony, 52–3, 63, 66–74, 87–8, 148–9, 155, 166, 197, 227 n., 231–44, 256, 263
Dialectical reason, 245–69
DIAMOND, S., 145 n.
DIBBLE, CH. E., 46 n.
DICKENS, CH., 17, 150
DIETERLEN, G., 39, 43, 104, 163, 166, 189
Dinka, 121, 128–9 n.

Diseases, 139, 164–5
Dobu, 110–1, 177
Dogon, 39, 104 n., 163, 189
Dogs, names given to, 167, 181–2, 204–8, 213
DORSEY, G.A., 128
DORSEY, J.O., 69, 148–9
Drysdale river, 168, 174, 176
DUPIRE, M., 145
DURKHEIM, E., 39, 40, 57, 76, 91, 102, 162, 214, 238–9, 241, 268

Eagle hunting, 46–51, 225
EGGAN, F., 71
Elema, 106–7
ELKIN, A.P., 65, 81–2, 84, 100, 102, 185, 218, 242, 265
ELMENDORF, W.W., 177 n., 196–7 n.
ELMORE, F.H., 40
Endogamy, 111–33
Eskimo, 40, 50, 64
EVANS-PRITCHARD, E.E., 11, 56, 60 n., 104, 161 n., 189, 224
Exogamy, 77–133, 231
Experimenting, 13–15, 73–4, 220–3
Extension, 20, 136, 153

Fang, 3, 61, 98–9, 103–4
FIRTH, R., 228 n.
FISCHER, A., 98
FISCHER, J.L., 98
FLETCHER, A.C., 10, 56, 112
Flowers, names given to, 211–6
Forrest river, 65
FORTUNE, R.F., 43, 61, 111
FOURIE, L., 103
FOX, C.E., 78 n.
FOX, R.B., 5, 8, 14
Fox tribe, 31, 65, 99, 199 n.
FRAKE, CH.O., 5, 139
France, 70, 90, 105, 111, 193–4, 254–5, 258, 261–2 n.
FRAZER, J.G., 57–8, 74, 76, 78–9, 81, 102, 106, 116, 140, 142, 231
FREEMAN, J.D., 55
FREIRE-MARRECO, B., 6
French Revolution, 254–5, 258, 261–2 n.
FREUD, S., 253
Fronde, 254–5
Fulani, 39 n., 43, 145

Gahuku-Gama, 30
GALEN, 42
Games, 30–2, 126
GARDINER, A.H., 172, 185, 201–3, 211, 215 n.
GEDDES, W.R., 205
GILGES, W., 6
GILLEN, F.J., 81–2, 84, 86, 88, 114, 238, 240–1
GOBINEAU, Comte J.A. DE, 261–2 n.
GÖDEL, K., 262
GOETHE, W., 244
GOGH, V. VAN, 244
'Golden Bough', 48
Golden Rod (Solidago), 46–8
GOLDENWEISER, A.A., 178, 188, 196
Grammar. See Vocabulary
GREUZE, J.-B., 30
GRIAULE, M., 5, 39, 163, 231
Groote Eylandt, 155
GRZIMEK, B., 137 n.
Guarani, 44
GUILBAUD, G.TH., 82 n.

HADDON, A.C., 115–6
HAILE, Fa. B., 40, 128, 203
HALLE, M. See JAKOBSON
HALLOWELL, A.I., 96
HAMPATÉ BA, A., 39 n., 43
HANDY, E.S. CRAIGHILL, 2, 3, 37, 96, 144
Hanunóo, 3–5, 7, 55, 62, 138, 153
HARNEY, W.E., 166
HARRINGTON, J.P., 6, 7, 169
HARRIS, S.K., 40, 204
HART, C.W.M., 177, 190, 195, 199–200, 210–1
Hawaii, 3, 37, 96, 144
HEDIGER, H., 38
HEIM, R., 186
Helmene, 8
HENDERSON, J., 7
HENRY, J., 105 n.
HERMES TRISMEGISTUS, 42

HERNANDEZ, TH., 155, 168, 174, 176
HEYTING, A., 248 n.
Hidasta, 46, 48, 52–3, 225
History, 66–74, 155–60, 186–7, 231–44, 248–9, 250–1, 252–63
HOFFMAN, W.J., 57, 167, 229
HOLLIS, A.C., 112
Hopi, 5, 40, 48, 60–1, 71–2, 165, 176, 178, 180, 229
Horses, names given to, 206–8, 213
HOUIS, M., 209 n.
HUBERT, R., 11, 18 n.
HUGO, V., 244

Iakoute, 8, 9
Iatmul, 174
Iban, 54, 56
Information theory, 154, 268–9
Infrastructures, 90–6, 130–1, 213–4
Intichiuma, 226–8
Ioway, 167
Iroquois, 57, 70, 114, 177–8, 188, 196–8, 223
IVENS, W.G., 78 n.

JAKOBSON, R., 149
JENNESS, D., 37, 43, 60, 227, 239 n.
JOUVENEL, B. DE, 70

K. (W.), 12
Kaguru, 145
Kaitish, 81, 86–7, 113
Kalar, 9
Kaleidoscope, 36
Karadjera, 88
Karuba, 121
Kauralaig, 88, 100–1
Kavirondo, 151
Kazak, 9
KELLY, C. TENNANT, 158, 180–1 n.
Keres, 71, 227 n.
KINIETZ, W.V., 116, 167
Kiwai, 140
Koko Yao, 100–1, 105
KOPPERS, W., 120
KRAUSE, A., 1
KRIGE, E.J., 159 n.
KRIGE, J.D., 159 n.
KROEBER, A.L., 71, 128, 175–7, 196–7 n.
Kuruba, 121
Kwakiutl, 189

LA BARRE, W., 44
Lacandon, 187 n.
LA FLESCHE, F., 56, 59, 112, 142–3, 144–8, 170–1, 173
LA FORCE, Duc DE, 244
LAGUNA, F. DE, 60, 173
Laierdila, 100–1
Language, 1–3, 56–7, 66–7, 105–6, 129, 131, 155–60, 172–216, 228, 252, 264–5, 267
LAROCK, V., 209 n.
LAUGHLIN, W.S., 153
LEIGHTON, A.H., 62, 204
LEIGHTON, D.C., 62, 204
LENOTRE, G., 244
LEVY-BRUHL, L., 251, 268
LIENHARDT, G., 121, 128–9 n.
Lifu, 78–80
Linguistics, 66–7, 102, 155–60, 172–222, 231, 252
LITTRÉ, E., 205
LOEB, E.M., 9
Logic, logical thought, 35–76, 102–3, 105, 126, 129, 135–216, 261, 267 and *passim*
LONG, J.K., 163
Loritja. See Aluridja
Lovedu, 159 n.
Luapula, 61–3
Luchozi, 6
Lugbara, 179–80
Luvale, 64–5, 97

Mabuiag, 115
McCLELLAN, C., 99
McCONNEL, U., 174
McLENNAN, J.F., 118, 231
Magic and religion, 220–8
MAHONY, F. See FISCHER
Maithakudi, 100–1
Maize, 61, 73, 112
Malaita, 78–80

Malecite, 8
MALINOWSKI, B., 3, 74, 91, 250
Mandan, 52
MANNHARDT, W., 95
MANU, Laws of, 106, 126
Manufactured articles, 121–9, 143–4, 151, 174–5
Marriage rules, 81–4, 88, 103–6, 109–33, 155, 243, 264–6
MARSH, G.H., 153
MARX, K., 130, 246, 253
Mashona, 105
Matabele, 105
Mathematics, 248 n.
MAUSS, M., 11, 18 n., 39, 40, 57, 223, 268
Maya, 187 n., 189
MEGGITT, M.J., 222
MELIES, G., 17
Menomini, 57, 116, 167, 188, 229
Menstruation, 46–8, 51–2, 91, 144, 225
Mentality, primitive, 37–8, 251, 267–8
Metaphor, 51–2, 105–6, 150 n., 204–8, 212–3, 224–8, 239
Meteorology, 91–7
Metonymy, 52, 106, 150 n., 204–8, 212–3, 224–8
MICHELSON, T., 31–2, 65, 100, 199 n.
Micmac, 8
MIDDLETON, J., 179–80
MILL, J.S., 172
Mind, savage, 219–20, 222–3, 245, 249 n., 263, 267–9
Miwok, 175, 178, 181
Mixe, 189
Mocassin, 143
Models, small-scale, 23–5, 150 n.
Mohawk, 178
Mohican, 142
Montagnais, 8
MORGAN, L., 118
Morphology, 7–9
Mota, 76, 79–80, 177
Motivation, 154–60
Motlav, 78–80
Munda, 120
Murngin, 91–3, 96, 174
Muskogi, 117
Myths, mythical thought, 16–22, 25–6, 30–3, 51–2, 68–70, 90–3, 127–8, 131–6, 148–50, 165–6, 168–9, 218, 223, 228–44, 254–5 and *passim*

Naga, 73
Nandi, 114
Names, proper, 112–3, 149–50, 167–8, 172–216, 218
Naskapi, 8
Natchez, 120
Navaho, 5, 39, 40, 45–6, 48, 55, 62, 128, 169, 203
Ndembu, 97
NEEDHAM, R., 144, 192–3, 195, 198 n.
Negrito, 4
NELSON, E.W., 53 n.
Neolithic, 13–15, 172, 269
Ngarinyin. See Ungarinyin
NSIMBI, N.B., 179
Nuer, 56, 60 n., 63, 104, 189, 224
Numerology, 142–7

Observation, 3–6, 219–23
Oïrote, 9
Ojibwa, 37, 60, 96, 142
Okerkila, 100–1
Omaha, 42, 59, 61, 112, 140, 170–1, 178, 216
Omens, 54–6, 131–3
Oraon, 120
Ordinal names, 182, 187, 189–97
Organicism, 169
Organism, 103–4, 136, 148, 151–4, 169–73, 175–6
Osage, 56, 59, 61, 69–70, 140, 142–3, 145, 147, 149, 170–1, 173, 178
Ossete, 8

Painting, 22–30
Papago, 165 n.
Papuans, 257–8 n.

Paradigmatic. See Syntagmatic
Parents-in-law, taboo of, 265–6
Parsons, E.C., 230
Particularization, 168–216
Paso y Troncoso, F. del, 46 n.
Pawnee, 10, 52, 56, 139
Peasant societies, 90, 111
Peirce, Ch.S., 20, 215
Penan, 191, 194–8
Penobscot, 8, 166
Personality, 214–5
Pima, 165
Pinatubo, 4, 8
Pink, O., 174
Pliny, 42
Poetry, 148
Ponapy, 98, 105
Ponca, 142
Praxis, 118, 122, 129–30, 251–2, 263–5
Priouret, R., 70
Prohibited food, 61–2, 76–80, 88, 97–133, 177, 205, 226–8
Prohibitions, linguistic, 176–7, 183–4, 194–200, 209–10, 264–5
Psychoanalysis, 252–4
Pueblo, 40, 52–3, 71, 169, 227 n.
Pukui, M. Kawena, 2, 3, 37, 96, 144
Pygmies, 4

Radcliffe-Brown, A.R., 55, 112 n., 114, 167
Radin, P., 57 n., 170, 189
Rasmussen, K., 40
Read, K.E., 31
Reichard, G.A., 40, 45, 55
Reko, B.P., 46 n.
Religion. See Magic and religion
Rembrandt, 28
Retz, Cardinal de, 254–5
Right and left, 144–5
Risley, H.H., 120
Rites, ritual, 30–3, 42–3, 45–53, 75–133, 143–7, 151, 154, 209–11, 220–8, 231, 235–44, 264–5 and *passim*
Ritzenthaler, R., 102
Rivers, W.H.R., 76, 78, 116
Robbins, W.W., 6
Robertson Smith, W., 231
Rocal, G., 111
Rolland, E., 201 n., 212 n.
Roman de Renart, 205 n.
Roscoe, J., 113
Rousseau, J.-J., 38, 163, 247
Russell, B., 215
Russell, F., 165
Russians (Altai), 9
Russians (Siberia), 8
Russians (Sourgout), 8
Ryukyu islands, 5

Sacrifice, 223–8
Saibai, 115
St John Chrysostom, 105
Samoa, 105
Sartre, J.-P., 130, 245–6, 248–56, 257–8 n., 264
Sauk, 170, 173, 188
Saussure, F. de, 18, 149, 156, 158–9
Schoolcraft, R.H. See Williams, M.L.W.
Sebillot, P., 204 n.
SEDEIS (*Société d'études et de documentation économiques, industrielles et sociales*), 70
Seminole, 5, 182
Sense, 172, 210, 249, 253–4, 255
Senufo, 154
Sharp, R. Lauriston, 88, 100–1, 151 n., 167, 236
Sherente, 53
Siegfried, A., 70
Sign, Signification, 18–20, 36, 130–3, 140, 156–60, 172–3, 181–3, 185–6, 203–15, 219–23, 239, 250, 257, 259, 266–9
Silence, 65
Sillans, R., 5
Simpson, G.G., 12, 13, 63, 156
Sioux, 57 n., 59, 140, 167, 173, 176, 189
Skinner, A., 167, 173, 188, 229
Smells, 12–3

SMITH. A.H., 5
SMITH BOWEN, E., 6
Solomon Islands, 140
Species, notions of, 136–72, 175, 177, 185–7, 200–16, 224–8
SPECK, F.G., 8, 166
SPENCER, B., 81–2, 84, 86, 88, 114, 238, 240–1
SPENGLER, O., 244
STANNER, W.E.H., 94, 228
Statistics (distribution), 72, 81–2, 85–6, 112, 159–60, 186–7, 232
STEPHEN, A.M., 60
STREHLOW, C., 167–8, 239
STREHLOW, T.G.H., 89, 229, 235, 239, 241, 243
STURTEVANT, W.C., 5, 183
Subanum, 5, 139
Superstructures, 117, 130, 213–4, 254
Surrealists, 21
SWANTON, J.R., 60, 119, 165
Synchrony, 52–3, 63, 66–74, 148–9, 155, 166, 197, 227 n., 231–44, 254, 256, 263
Syntagmatic, paradigmatic, 150 n., 203, 206–8, 211, 215–6

Tanoan, 71
Tastes, 12–3
Taxonomy, 9–13, 15–6, 38–45, 137–9, 153–4, 156, 186–9, 203, 231
Teleology, 252
TERTULLIAN, 105
TESSMANN, G., 3, 61 n., 98–9, 104
Tewa, 5–7
THOMAS, N.W., 113
THOMSON D.F., 45, 167, 183–4, 188
Thunder Birds, 96, 229
THURNWALD, R., 200
THURSTON, E., 63 n., 121
Tikopia, 139, 228 n.
Tikuna, 106–7
Tiwi, 177, 190, 195, 199–200, 206, 209, 211, 212–3 n.
Tjongandji, 100–1
Tlingit, 26, 60, 99, 173
Toradja, 169
Toreya, 63
Totalization, detotalization, 146–9, 151–4, 169, 175–6, 178, 250–62
Totem, totemism, *passim*
TOZZER, A.M., 187 n., 189
Tree, 158–9
TREVOUX (dictionary), 201 n.
Trobriand islands, 140
Tupi Kawahib, 173
TURNER, G., 233
TURNER, V.W., 97
Tutu, 115
Twins, 180, 189–90
TYLOR, E.B., 153–4, 164

Ulawa, 78–80, 177
Unconscious, collective, 65
Ungarinyin, 56, 184
Universalization, 164–7
Unmatjera, 86–7, 113

Vagina dentata, 106
VAN GENNEP, A., 109, 162–3
VAN GULIK, R.H., 106, 165 n.
VANZOLINI, P.E., 40 n.
VENDRYES, J., 203
VESTAL, P.A., 40, 48
Vocabulary, 138–9, 143, 154–60, 231–2
VOGT, E.Z., 234
VOTH, H.R., 48, 61, 165, 176, 230

Wakelbura, 102
WALKER, A. RAPONDA, 5
WALLIS, W.D., 190
Walpari, 114
WARNER, W. LLOYD, 91–3, 96, 174
Warramunga, 81, 85–7, 114, 184, 238
Water-colours (Aranda), 89, 244
WATERMAN, T.T., 168, 196–7 n.
Wawilak sisters, 91–3
WEYDEN, R. VAN DER, 28
WHEELWRIGHT, M.C., 128, 203
WHITE, C.M.N., 65, 98
WHITE, L.A., 227 n.

Wik Munkan, 45, 167 n., 174, 183, 186–8, 212
Williams, M. L. W., 56
Wilson, G. L., 48, 50
Winnebago, 57, 140, 142, 167, 170
Wirz, P., 63 n.
Witkowski, G. J., 201
Woensdregt, J., 169
Wolverine, 50–3
Wormwood. See *Artemisia*
Worsley, P., 156
Wotjobaluk, 57, 105
Wyman, L. C., 40, 204

Yathaikeno, 100–1
Yoruba, 105, 131–3
Yuma, 180
Yurlunggur (snake), 91–3
Yurok, 168, 177, 189, 196–7

Zahan, D., 39, 163
Zegwaard, G. A., 61
Zelenine, D., 9
Zuni, 40, 71–2